UNCANNY X-FORCE

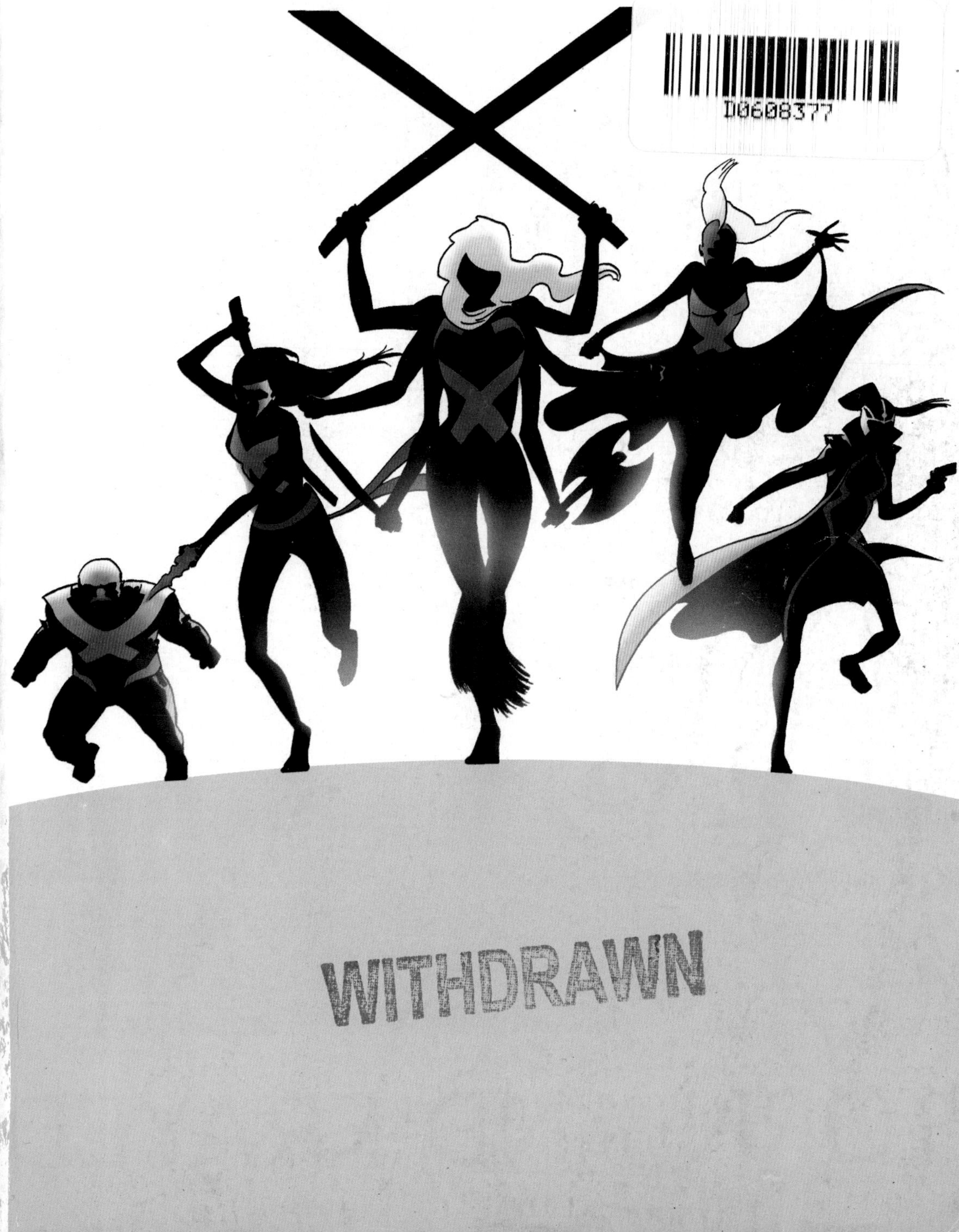

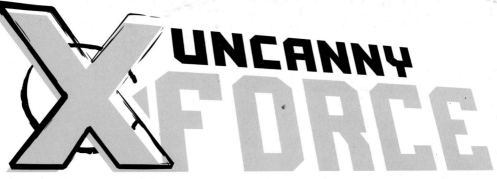

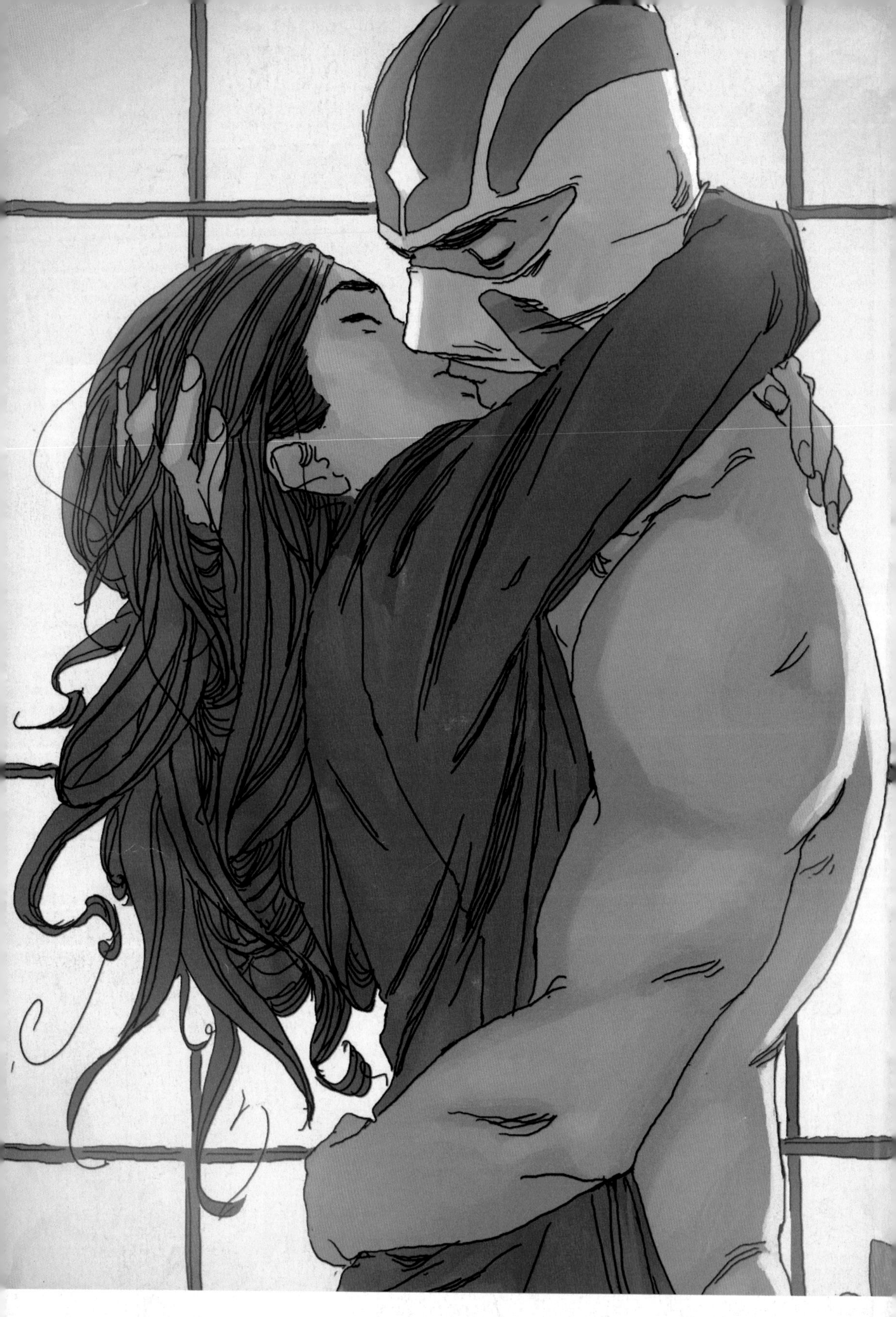

TORN AND FRAYED

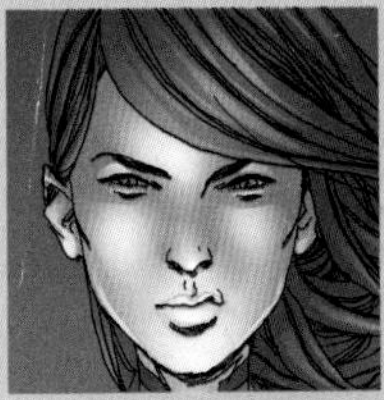

PSYLOCKE

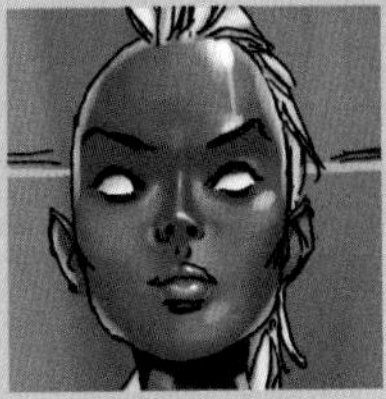

STORM

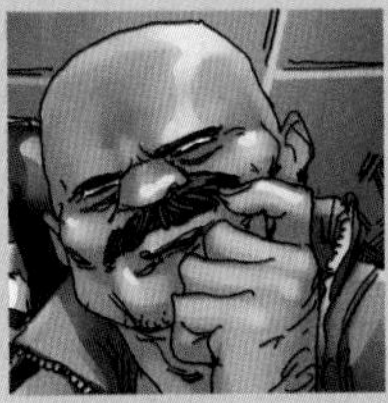

PUCK

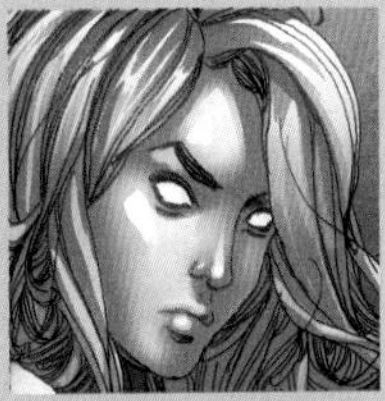

SPIRAL

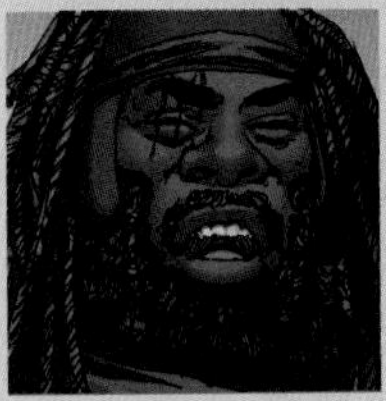

BISHOP

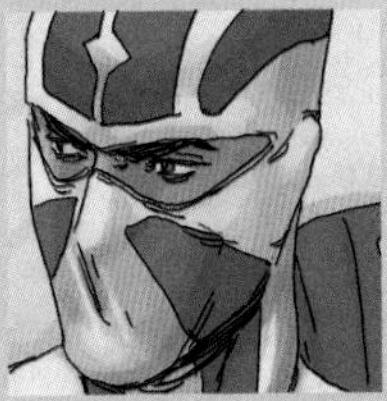

FANTOMEX

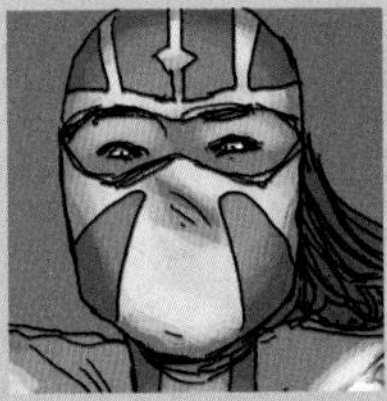

CLUSTER

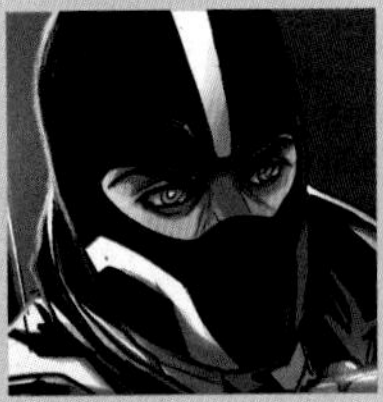

WEAPON XIII

Elizabeth Braddock, a.k.a. Psylocke, spent last summer in Paris with the three individuals spawned from Fantomex's triple brain — Fantomex, Cluster, and the sinister Weapon XIII. But by the end of the season, Betsy left the trio behind and returned to the X-Men without explanation, remaining tight-lipped about her recent experiences.

Now, Cluster has reappeared with dire news: Weapon XIII has kidnapped Fantomex. Reluctantly, Betsy has agreed to help Cluster rescue her former beau — but a mission like this is likely to bring long-buried secrets to the surface...

SAM HUMPHRIES
WRITER

ADRIAN ALPHONA & DALIBOR TALAJIĆ
ARTISTS, #7-9

CHRIS SOTOMAYOR & LEE LOUGHRIDGE
COLOR ARTISTS, #7-9

RAMON PÉREZ
ARTIST, #10-11

ADRIAN ALPHONA
ARTIST, #12

JAY DAVID RAMOS & RACHELLE ROSENBERG
COLOR ARTISTS, #10-12

VC'S CORY PETIT
WITH JOE SABINO (#7)
LETTERERS

KRIS ANKA
COVER ART

JENNIFER M. SMITH & XANDER JAROWEY
ASSISTANT EDITORS

DANIEL KETCHUM
EDITOR

NICK LOWE
X-MEN GROUP EDITOR

COLLECTION EDITOR: **JENNIFER GRÜNWALD** • ASSISTANT EDITORS: **ALEX STARBUCK** & **NELSON RIBEIRO** • EDITOR, SPECIAL PROJECTS: **MARK D. BEAZLEY**
SENIOR EDITOR, SPECIAL PROJECTS: **JEFF YOUNGQUIST** • SVP OF PRINT & DIGITAL PUBLISHING SALES: **DAVID GABRIEL** • BOOK DESIGN: **JEFF POWELL**
EDITOR IN CHIEF: **AXEL ALONSO** • CHIEF CREATIVE OFFICER: **JOE QUESADA** • PUBLISHER: **DAN BUCKLEY** • EXECUTIVE PRODUCER: **ALAN FINE**

UNCANNY X-FORCE VOL. 2: TORN AND FRAYED. Contains material originally published in magazine form as UNCANNY X-FORCE #7-12. First printing 2013. ISBN# 978-0-7851-6740-2. Published by MARVEL WORLDWIDE, INC., a subsidiary of MARVEL ENTERTAINMENT, LLC. OFFICE OF PUBLICATION: 135 West 50th Street, New York, NY 10020.

Printed in the U.S.A. ALAN FINE, EVP - Office of the President, Marvel Worldwide, Inc. and EVP & CMO Marvel Characters B.V.; DAN BUCKLEY, Publisher & President - Print, Animation & Digital Divisions; JOE QUESADA, Chief Creative Officer; TOM BREVOORT, SVP of Publishing; DAVID BOGART, SVP of Operations & Procurement, Publishing; C.B. CEBULSKI, SVP of Creator & Content Development; DAVID GABRIEL, SVP of Print & Digital Publishing Sales; JIM O'KEEFE, VP of Operations & Logistics; DAN CARR, Executive Director of Publishing Technology; SUSAN CRESPI, Editorial Operations Manager; ALEX MORALES, Publishing Operations Manager; STAN LEE, Chairman Emeritus. For information regarding advertising in Marvel Comics or on Marvel.com, please contact Niza Disla, Director of Marvel Partnerships, at ndisla@marvel.com. For Marvel subscription inquiries, please call 800-217-9158. **Manufactured between 9/27/2013 and 11/4/2013 by QUAD/GRAPHICS, VERSAILLES, KY, USA.**

10 9 8 7 6 5 4 3 2 1

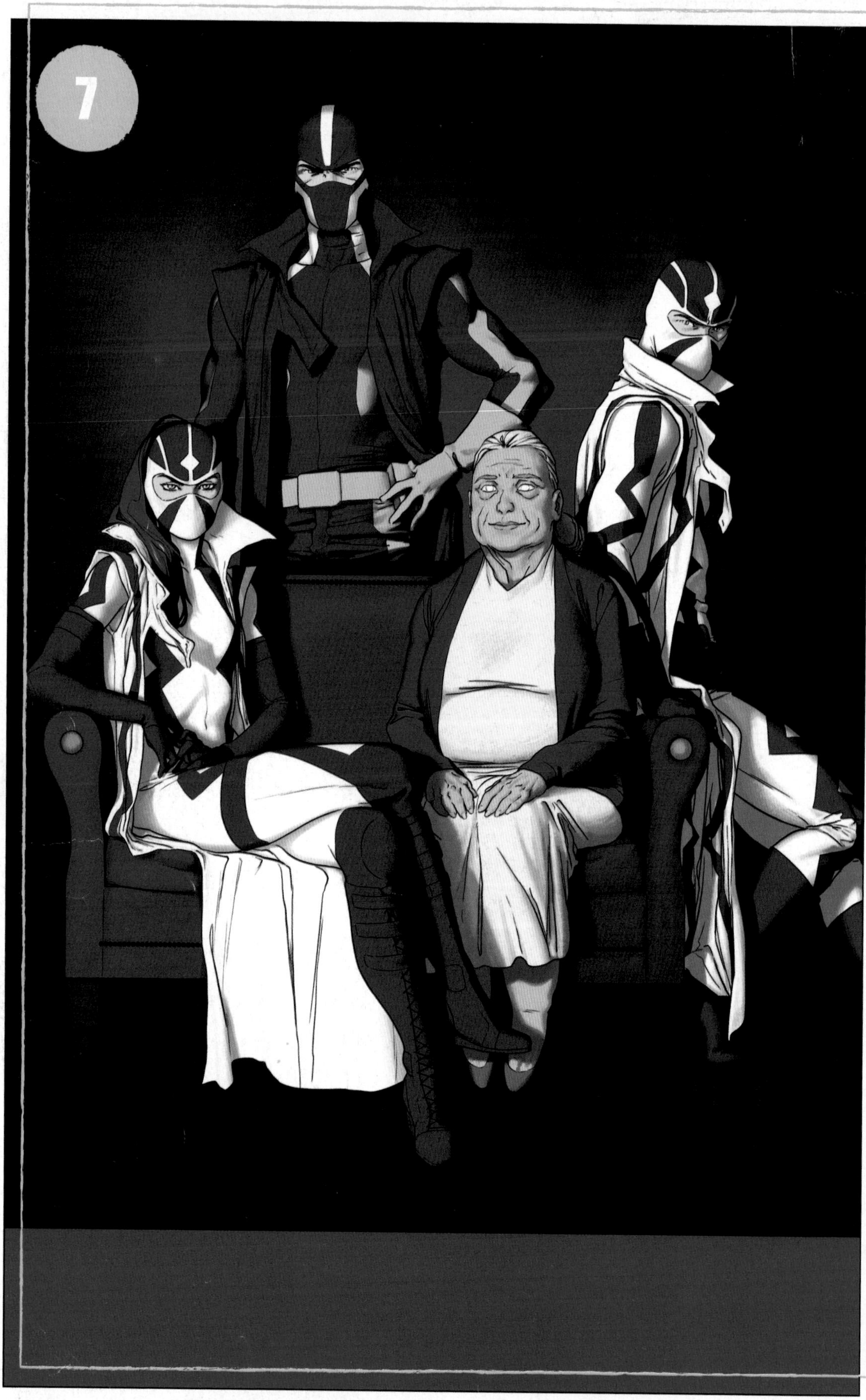
7

GOLD DUST WOMAN

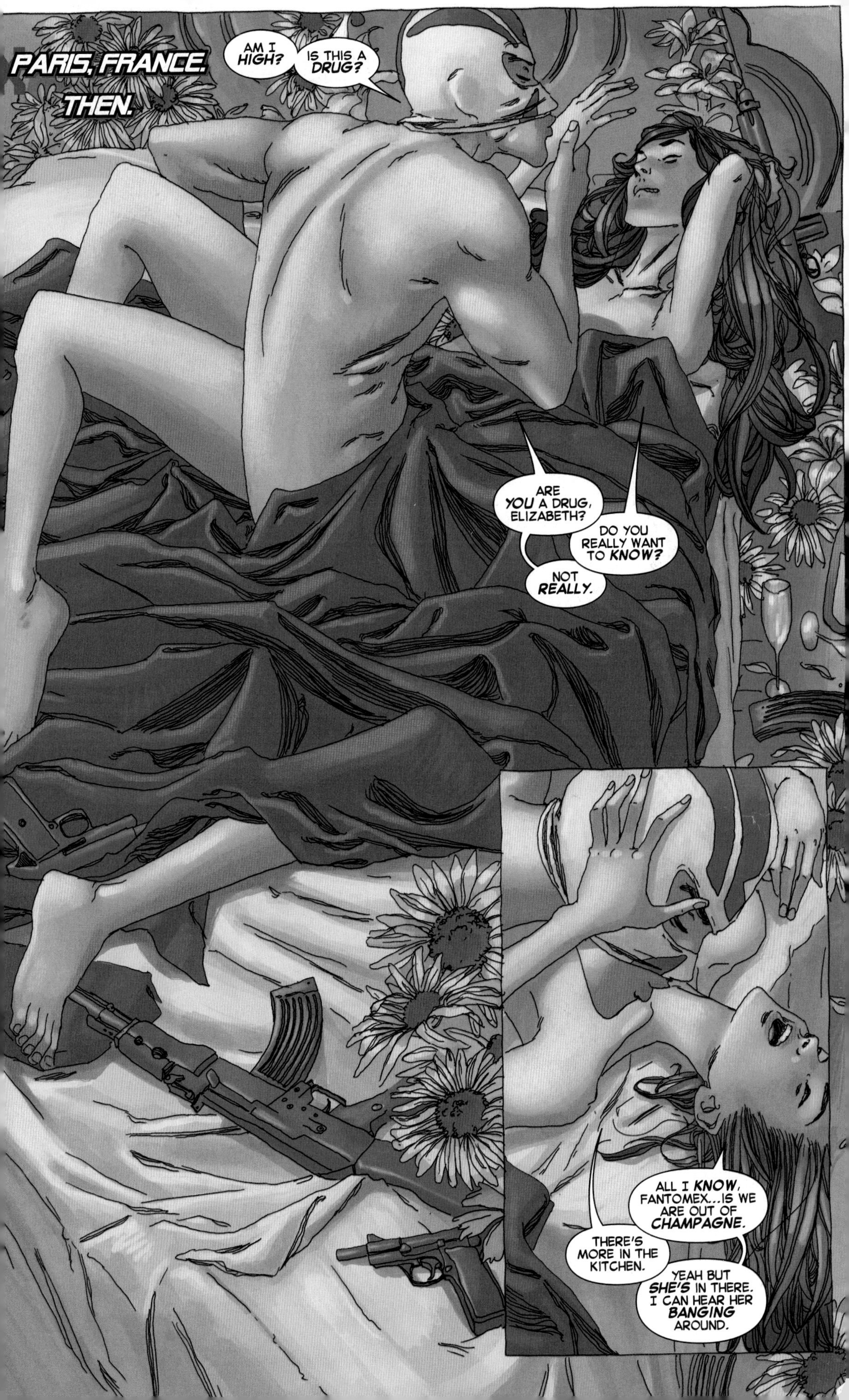
PARIS, FRANCE.
THEN.
AM I HIGH?
IS THIS A DRUG?
ARE YOU A DRUG, ELIZABETH?
DO YOU REALLY WANT TO KNOW?
NOT REALLY.
ALL I KNOW, FANTOMEX...IS WE ARE OUT OF CHAMPAGNE.
THERE'S MORE IN THE KITCHEN.
YEAH BUT SHE'S IN THERE. I CAN HEAR HER BANGING AROUND.

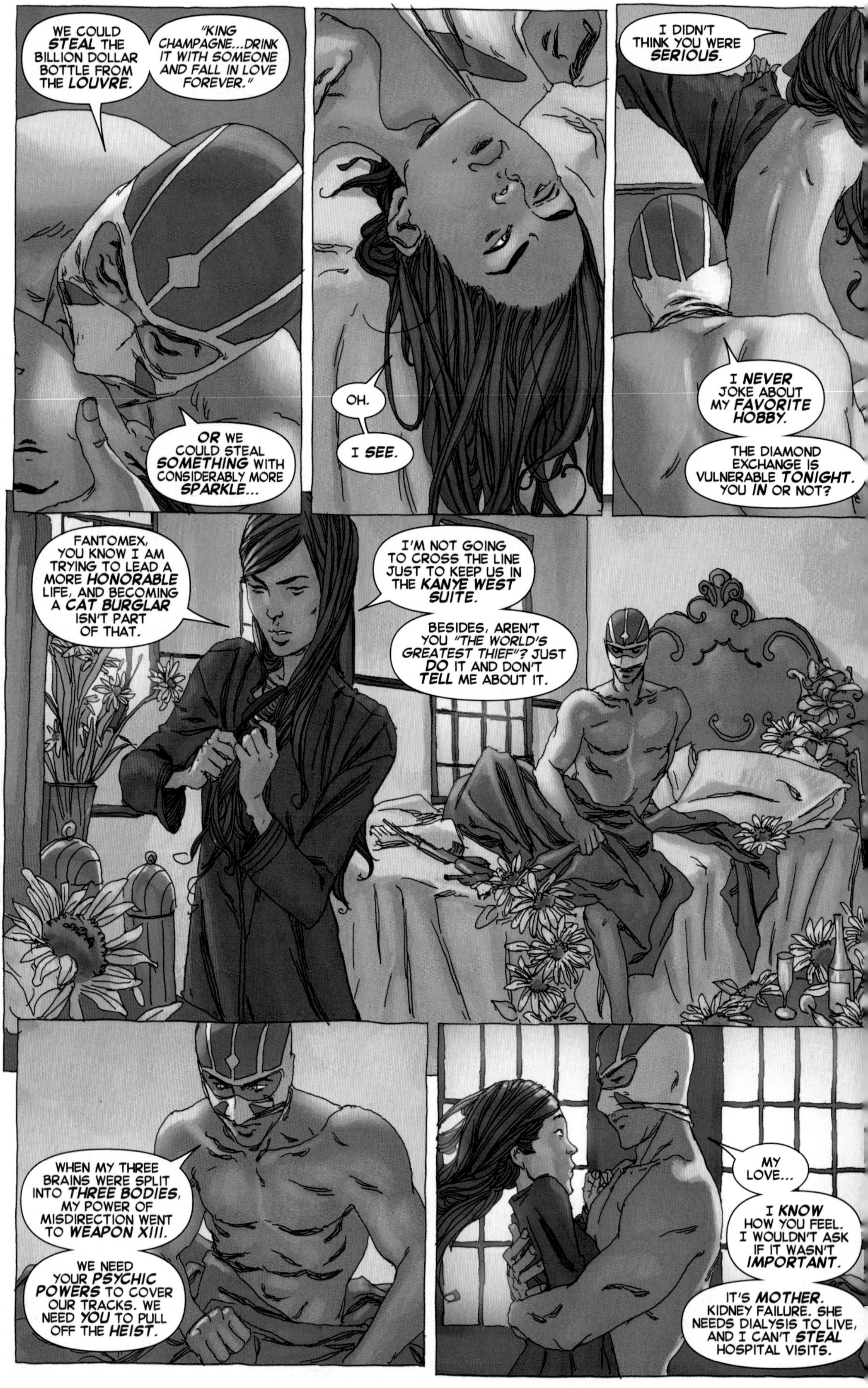

WE COULD STEAL THE BILLION DOLLAR BOTTLE FROM THE LOUVRE.
"KING CHAMPAGNE...DRINK IT WITH SOMEONE AND FALL IN LOVE FOREVER."
OR WE COULD STEAL SOMETHING WITH CONSIDERABLY MORE SPARKLE...
OH.
I SEE.
I DIDN'T THINK YOU WERE SERIOUS.
I NEVER JOKE ABOUT MY FAVORITE HOBBY.
THE DIAMOND EXCHANGE IS VULNERABLE TONIGHT. YOU IN OR NOT?
FANTOMEX, YOU KNOW I AM TRYING TO LEAD A MORE HONORABLE LIFE, AND BECOMING A CAT BURGLAR ISN'T PART OF THAT.
I'M NOT GOING TO CROSS THE LINE JUST TO KEEP US IN THE KANYE WEST SUITE.
BESIDES, AREN'T YOU "THE WORLD'S GREATEST THIEF"? JUST DO IT AND DON'T TELL ME ABOUT IT.
WHEN MY THREE BRAINS WERE SPLIT INTO THREE BODIES, MY POWER OF MISDIRECTION WENT TO WEAPON XIII.
WE NEED YOUR PSYCHIC POWERS TO COVER OUR TRACKS. WE NEED YOU TO PULL OFF THE HEIST.
MY LOVE...
I KNOW HOW YOU FEEL. I WOULDN'T ASK IF IT WASN'T IMPORTANT.
IT'S MOTHER. KIDNEY FAILURE. SHE NEEDS DIALYSIS TO LIVE, AND I CAN'T STEAL HOSPITAL VISITS.

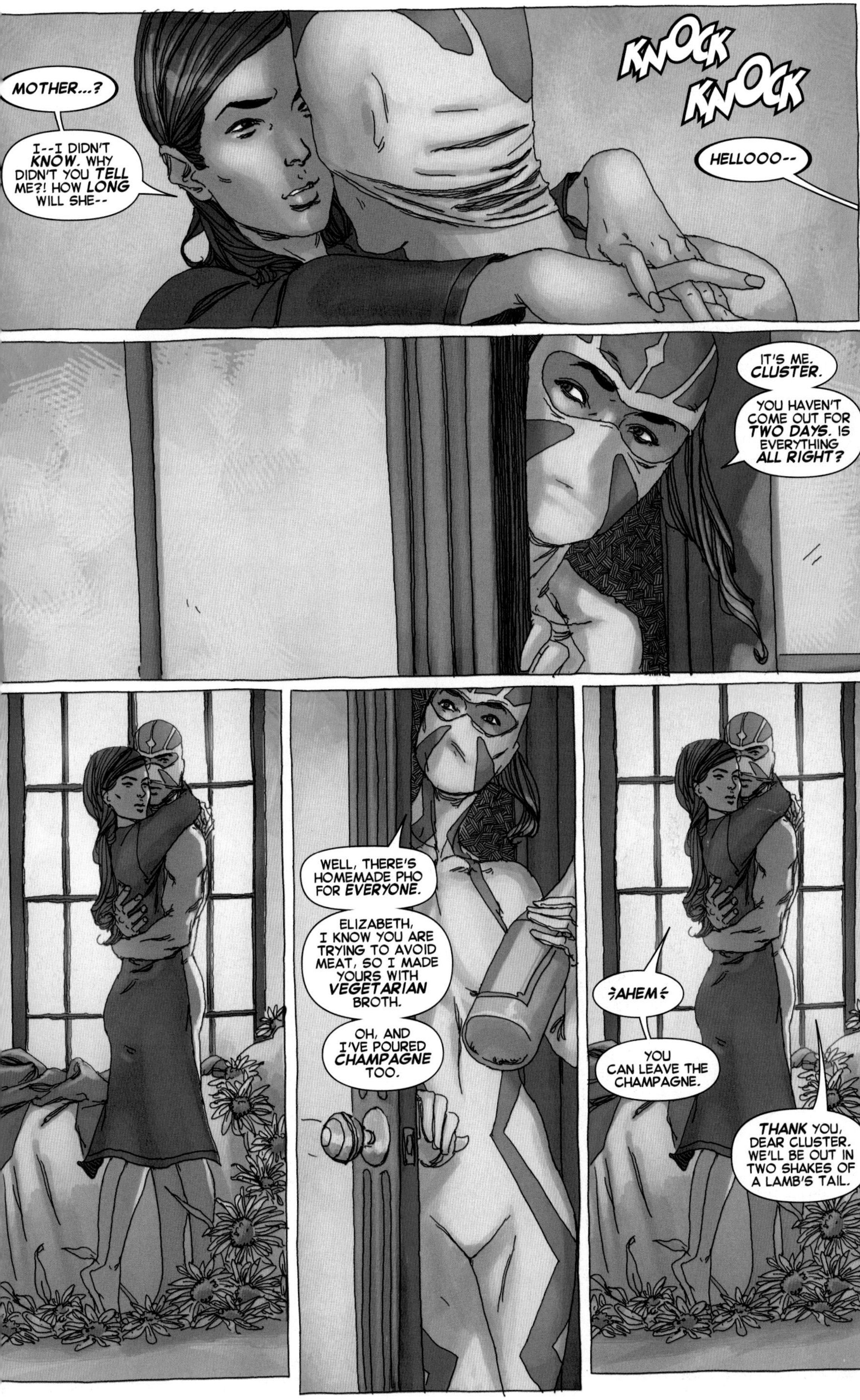
MOTHER...?
I--I DIDN'T KNOW. WHY DIDN'T YOU TELL ME?! HOW LONG WILL SHE--
KNOCK KNOCK
HELLOOO--
IT'S ME. CLUSTER.
YOU HAVEN'T COME OUT FOR TWO DAYS. IS EVERYTHING ALL RIGHT?
WELL, THERE'S HOMEMADE PHO FOR EVERYONE.
ELIZABETH, I KNOW YOU ARE TRYING TO AVOID MEAT, SO I MADE YOURS WITH VEGETARIAN BROTH.
OH, AND I'VE POURED CHAMPAGNE TOO.
AHEM
YOU CAN LEAVE THE CHAMPAGNE.
THANK YOU, DEAR CLUSTER. WE'LL BE OUT IN TWO SHAKES OF A LAMB'S TAIL.

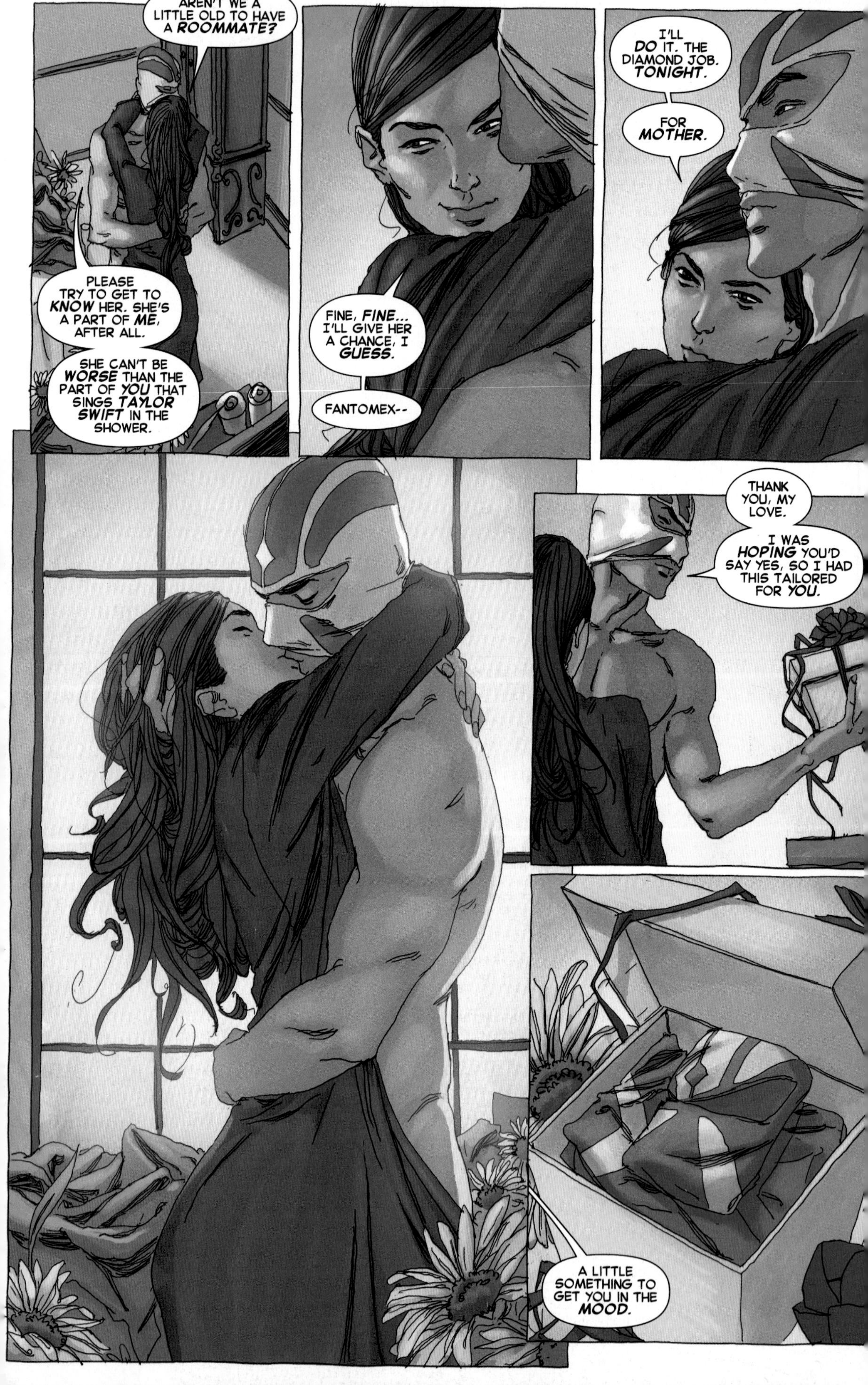

AREN'T WE A LITTLE OLD TO HAVE A ROOMMATE?
PLEASE TRY TO GET TO KNOW HER. SHE'S A PART OF ME, AFTER ALL.
SHE CAN'T BE WORSE THAN THE PART OF YOU THAT SINGS TAYLOR SWIFT IN THE SHOWER.
FINE, FINE... I'LL GIVE HER A CHANCE, I GUESS.
FANTOMEX--
I'LL DO IT. THE DIAMOND JOB. TONIGHT.
FOR MOTHER.
THANK YOU, MY LOVE.
I WAS HOPING YOU'D SAY YES, SO I HAD THIS TAILORED FOR YOU.
A LITTLE SOMETHING TO GET YOU IN THE MOOD.

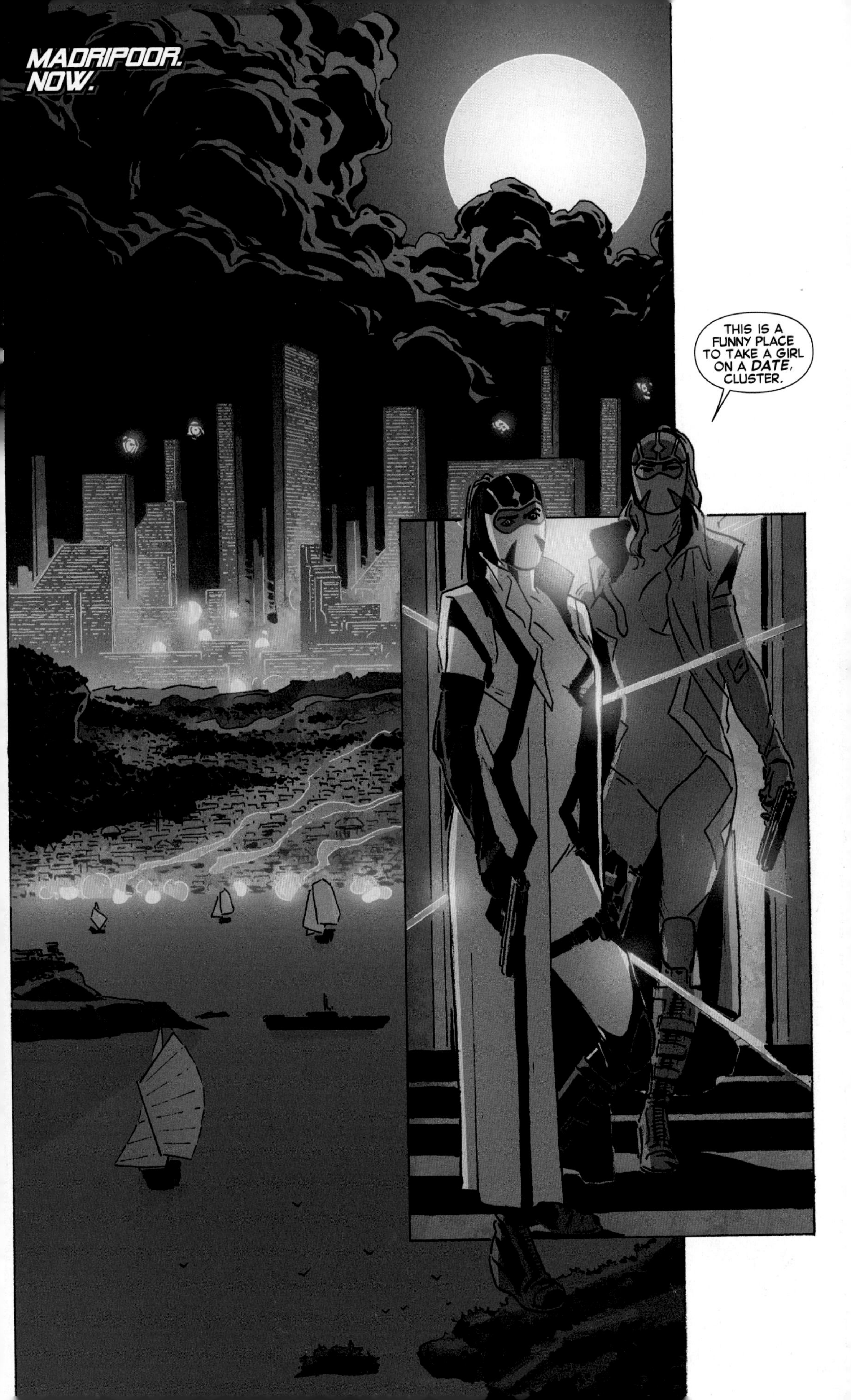
MADRIPOOR.
NOW.
THIS IS A FUNNY PLACE TO TAKE A GIRL ON A DATE, CLUSTER.

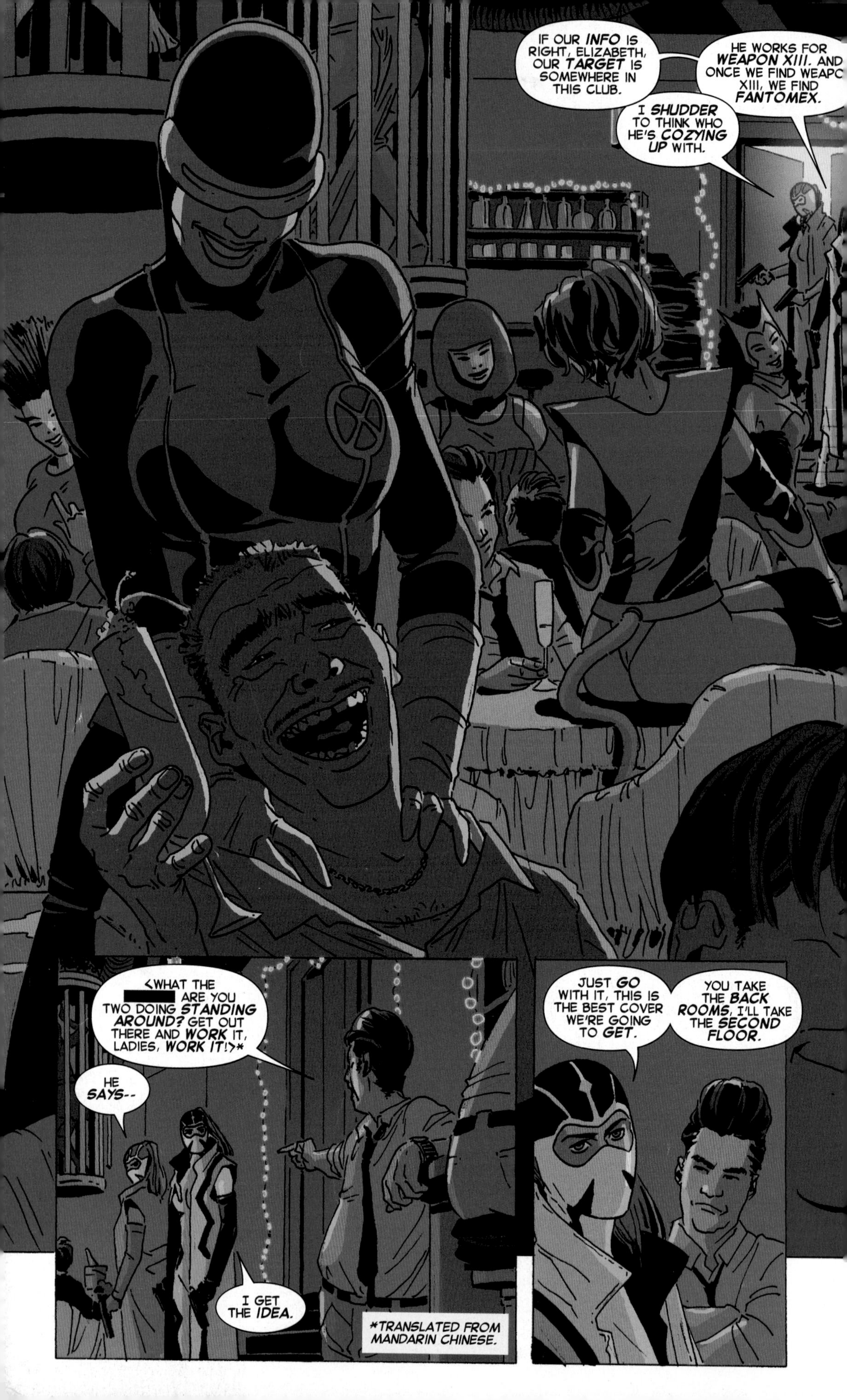
IF OUR INFO IS RIGHT, ELIZABETH, OUR TARGET IS SOMEWHERE IN THIS CLUB.
HE WORKS FOR WEAPON XIII. AND ONCE WE FIND WEAPO XIII, WE FIND FANTOMEX.
I SHUDDER TO THINK WHO HE'S COZYING UP WITH.
<WHAT THE [redacted] ARE YOU TWO DOING STANDING AROUND? GET OUT THERE AND WORK IT, LADIES, WORK IT!>*
HE SAYS--
I GET THE IDEA.
*TRANSLATED FROM MANDARIN CHINESE.
JUST GO WITH IT, THIS IS THE BEST COVER WE'RE GOING TO GET.
YOU TAKE THE BACK ROOMS, I'LL TAKE THE SECOND FLOOR.

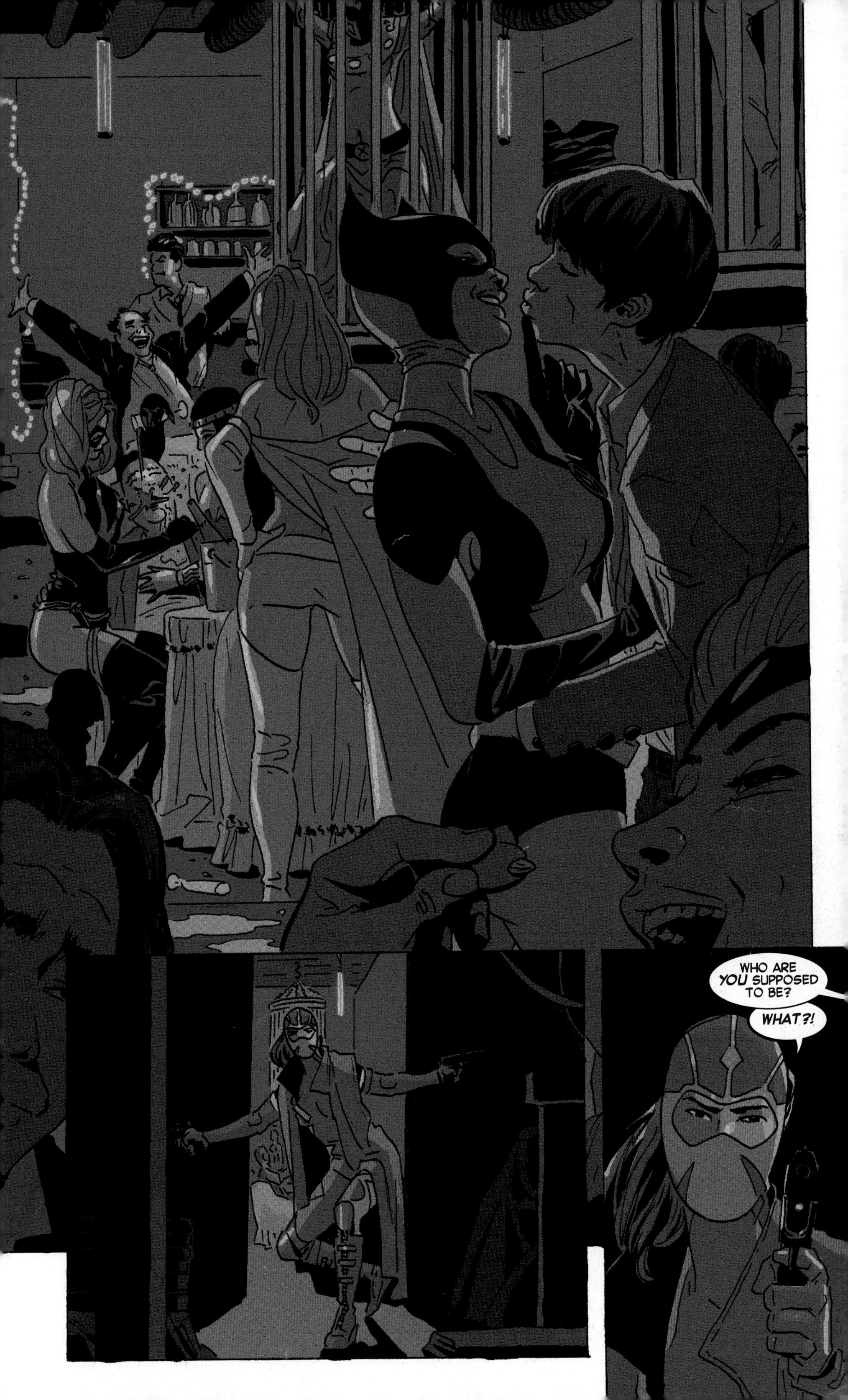
WHO ARE YOU SUPPOSED TO BE?
WHAT?!

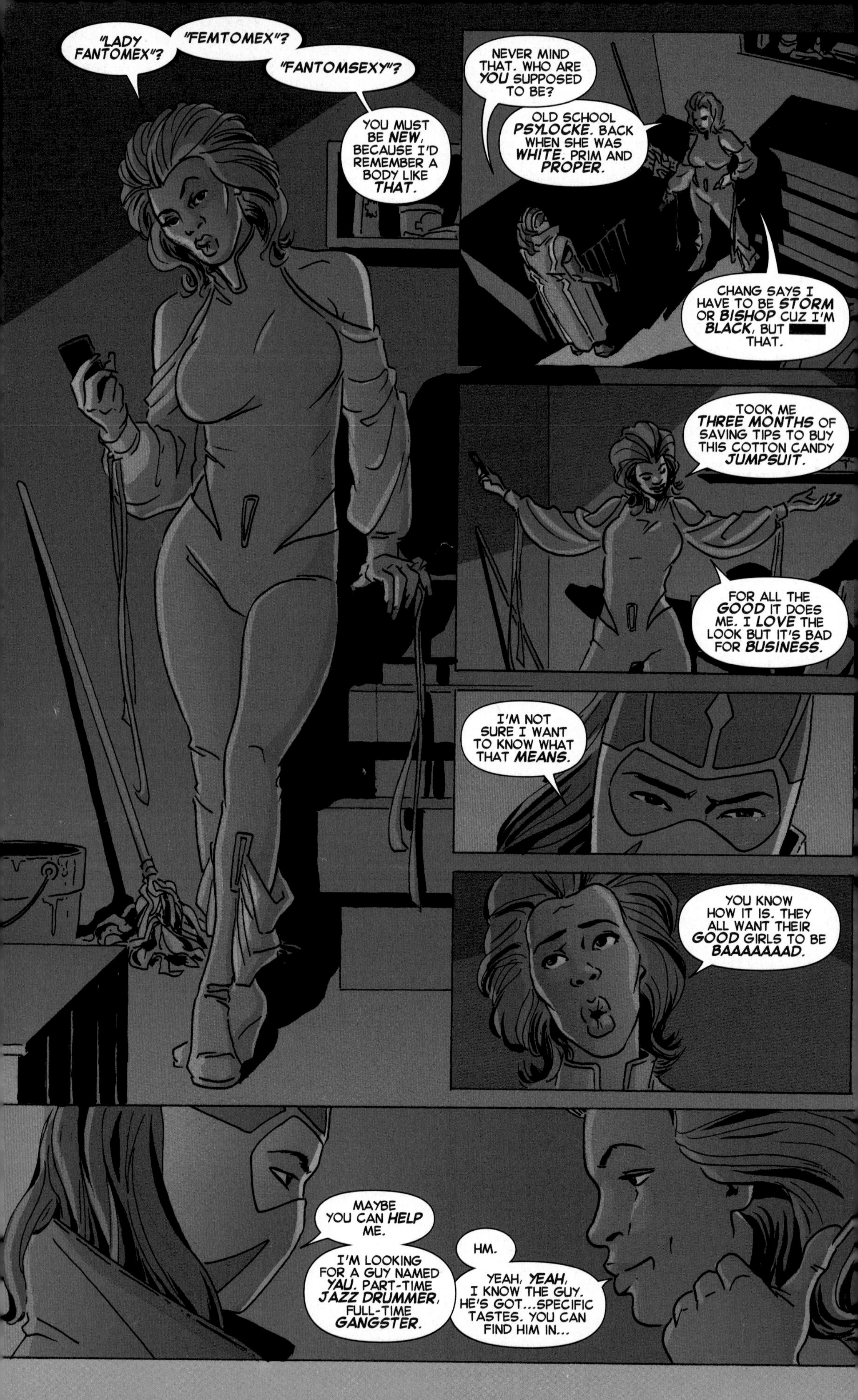
"LADY FANTOMEX"?
"FEMTOMEX"?
"FANTOMSEXY"?
YOU MUST BE NEW, BECAUSE I'D REMEMBER A BODY LIKE THAT.
NEVER MIND THAT. WHO ARE YOU SUPPOSED TO BE?
OLD SCHOOL PSYLOCKE. BACK WHEN SHE WAS WHITE. PRIM AND PROPER.
CHANG SAYS I HAVE TO BE STORM OR BISHOP CUZ I'M BLACK, BUT [redacted] THAT.
TOOK ME THREE MONTHS OF SAVING TIPS TO BUY THIS COTTON CANDY JUMPSUIT.
FOR ALL THE GOOD IT DOES ME. I LOVE THE LOOK BUT IT'S BAD FOR BUSINESS.
I'M NOT SURE I WANT TO KNOW WHAT THAT MEANS.
YOU KNOW HOW IT IS. THEY ALL WANT THEIR GOOD GIRLS TO BE BAAAAAAAD.
MAYBE YOU CAN HELP ME.
I'M LOOKING FOR A GUY NAMED YAU. PART-TIME JAZZ DRUMMER, FULL-TIME GANGSTER.
HM.
YEAH, YEAH, I KNOW THE GUY. HE'S GOT...SPECIFIC TASTES. YOU CAN FIND HIM IN...

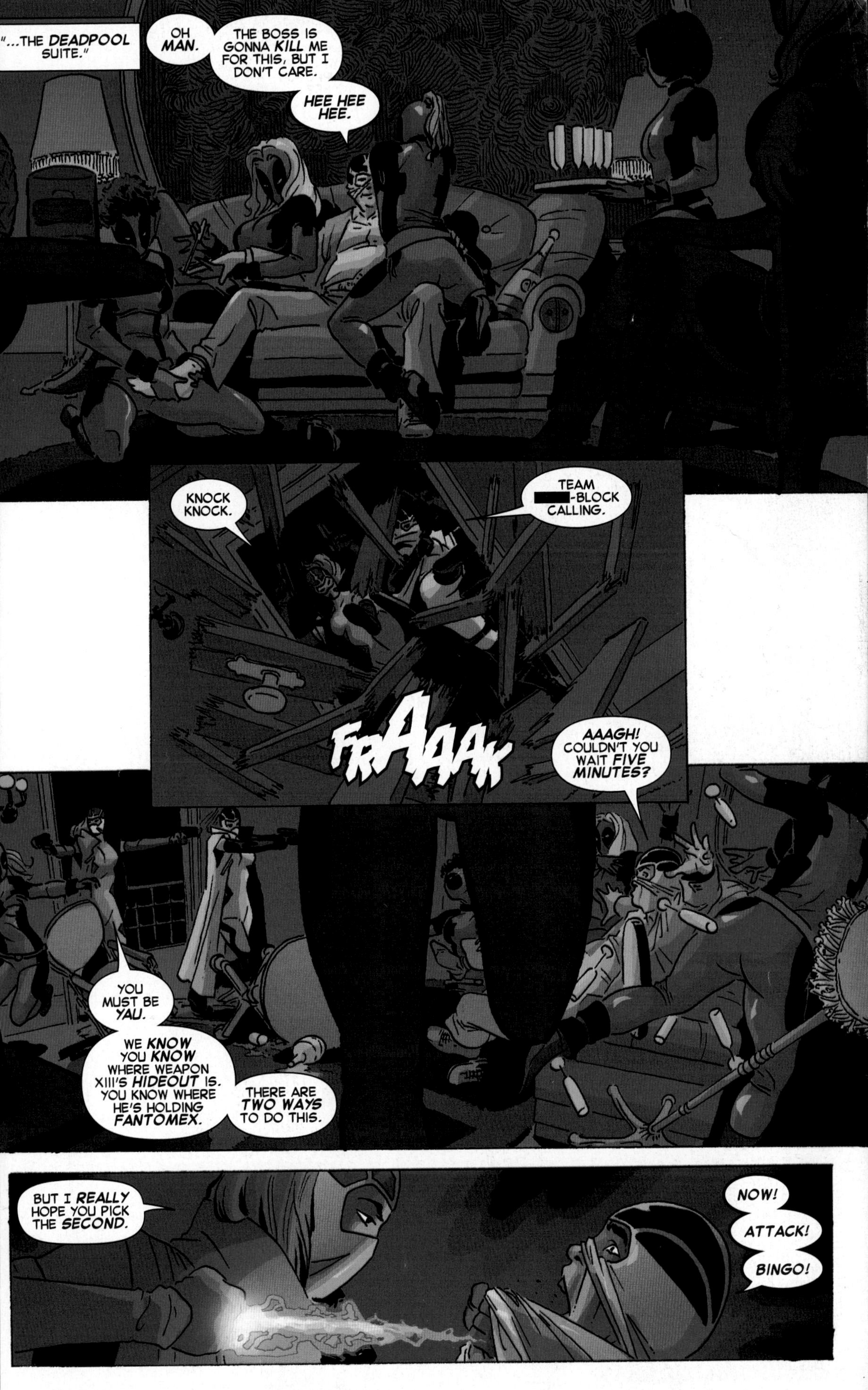
"...THE DEADPOOL SUITE."
OH MAN.
THE BOSS IS GONNA KILL ME FOR THIS, BUT I DON'T CARE.
HEE HEE HEE.
KNOCK KNOCK.
TEAM [redacted]-BLOCK CALLING.
FRAAAK
AAAGH! COULDN'T YOU WAIT FIVE MINUTES?
YOU MUST BE YAU.
WE KNOW YOU KNOW WHERE WEAPON XIII'S HIDEOUT IS. YOU KNOW WHERE HE'S HOLDING FANTOMEX.
THERE ARE TWO WAYS TO DO THIS.
BUT I REALLY HOPE YOU PICK THE SECOND.
NOW!
ATTACK!
BINGO!

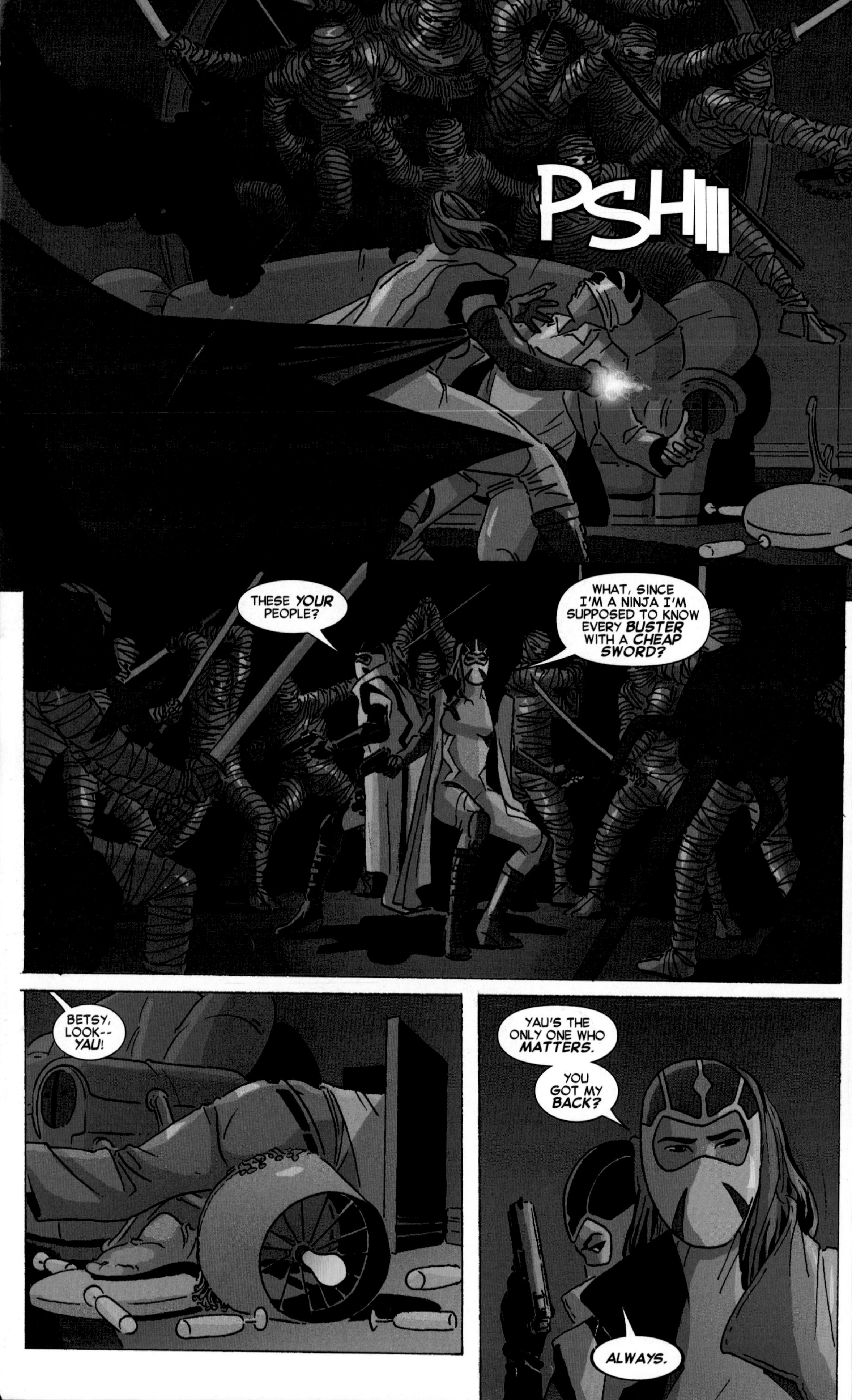
PSHIIII
THESE YOUR PEOPLE?
WHAT, SINCE I'M A NINJA I'M SUPPOSED TO KNOW EVERY BUSTER WITH A CHEAP SWORD?
BETSY, LOOK-- YAU!
YAU'S THE ONLY ONE WHO MATTERS.
YOU GOT MY BACK?
ALWAYS.

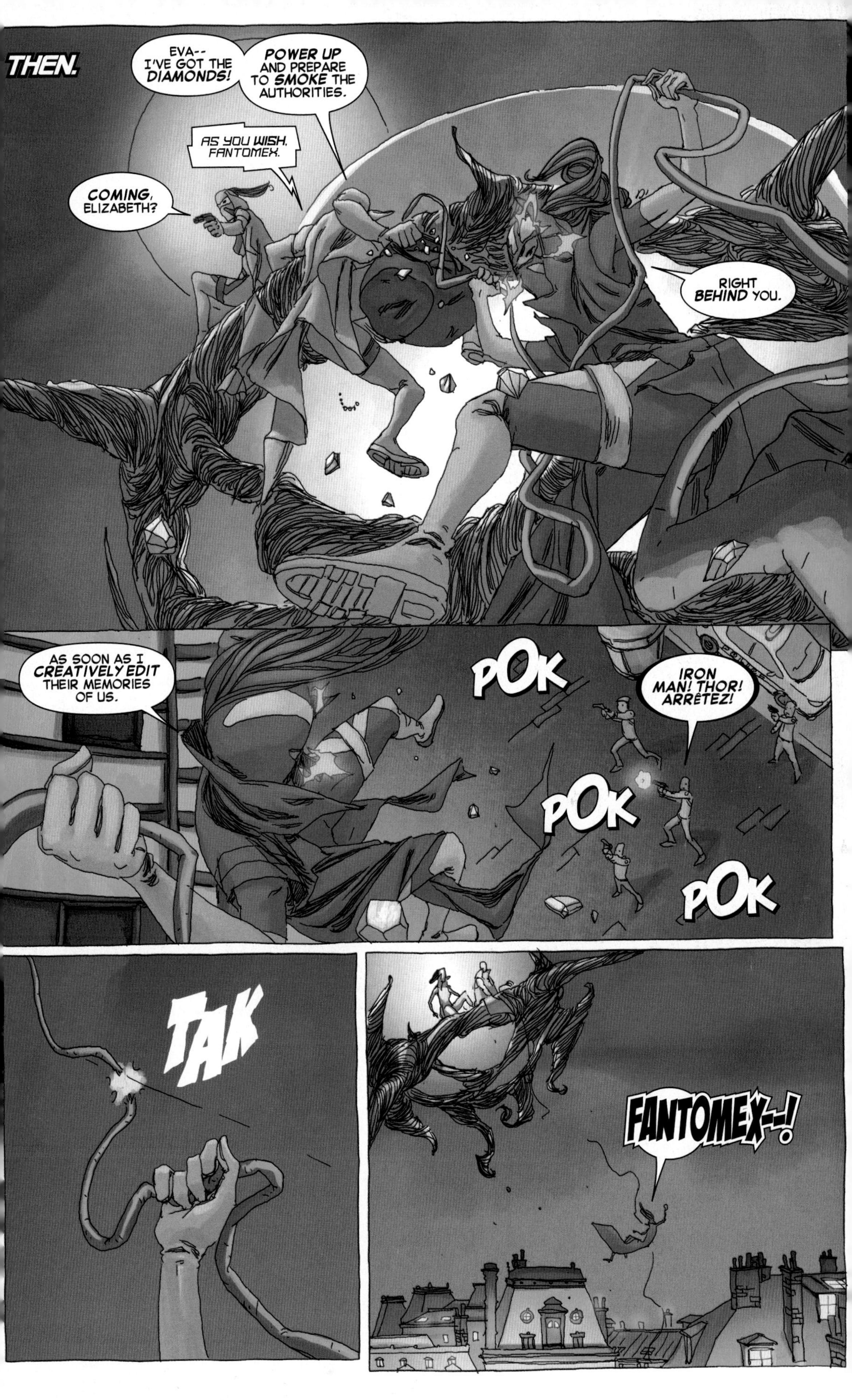
THEN.
EVA-- I'VE GOT THE DIAMONDS!
POWER UP AND PREPARE TO SMOKE THE AUTHORITIES.
AS YOU WISH, FANTOMEX.
COMING, ELIZABETH?
RIGHT BEHIND YOU.
AS SOON AS I CREATIVELY EDIT THEIR MEMORIES OF US.
POK
IRON MAN! THOR! ARRÊTEZ!
POK
POK
TAK
FANTOMEX--!

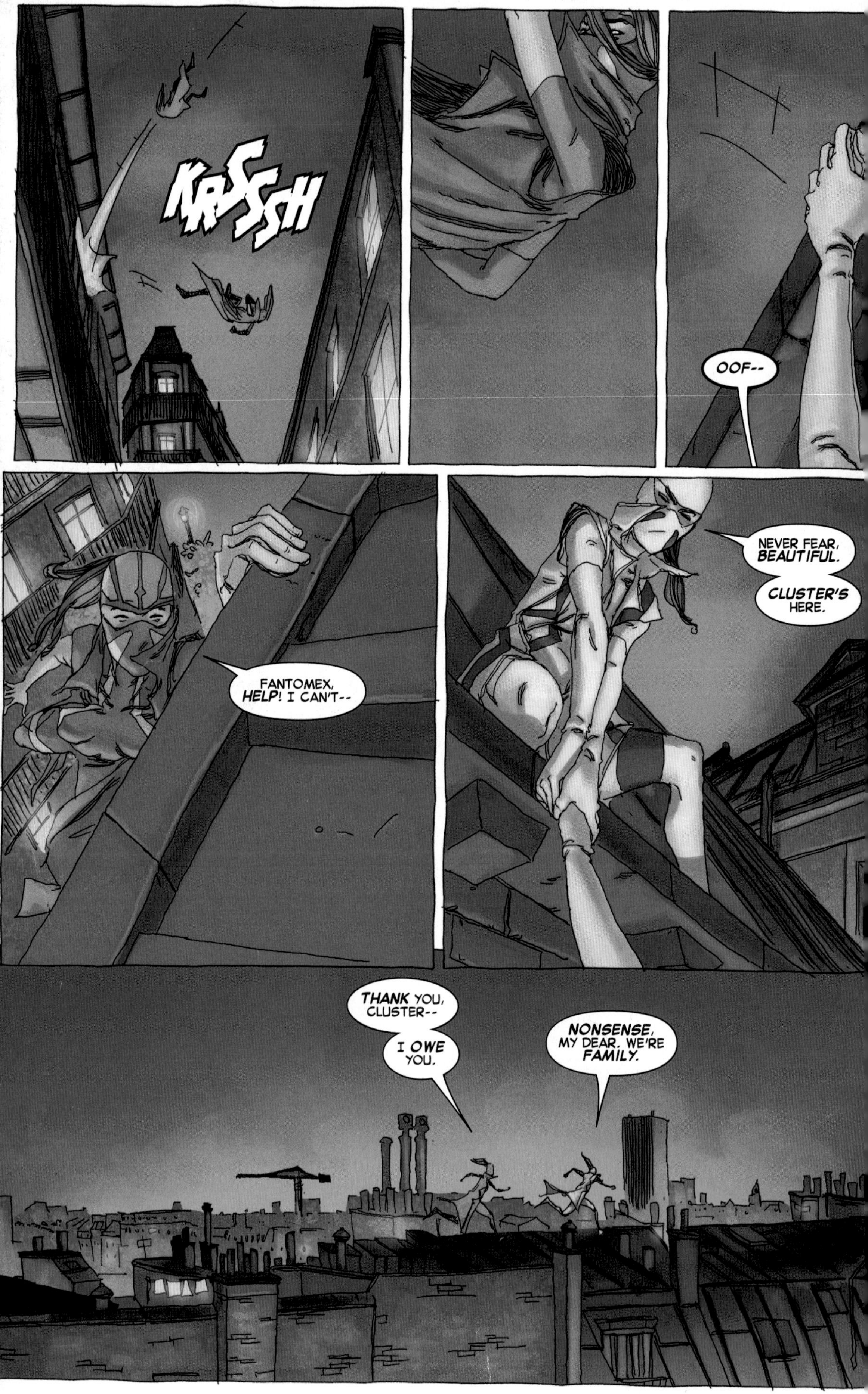
KRSSSH
OOF--
FANTOMEX, HELP! I CAN'T--
NEVER FEAR, BEAUTIFUL.
CLUSTER'S HERE.
THANK YOU, CLUSTER--
I OWE YOU.
NONSENSE, MY DEAR. WE'RE FAMILY.

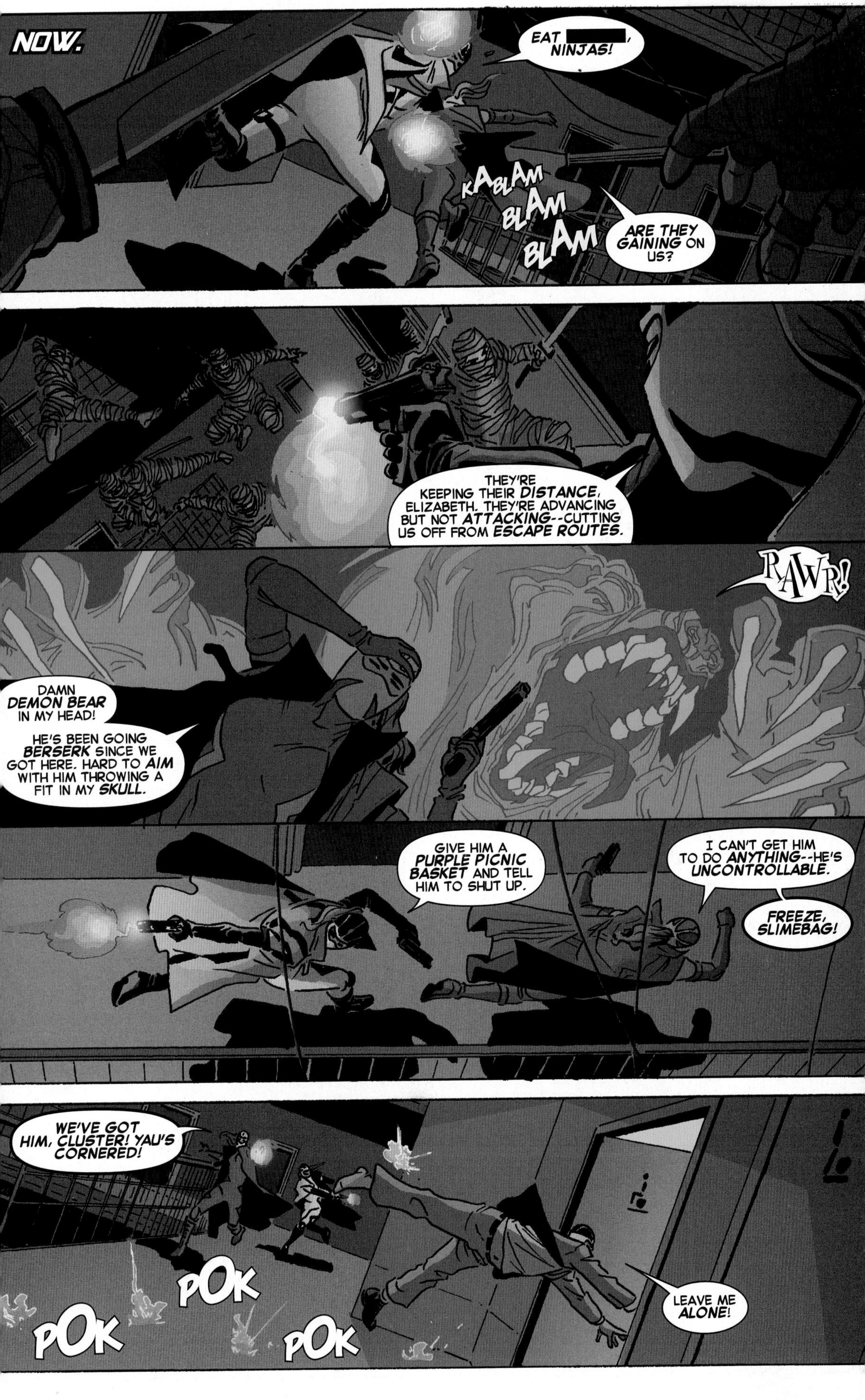
NOW.
EAT [redacted], NINJAS!
KABLAM
BLAM
BLAM
ARE THEY GAINING ON US?
THEY'RE KEEPING THEIR DISTANCE, ELIZABETH. THEY'RE ADVANCING BUT NOT ATTACKING--CUTTING US OFF FROM ESCAPE ROUTES.
RAWR!
DAMN DEMON BEAR IN MY HEAD!
HE'S BEEN GOING BERSERK SINCE WE GOT HERE. HARD TO AIM WITH HIM THROWING A FIT IN MY SKULL.
GIVE HIM A PURPLE PICNIC BASKET AND TELL HIM TO SHUT UP.
I CAN'T GET HIM TO DO ANYTHING--HE'S UNCONTROLLABLE.
FREEZE, SLIMEBAG!
WE'VE GOT HIM, CLUSTER! YAU'S CORNERED!
POK
POK
POK
LEAVE ME ALONE!

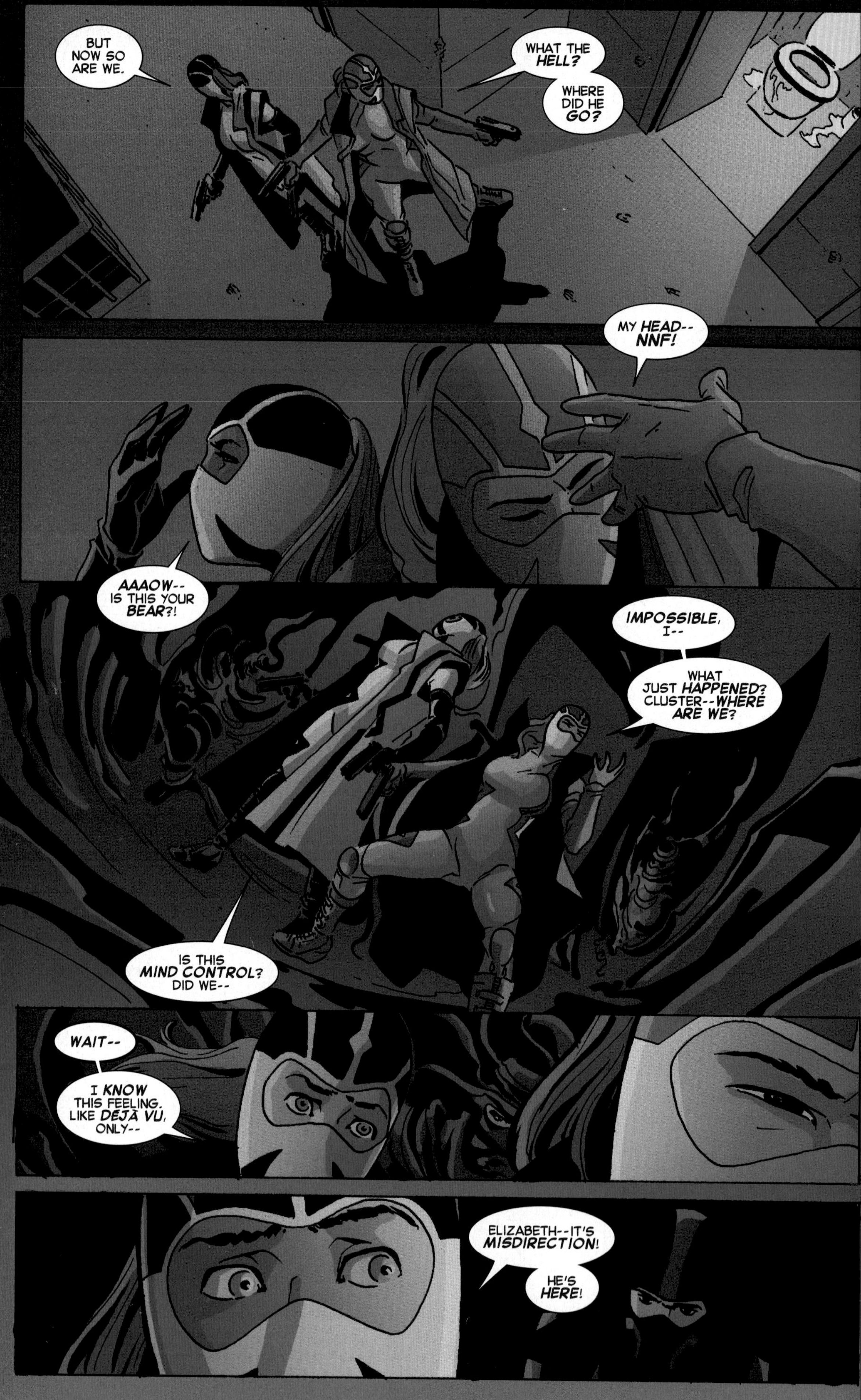

BUT NOW SO ARE WE.
WHAT THE HELL?
WHERE DID HE GO?
MY HEAD-- NNF!
AAAOW-- IS THIS YOUR BEAR?!
IMPOSSIBLE. I--
WHAT JUST HAPPENED? CLUSTER--WHERE ARE WE?
IS THIS MIND CONTROL? DID WE--
WAIT--
I KNOW THIS FEELING. LIKE DÉJÀ VU, ONLY--
ELIZABETH--IT'S MISDIRECTION!
HE'S HERE!

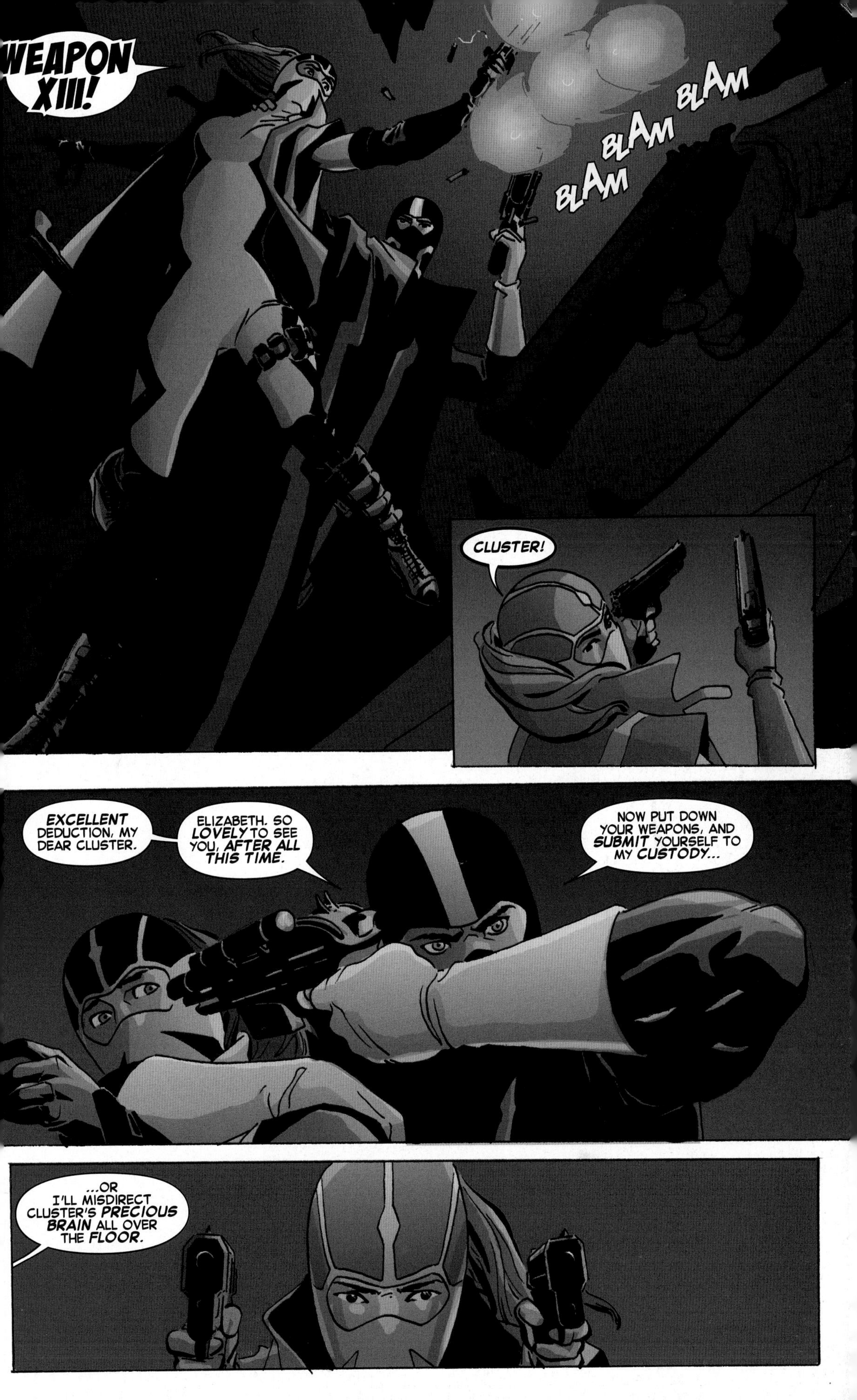
WEAPON XIII!
BLAM BLAM BLAM BLAM
CLUSTER!
EXCELLENT DEDUCTION, MY DEAR CLUSTER.
ELIZABETH. SO LOVELY TO SEE YOU, AFTER ALL THIS TIME.
NOW PUT DOWN YOUR WEAPONS, AND SUBMIT YOURSELF TO MY CUSTODY...
...OR I'LL MISDIRECT CLUSTER'S PRECIOUS BRAIN ALL OVER THE FLOOR.

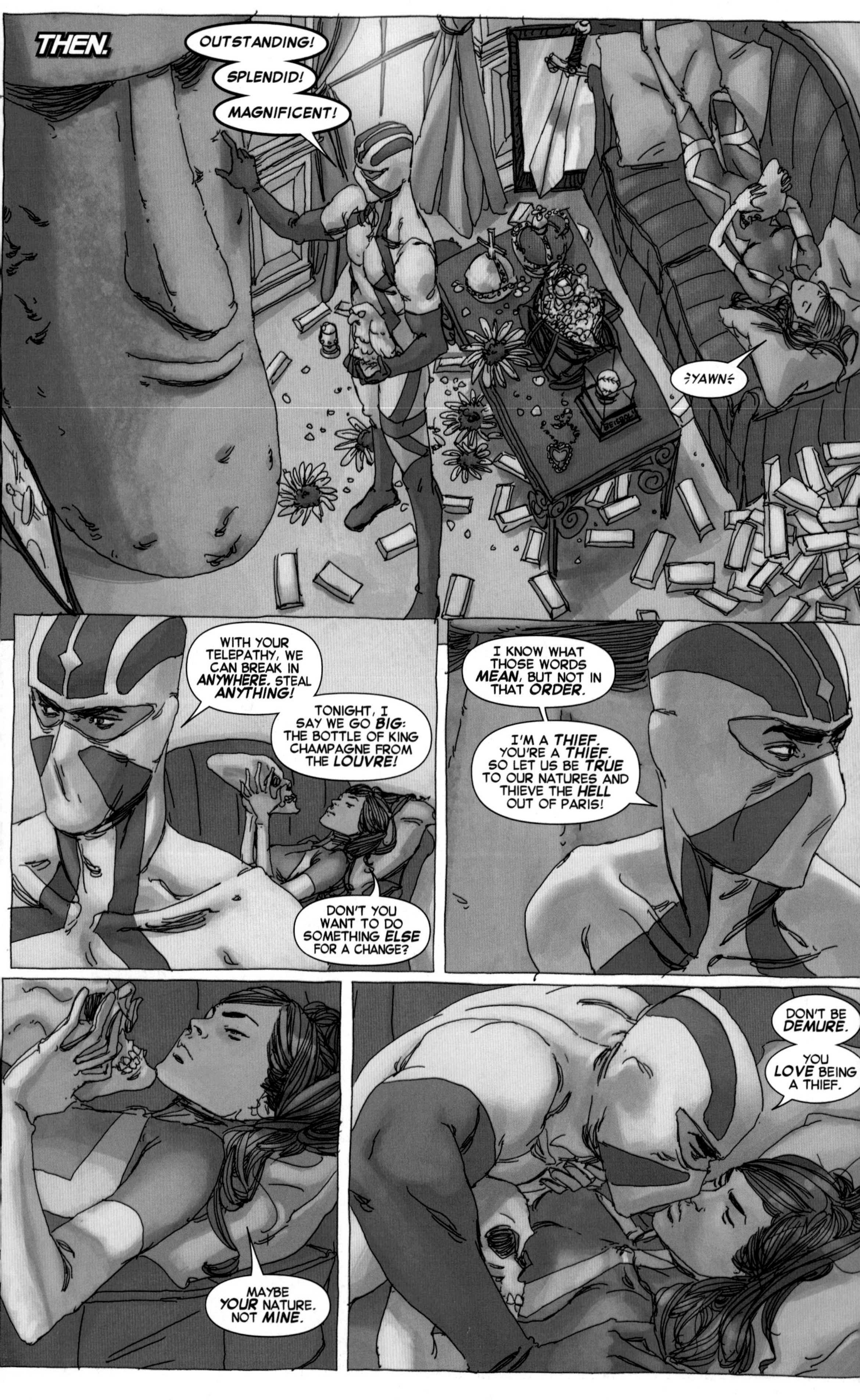
THEN.
OUTSTANDING!
SPLENDID!
MAGNIFICENT!
≶YAWN≶
WITH YOUR TELEPATHY, WE CAN BREAK IN ANYWHERE. STEAL ANYTHING!
TONIGHT, I SAY WE GO BIG: THE BOTTLE OF KING CHAMPAGNE FROM THE LOUVRE!
DON'T YOU WANT TO DO SOMETHING ELSE FOR A CHANGE?
I KNOW WHAT THOSE WORDS MEAN, BUT NOT IN THAT ORDER.
I'M A THIEF. YOU'RE A THIEF. SO LET US BE TRUE TO OUR NATURES AND THIEVE THE HELL OUT OF PARIS!
MAYBE YOUR NATURE. NOT MINE.
DON'T BE DEMURE.
YOU LOVE BEING A THIEF.

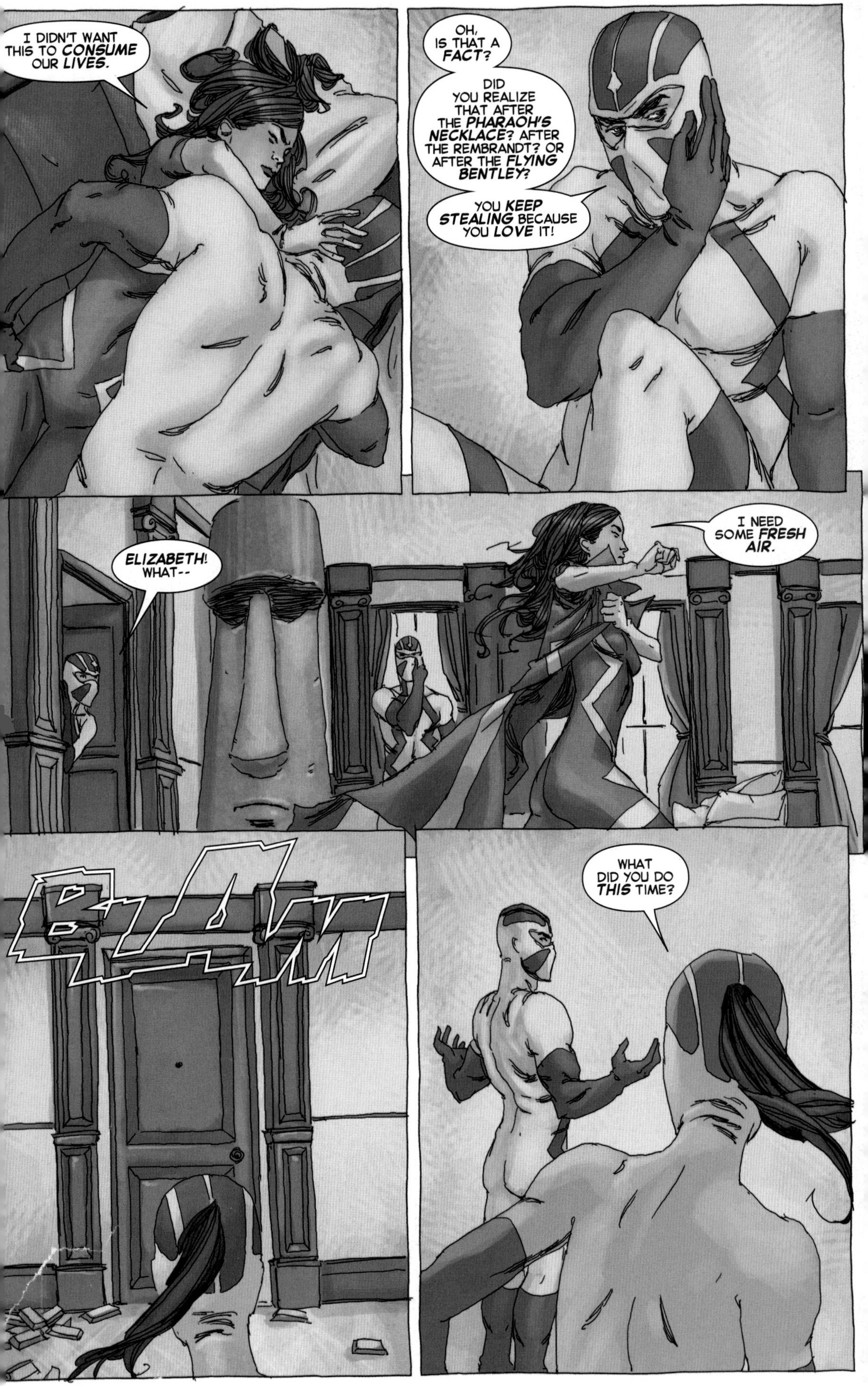
I DIDN'T WANT THIS TO CONSUME OUR LIVES.
OH, IS THAT A FACT?
DID YOU REALIZE THAT AFTER THE PHARAOH'S NECKLACE? AFTER THE REMBRANDT? OR AFTER THE FLYING BENTLEY?
YOU KEEP STEALING BECAUSE YOU LOVE IT!
ELIZABETH! WHAT--
I NEED SOME FRESH AIR.
BLAM
WHAT DID YOU DO THIS TIME?

ELIZABETH!

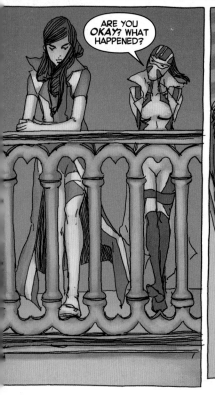

ARE YOU *OKAY*? WHAT HAPPENED?

WHY DOES HE HAVE TO BE SUCH A *JERK* ALL THE TIME?

SHE ISN'T SICK AT *ALL*, IS SHE? HIS *MOTHER.*

I MEAN... *YOUR* MOTHER. *WHATEVER.*

PLEASE UNDERSTAND... THIS HAS BEEN AN *ADJUSTMENT* FOR ALL OF US.

ME, FANTOMEX, WEAPON XIII...WE ALL USED TO BE *ONE* PERSON. WE HAD *BALANCE.* WHEN THEY *DIVIDED* US, WELL...I GUESS FANTOMEX GOT ALL THE *SCOUNDREL* PARTS.

BUT *I'VE* GOT...

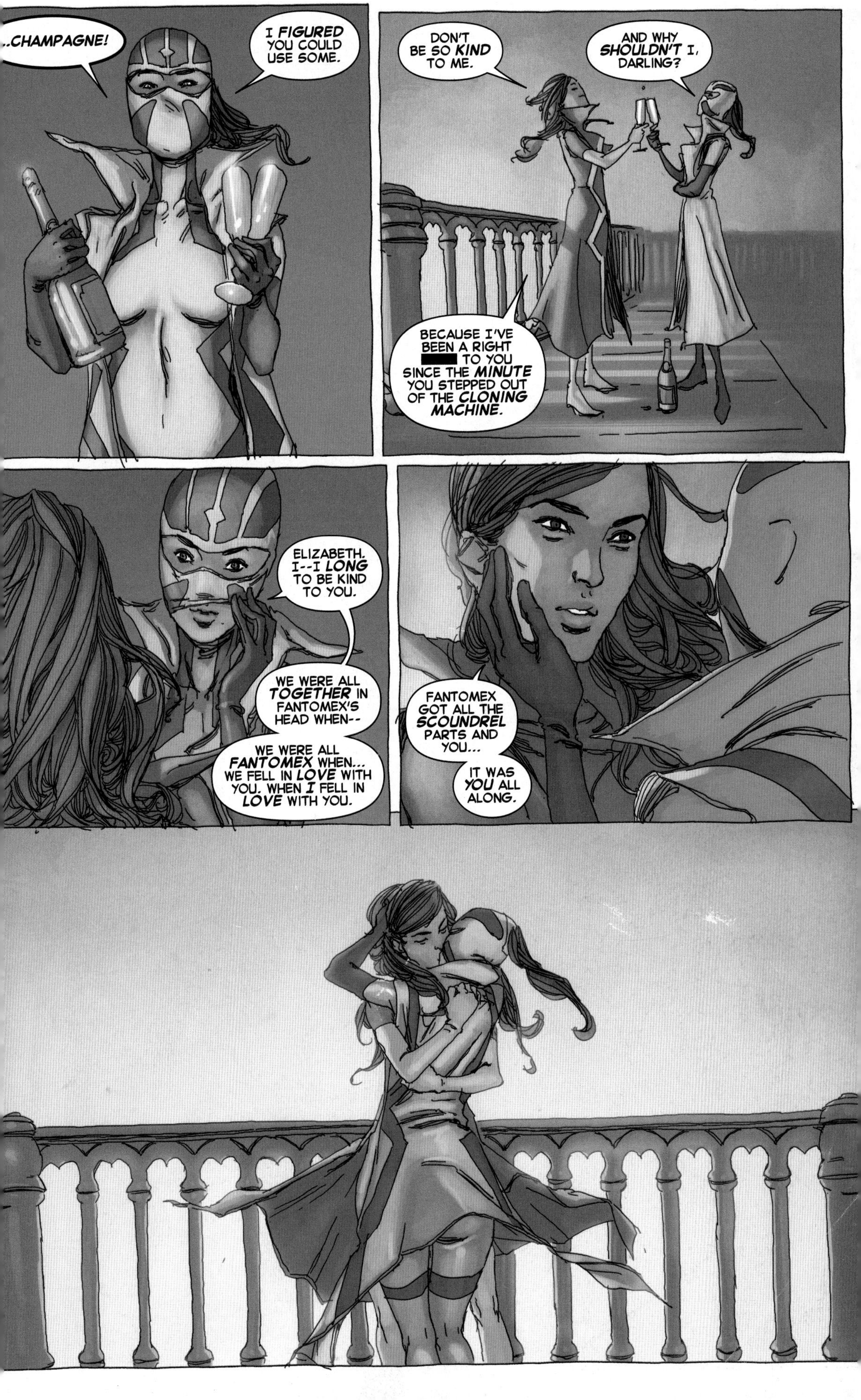
..CHAMPAGNE!
I FIGURED YOU COULD USE SOME.
DON'T BE SO KIND TO ME.
AND WHY SHOULDN'T I, DARLING?
BECAUSE I'VE BEEN A RIGHT [redacted] TO YOU SINCE THE MINUTE YOU STEPPED OUT OF THE CLONING MACHINE.
ELIZABETH. I--I LONG TO BE KIND TO YOU.
WE WERE ALL TOGETHER IN FANTOMEX'S HEAD WHEN--
WE WERE ALL FANTOMEX WHEN... WE FELL IN LOVE WITH YOU. WHEN I FELL IN LOVE WITH YOU.
FANTOMEX GOT ALL THE SCOUNDREL PARTS AND YOU...
IT WAS YOU ALL ALONG.

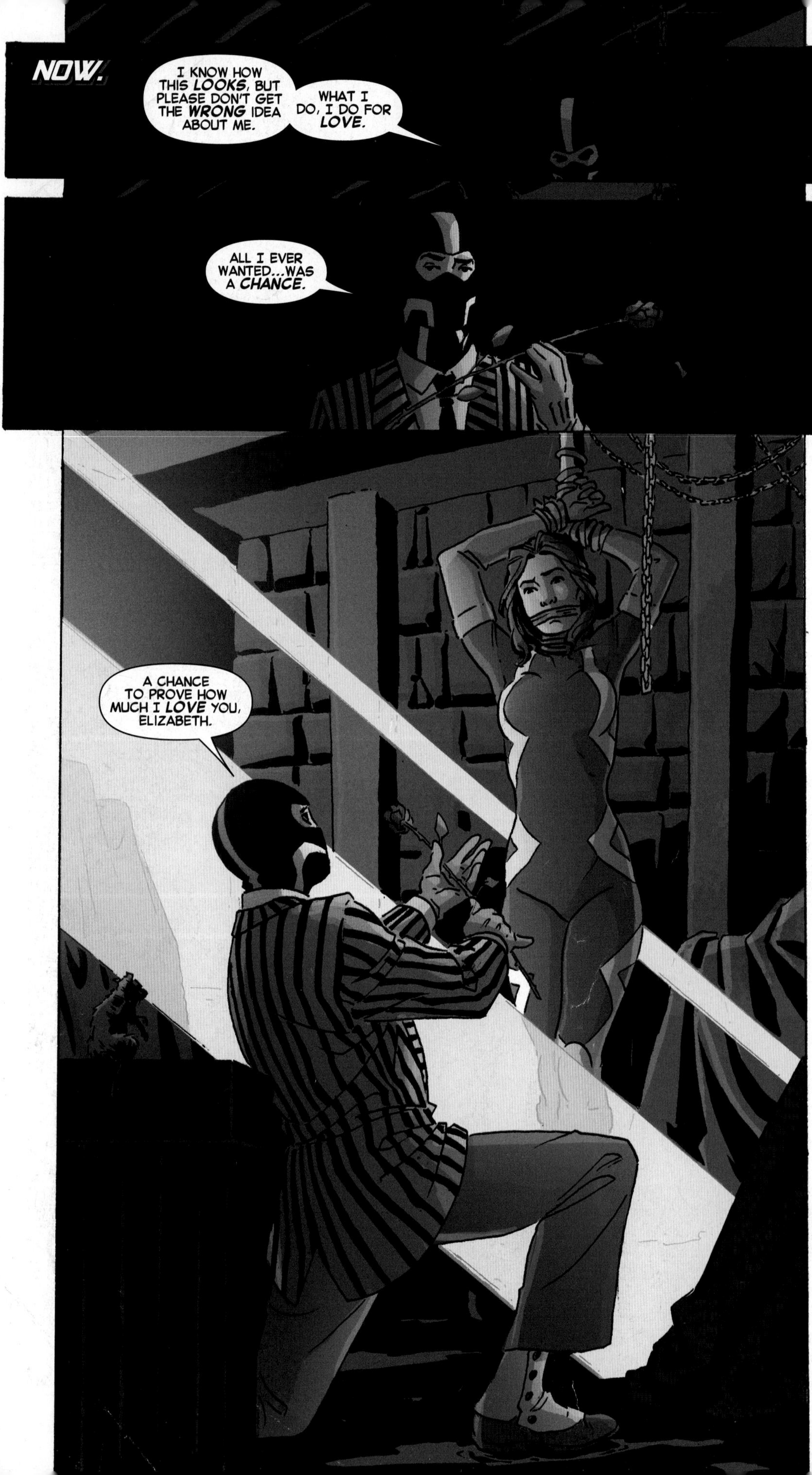

NOW.
I KNOW HOW THIS LOOKS, BUT PLEASE DON'T GET THE WRONG IDEA ABOUT ME.
WHAT I DO, I DO FOR LOVE.
ALL I EVER WANTED...WAS A CHANCE.
A CHANCE TO PROVE HOW MUCH I LOVE YOU, ELIZABETH.

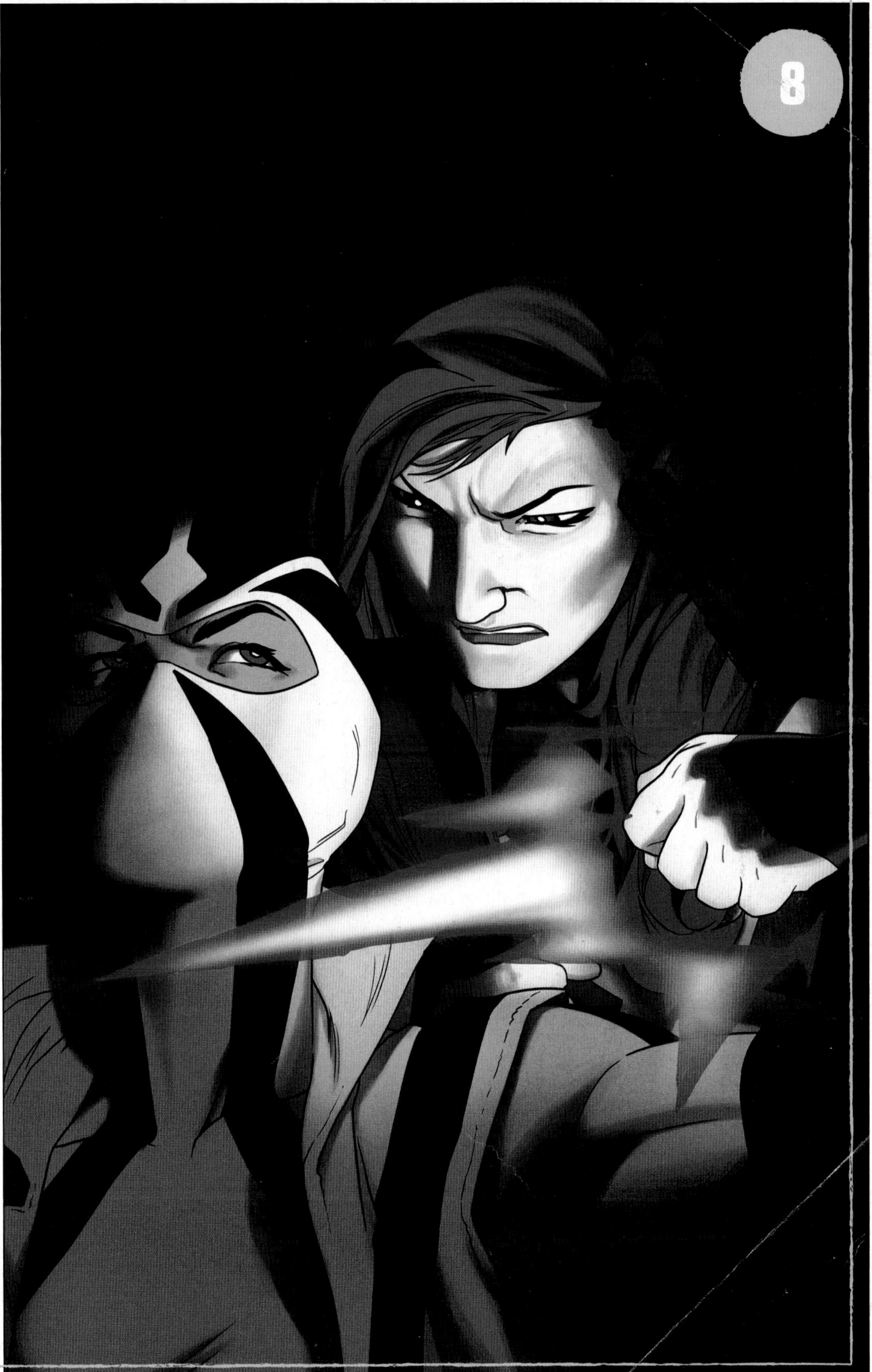
8

NEVER GOING BACK AGAIN

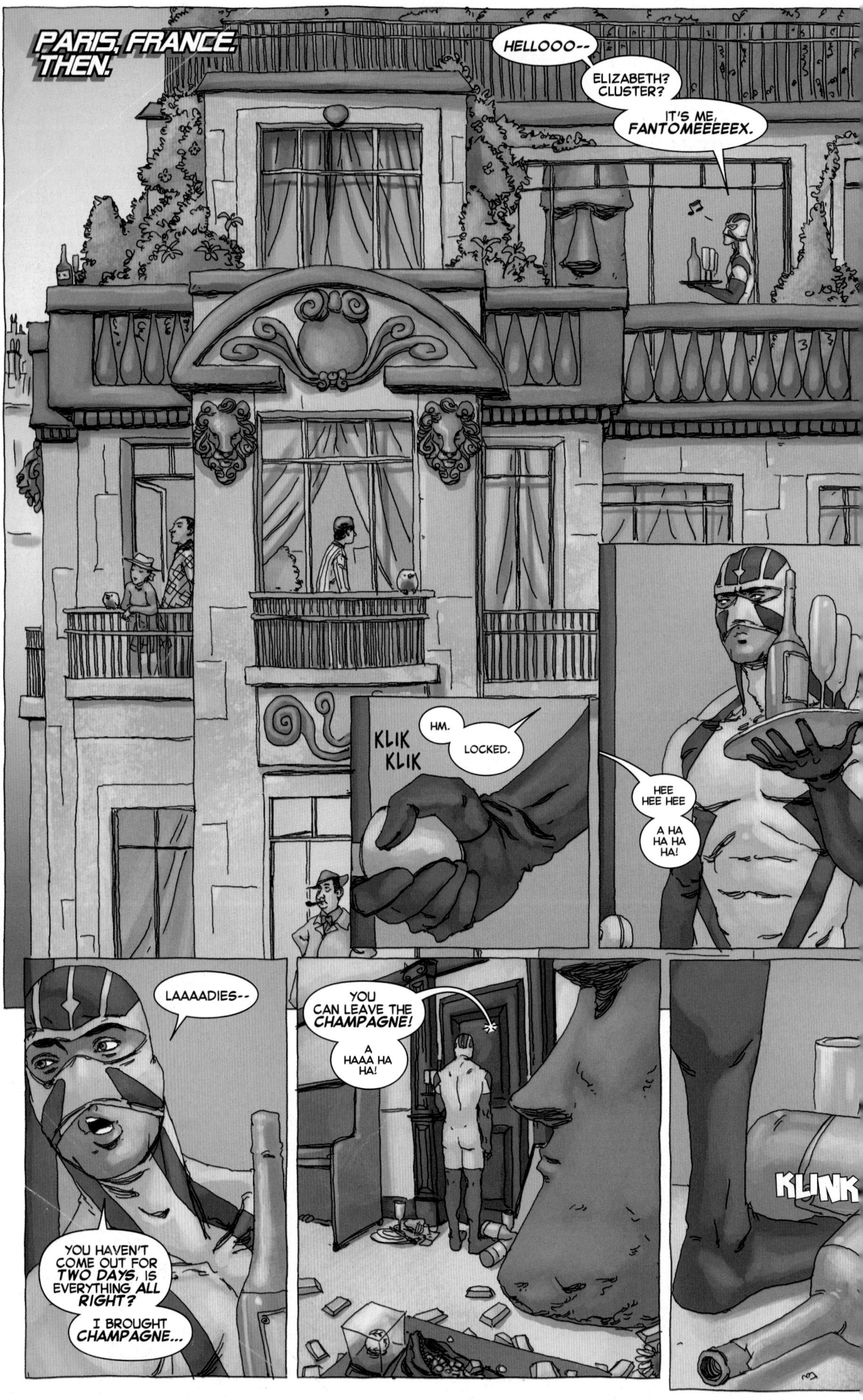
PARIS, FRANCE. THEN.
HELLOOO--
ELIZABETH? CLUSTER?
IT'S ME, FANTOMEEEEEX.
KLIK KLIK
HM.
LOCKED.
HEE HEE HEE
A HA HA HA HA!
LAAAADIES--
YOU HAVEN'T COME OUT FOR TWO DAYS, IS EVERYTHING ALL RIGHT?
I BROUGHT CHAMPAGNE...
YOU CAN LEAVE THE CHAMPAGNE!
A HAAA HA HA!
KLINK

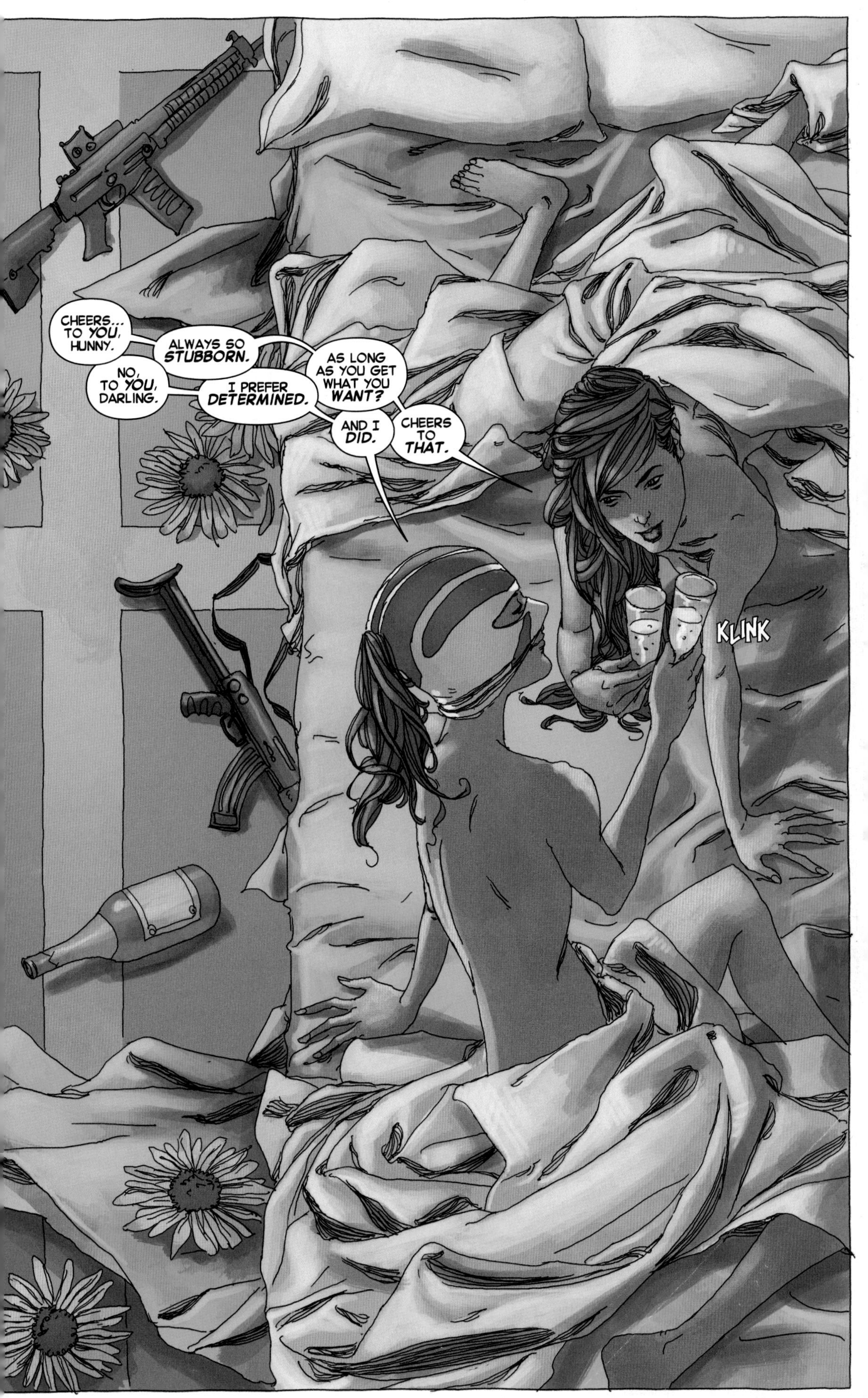

CHEERS... TO YOU, HUNNY.
ALWAYS SO STUBBORN.
NO, TO YOU, DARLING.
I PREFER DETERMINED.
AS LONG AS YOU GET WHAT YOU WANT?
AND I DID.
CHEERS TO THAT.
KLINK

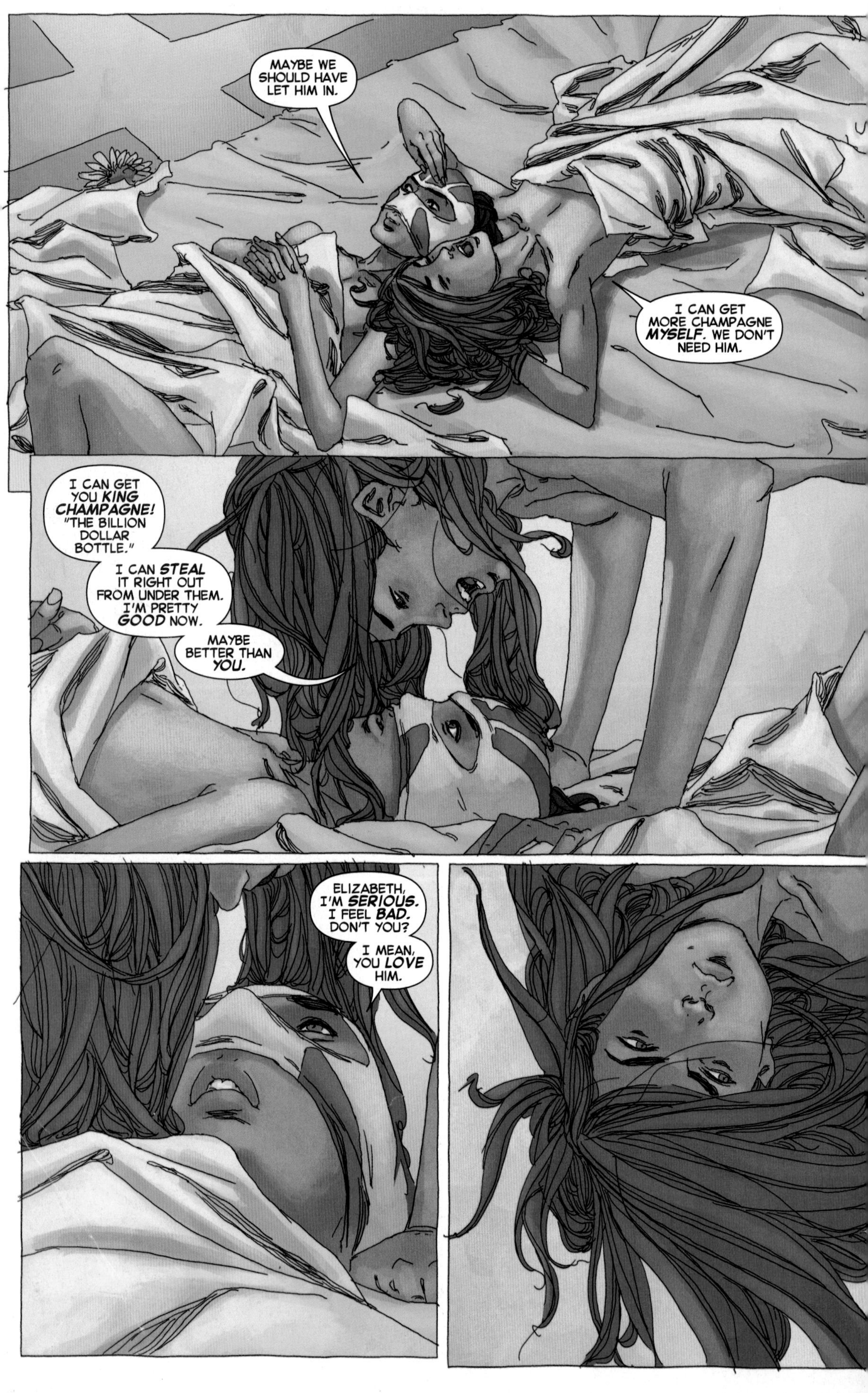
MAYBE WE SHOULD HAVE LET HIM IN.
I CAN GET MORE CHAMPAGNE MYSELF. WE DON'T NEED HIM.
I CAN GET YOU KING CHAMPAGNE! "THE BILLION DOLLAR BOTTLE."
I CAN STEAL IT RIGHT OUT FROM UNDER THEM. I'M PRETTY GOOD NOW.
MAYBE BETTER THAN YOU.
ELIZABETH, I'M SERIOUS. I FEEL BAD. DON'T YOU?
I MEAN, YOU LOVE HIM.

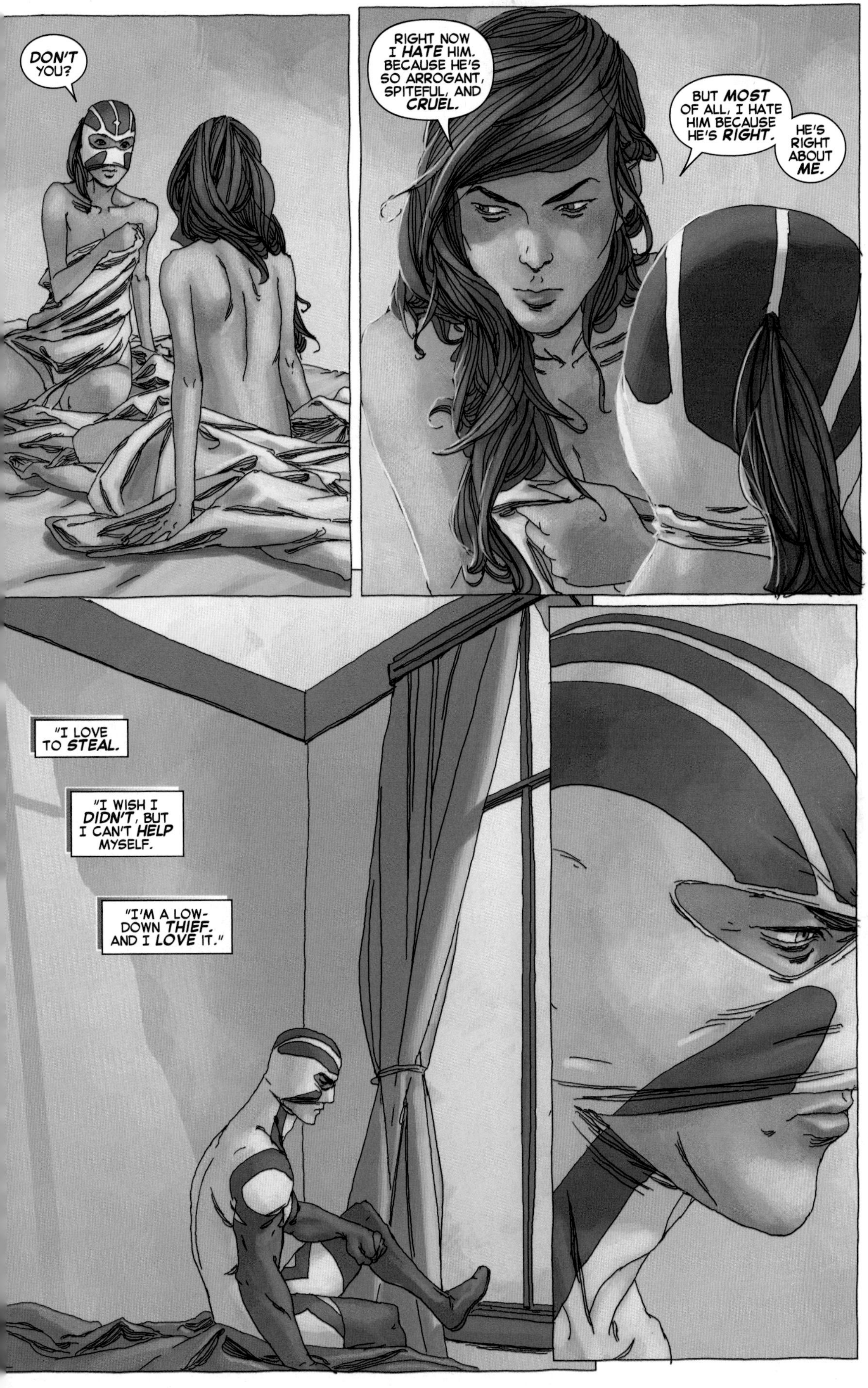
DON'T YOU?
RIGHT NOW I HATE HIM. BECAUSE HE'S SO ARROGANT, SPITEFUL, AND CRUEL.
BUT MOST OF ALL, I HATE HIM BECAUSE HE'S RIGHT.
HE'S RIGHT ABOUT ME.
"I LOVE TO STEAL.
"I WISH I DIDN'T, BUT I CAN'T HELP MYSELF.
"I'M A LOW-DOWN THIEF. AND I LOVE IT."

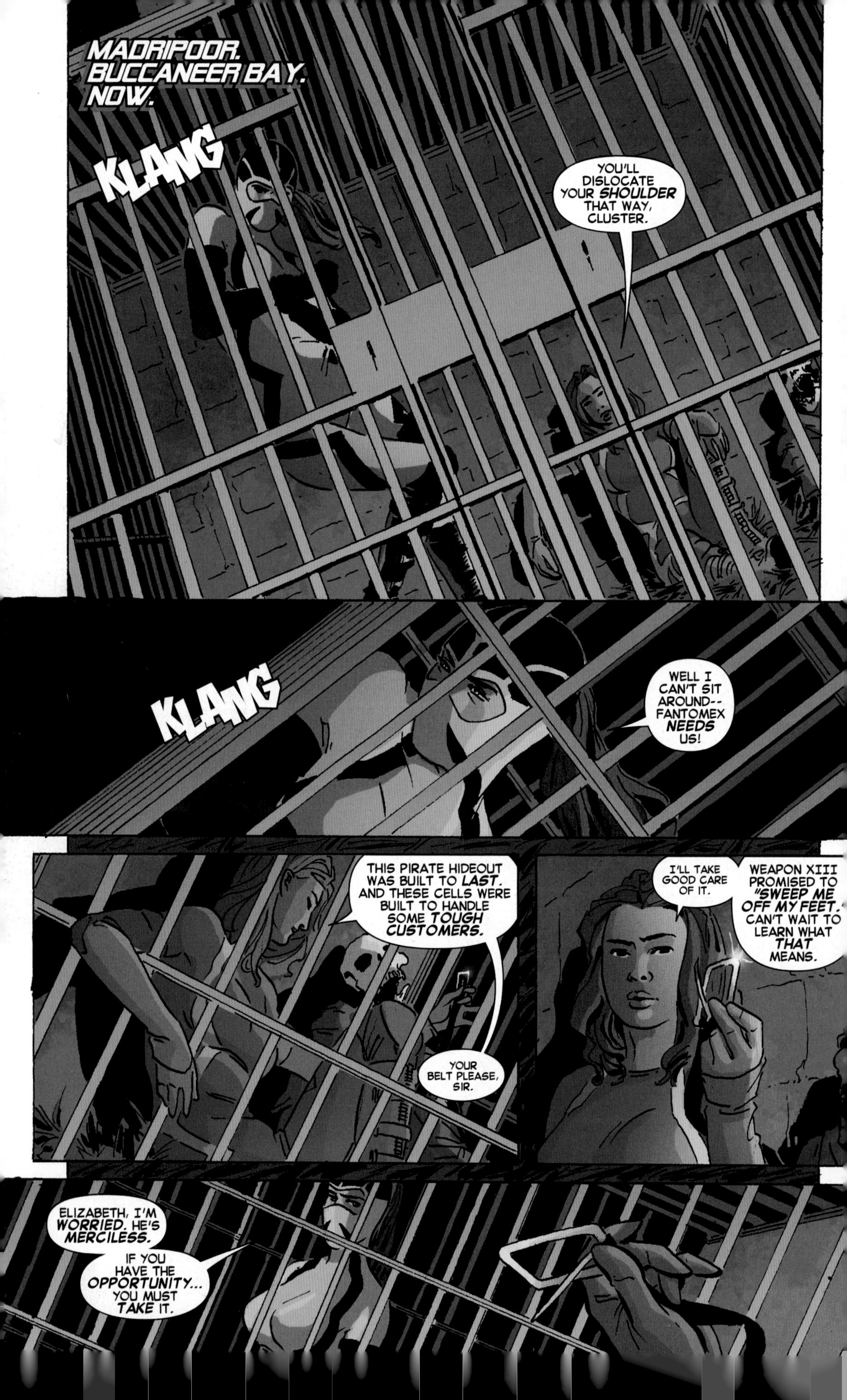
MADRIPOOR. BUCCANEER BAY. NOW.
KLANG
YOU'LL DISLOCATE YOUR SHOULDER THAT WAY, CLUSTER.
KLANG
WELL I CAN'T SIT AROUND-- FANTOMEX NEEDS US!
THIS PIRATE HIDEOUT WAS BUILT TO LAST. AND THESE CELLS WERE BUILT TO HANDLE SOME TOUGH CUSTOMERS.
YOUR BELT PLEASE, SIR.
I'LL TAKE GOOD CARE OF IT.
WEAPON XIII PROMISED TO "SWEEP ME OFF MY FEET." CAN'T WAIT TO LEARN WHAT THAT MEANS.
ELIZABETH, I'M WORRIED. HE'S MERCILESS.
IF YOU HAVE THE OPPORTUNITY... YOU MUST TAKE IT.

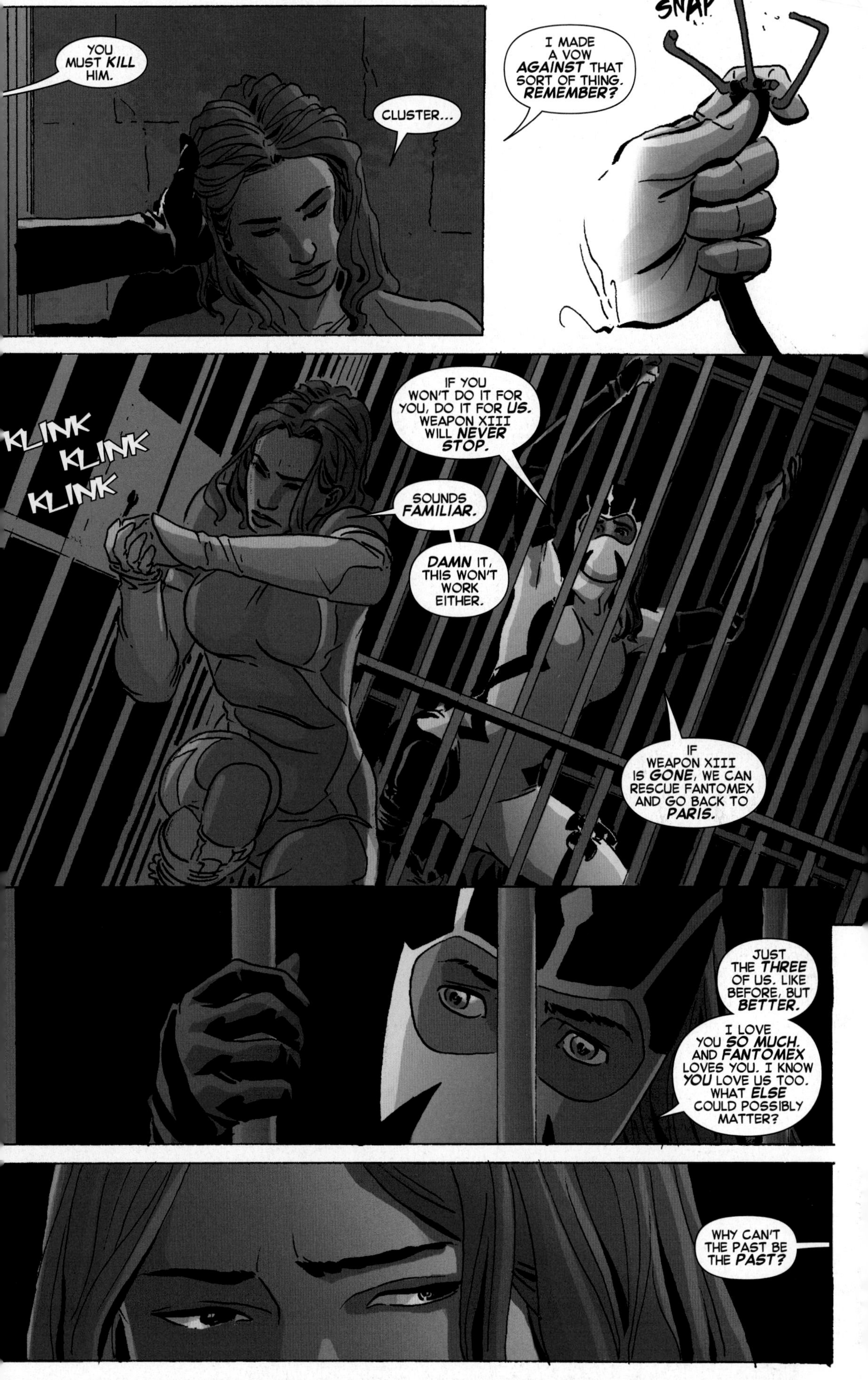
YOU MUST KILL HIM.
CLUSTER...
I MADE A VOW AGAINST THAT SORT OF THING. REMEMBER?
SNAP
KLINK KLINK KLINK
IF YOU WON'T DO IT FOR YOU, DO IT FOR US. WEAPON XIII WILL NEVER STOP.
SOUNDS FAMILIAR.
DAMN IT, THIS WON'T WORK EITHER.
IF WEAPON XIII IS GONE, WE CAN RESCUE FANTOMEX AND GO BACK TO PARIS.
JUST THE THREE OF US. LIKE BEFORE, BUT BETTER.
I LOVE YOU SO MUCH. AND FANTOMEX LOVES YOU. I KNOW YOU LOVE US TOO. WHAT ELSE COULD POSSIBLY MATTER?
WHY CAN'T THE PAST BE THE PAST?

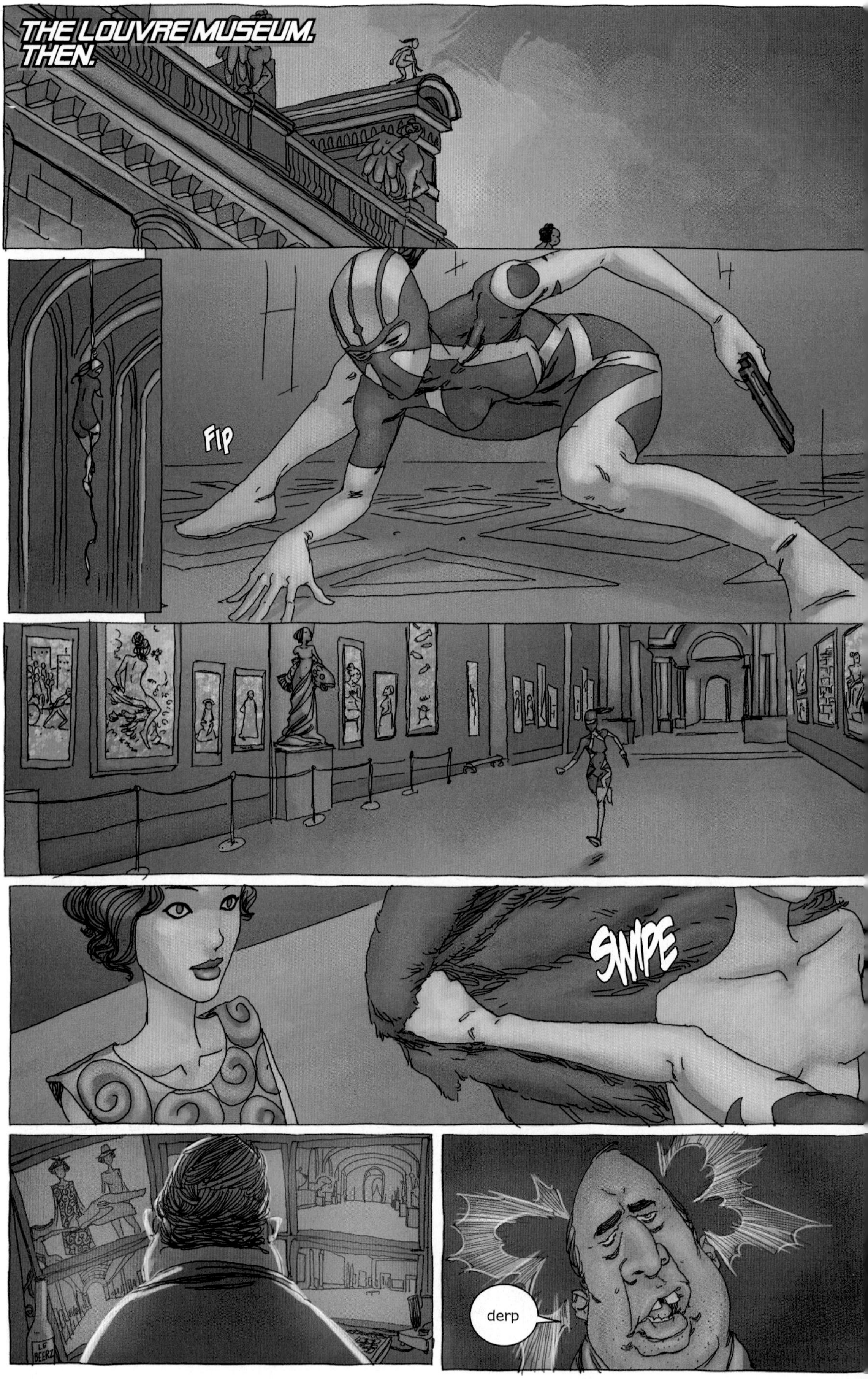
THE LOUVRE MUSEUM.
THEN.
FIP
SWIPE
LE BEERZ
derp

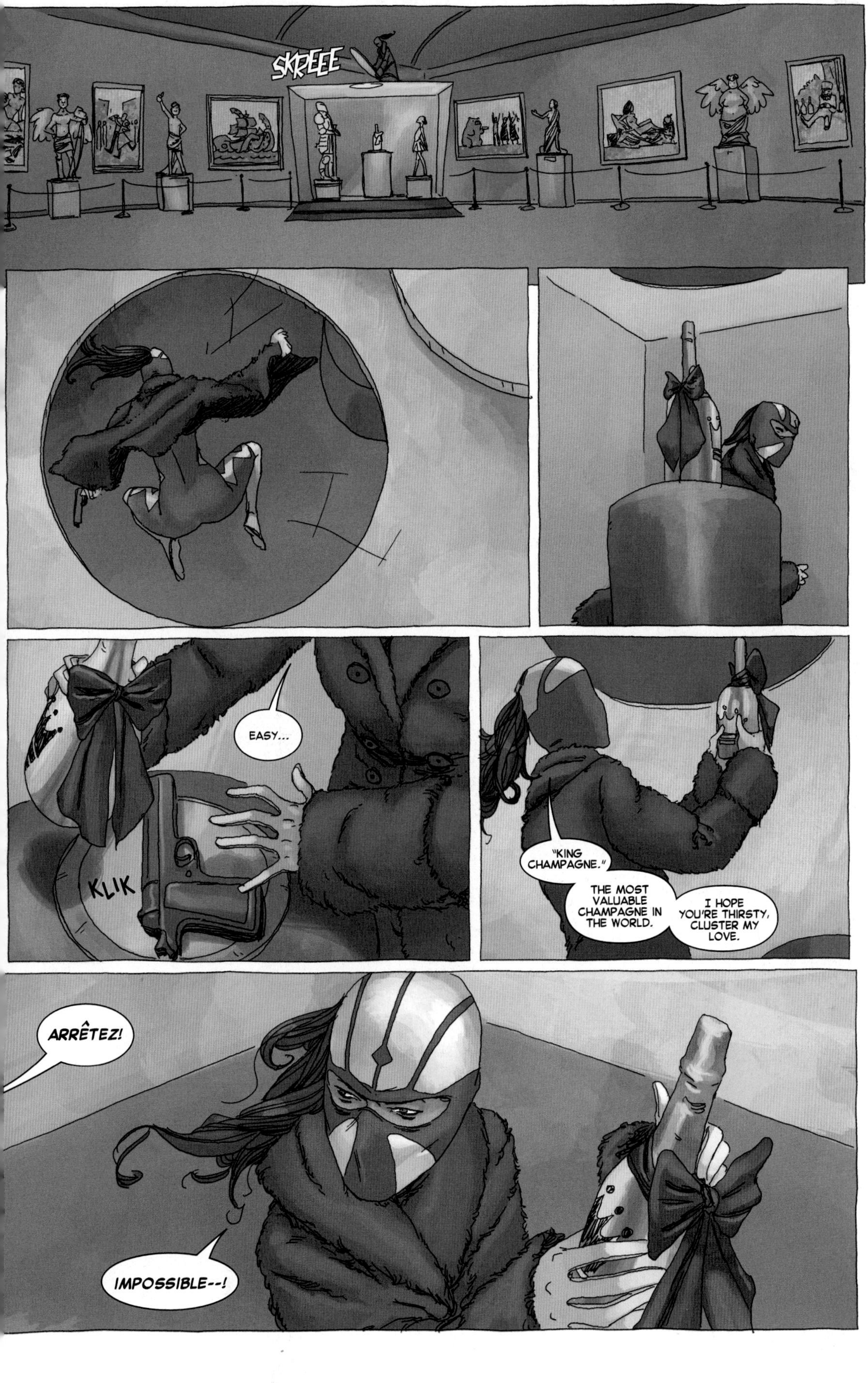
SKREEE
EASY...
KLIK
"KING CHAMPAGNE."
THE MOST VALUABLE CHAMPAGNE IN THE WORLD.
I HOPE YOU'RE THIRSTY, CLUSTER MY LOVE.
ARRÊTEZ!
IMPOSSIBLE--!

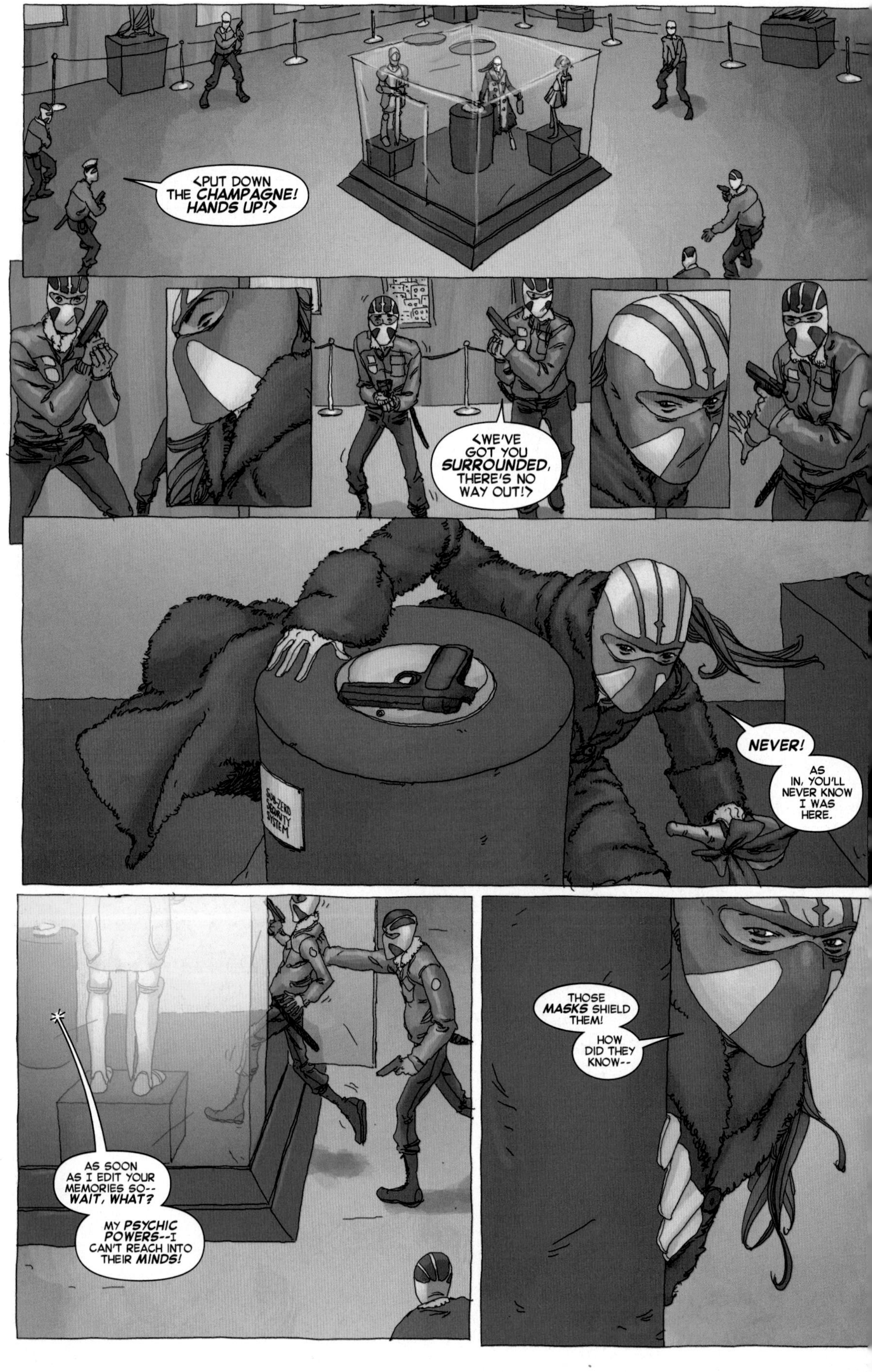
<PUT DOWN THE CHAMPAGNE! HANDS UP!>
<WE'VE GOT YOU SURROUNDED, THERE'S NO WAY OUT!>
NEVER!
AS IN, YOU'LL NEVER KNOW I WAS HERE.
SUB-ZERO SECURITY SYSTEM
AS SOON AS I EDIT YOUR MEMORIES SO-- WAIT, WHAT?
MY PSYCHIC POWERS--I CAN'T REACH INTO THEIR MINDS!
THOSE MASKS SHIELD THEM!
HOW DID THEY KNOW--

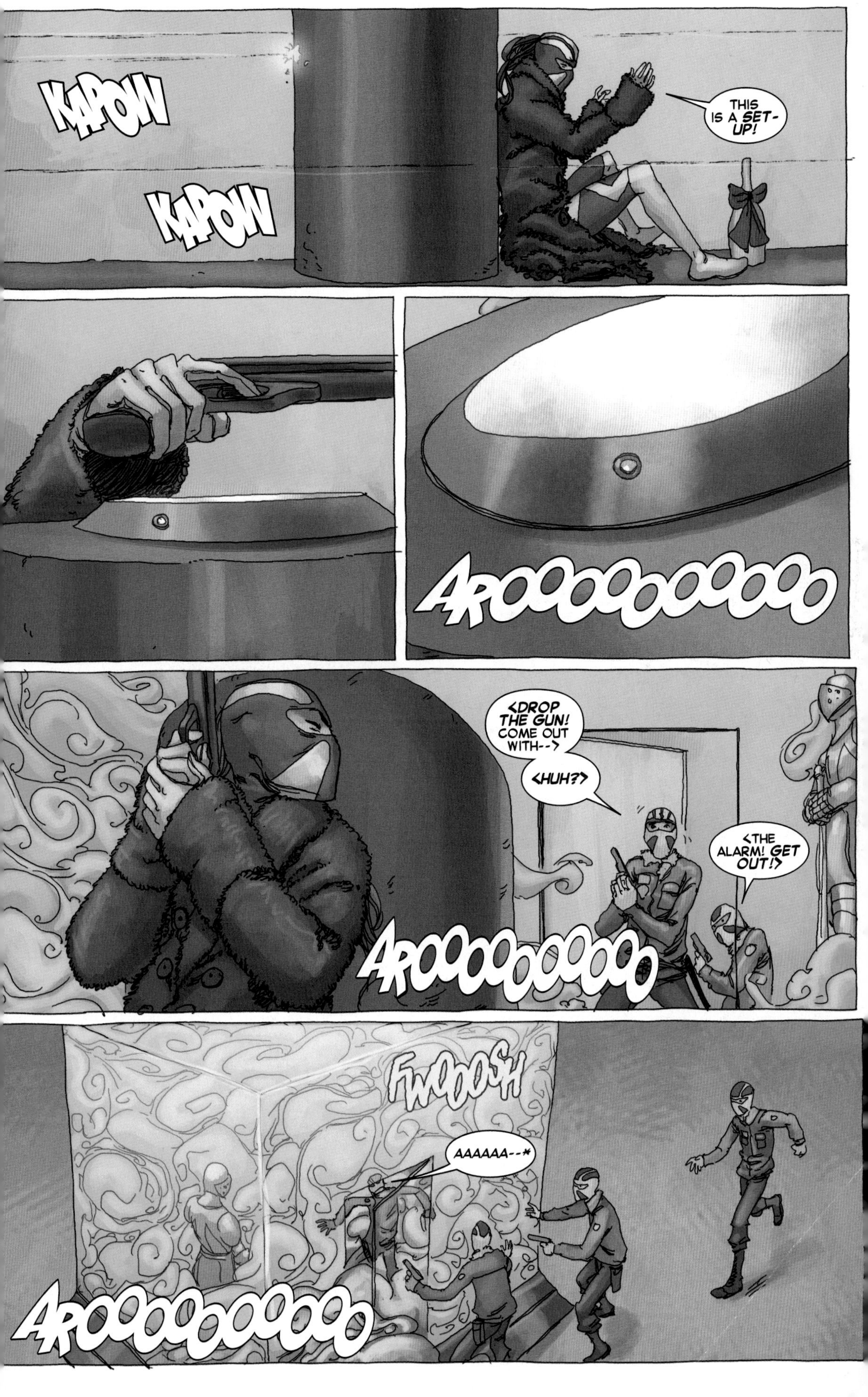
KAPOW
KAPOW
THIS IS A SET-UP!
AROOOOOOOOOO
<DROP THE GUN! COME OUT WITH-->
<HUH?>
<THE ALARM! GET OUT!>
AROOOOOOOOOO
FWOOOSH
AAAAAA--*
AROOOOOOOOOOO

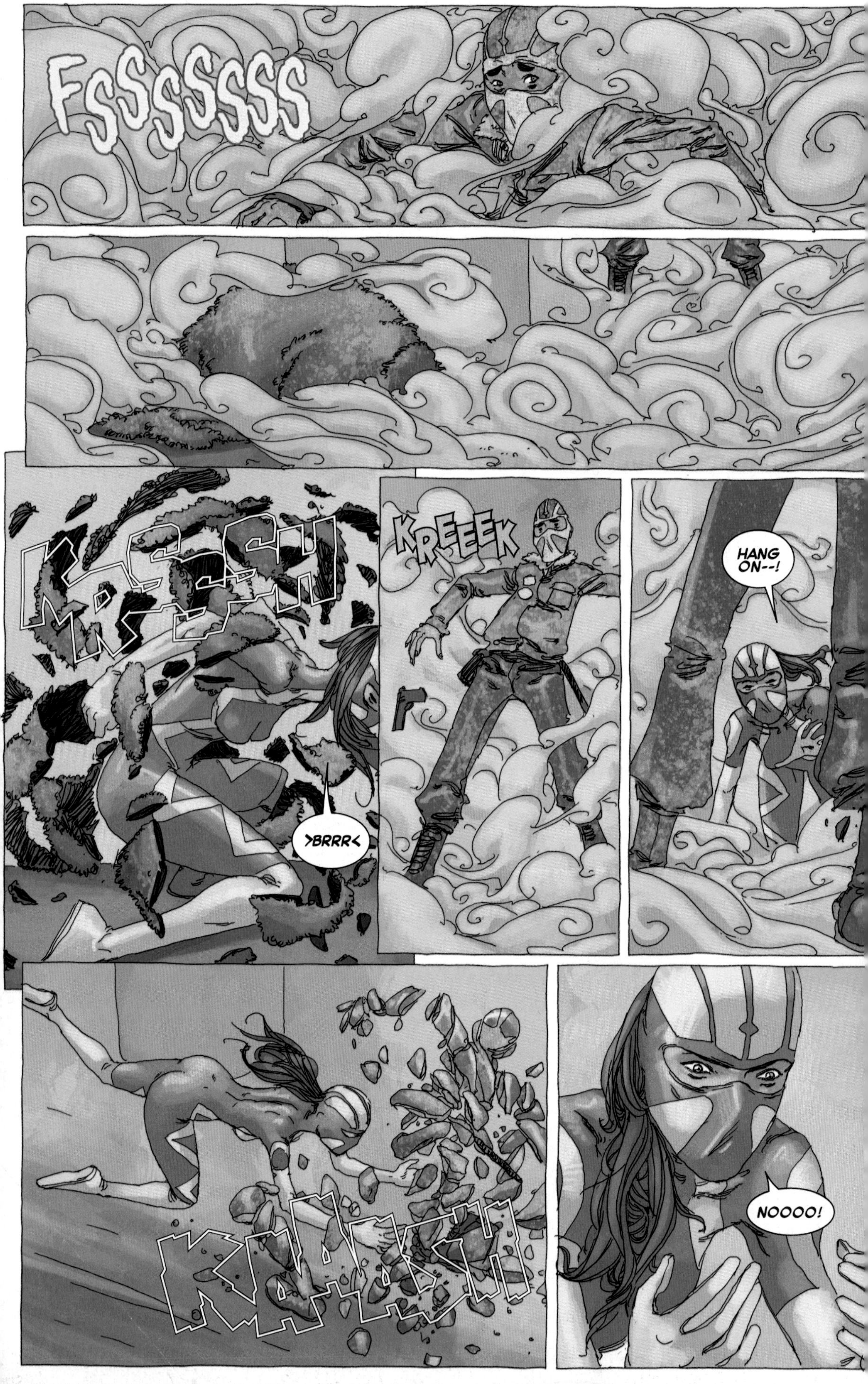
FSSSSSSS
KRSSH
>BRRR<
KREEEK
HANG ON--!
KRAKSH
NOOOO!

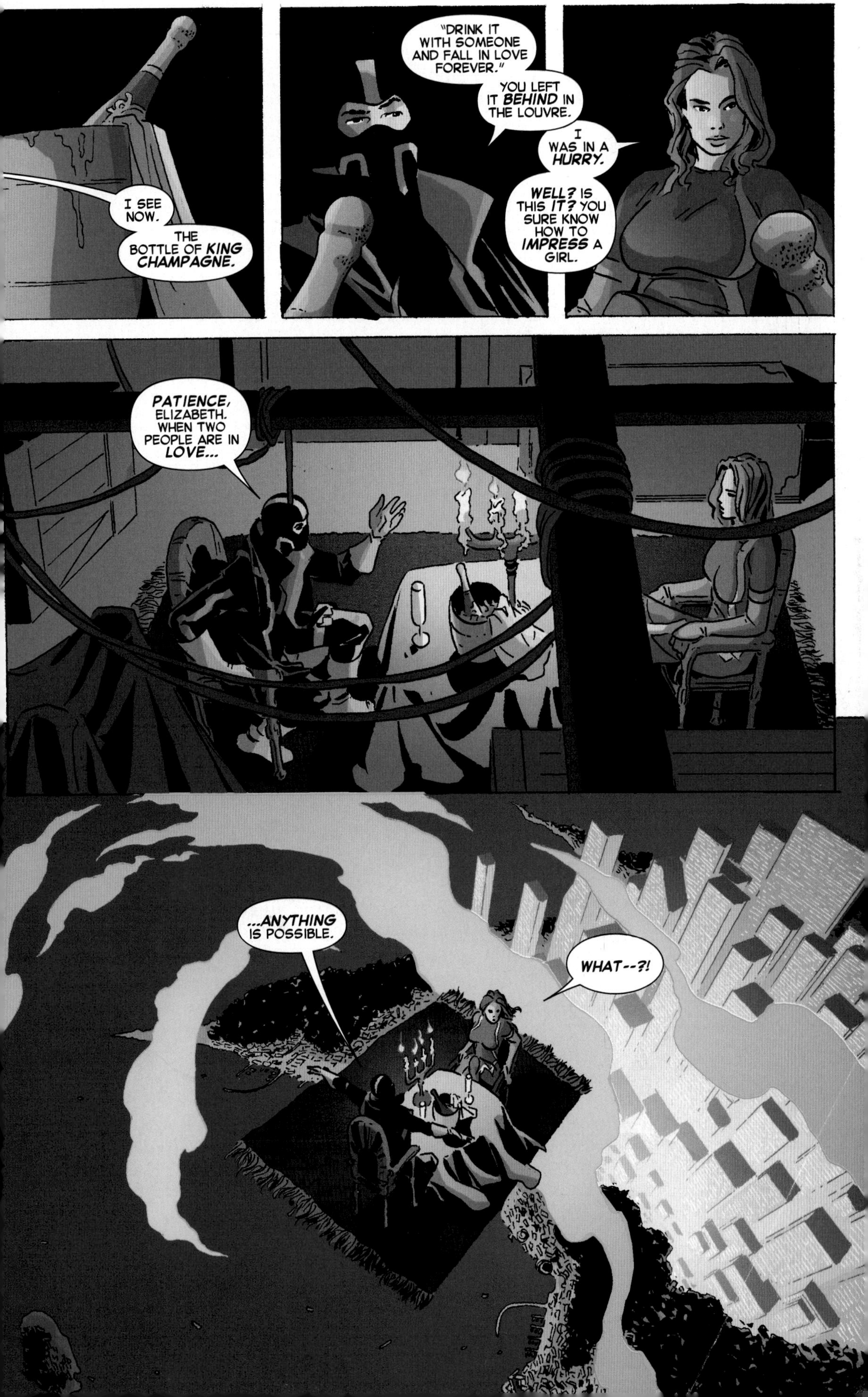

I SEE NOW.
THE BOTTLE OF KING CHAMPAGNE.
"DRINK IT WITH SOMEONE AND FALL IN LOVE FOREVER."
YOU LEFT IT BEHIND IN THE LOUVRE.
I WAS IN A HURRY.
WELL? IS THIS IT? YOU SURE KNOW HOW TO IMPRESS A GIRL.
PATIENCE, ELIZABETH. WHEN TWO PEOPLE ARE IN LOVE...
...ANYTHING IS POSSIBLE.
WHAT--?!

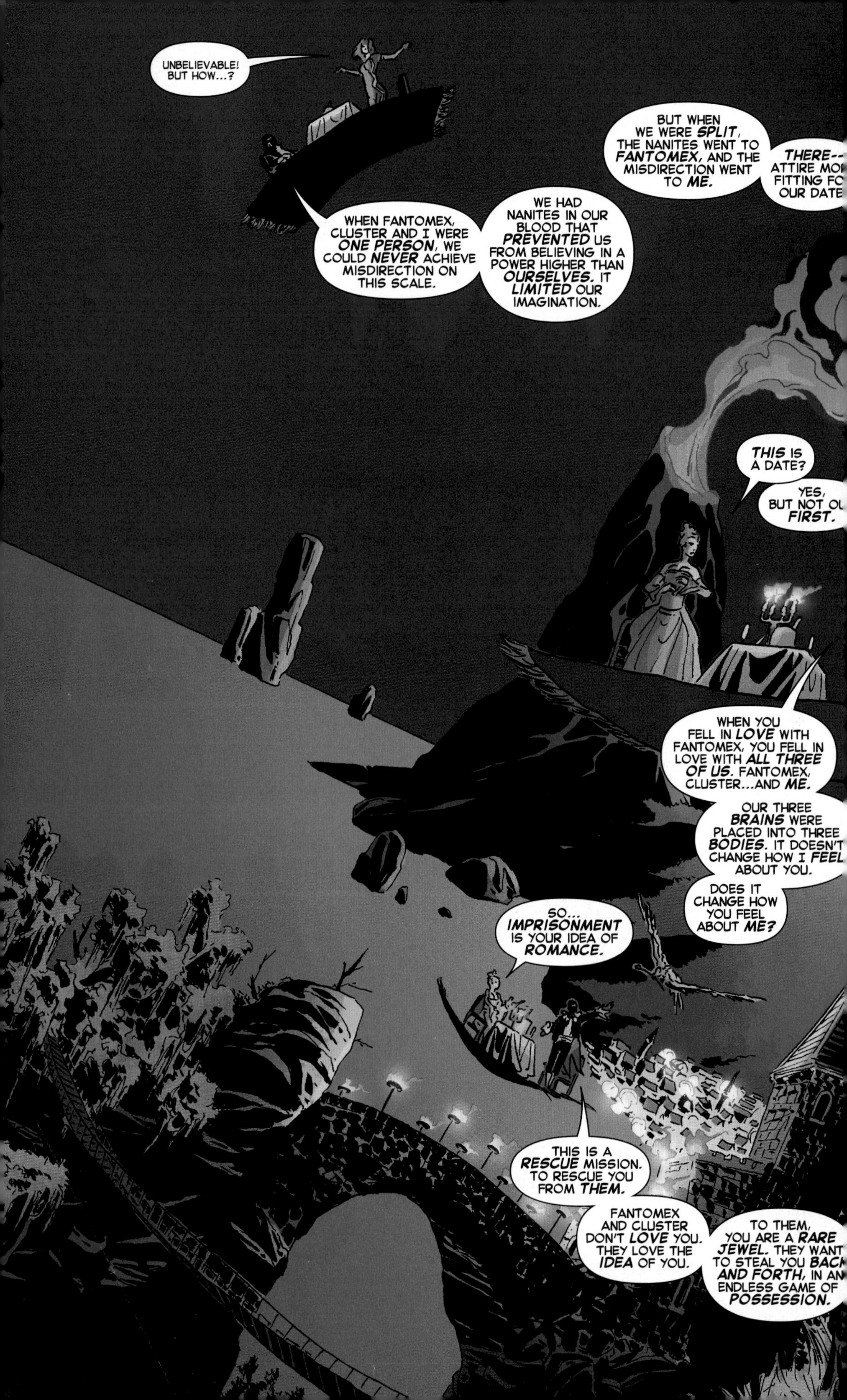

UNBELIEVABLE! BUT HOW...?
WHEN FANTOMEX, CLUSTER AND I WERE ONE PERSON, WE COULD NEVER ACHIEVE MISDIRECTION ON THIS SCALE.
WE HAD NANITES IN OUR BLOOD THAT PREVENTED US FROM BELIEVING IN A POWER HIGHER THAN OURSELVES. IT LIMITED OUR IMAGINATION.
BUT WHEN WE WERE SPLIT, THE NANITES WENT TO FANTOMEX, AND THE MISDIRECTION WENT TO ME.
THERE-- ATTIRE MO FITTING FO OUR DATE
THIS IS A DATE?
YES, BUT NOT OU FIRST.
WHEN YOU FELL IN LOVE WITH FANTOMEX, YOU FELL IN LOVE WITH ALL THREE OF US. FANTOMEX, CLUSTER...AND ME.
OUR THREE BRAINS WERE PLACED INTO THREE BODIES. IT DOESN'T CHANGE HOW I FEEL ABOUT YOU.
DOES IT CHANGE HOW YOU FEEL ABOUT ME?
SO... IMPRISONMENT IS YOUR IDEA OF ROMANCE.
THIS IS A RESCUE MISSION. TO RESCUE YOU FROM THEM.
FANTOMEX AND CLUSTER DON'T LOVE YOU. THEY LOVE THE IDEA OF YOU.
TO THEM, YOU ARE A RARE JEWEL. THEY WANT TO STEAL YOU BACK AND FORTH, IN AN ENDLESS GAME OF POSSESSION.

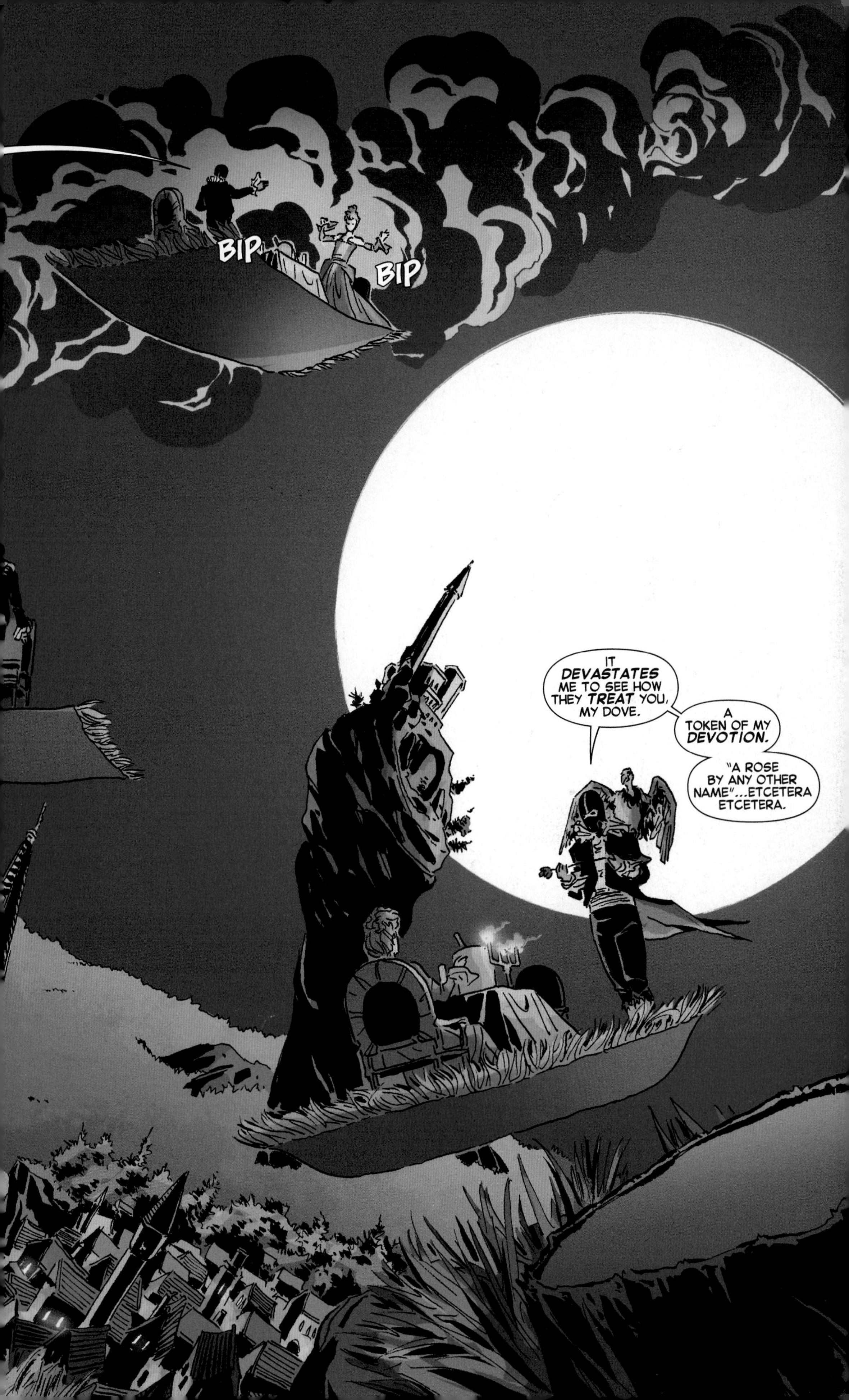
BIP
BIP
IT DEVASTATES ME TO SEE HOW THEY TREAT YOU, MY DOVE.
A TOKEN OF MY DEVOTION.
"A ROSE BY ANY OTHER NAME"...ETCETERA ETCETERA.

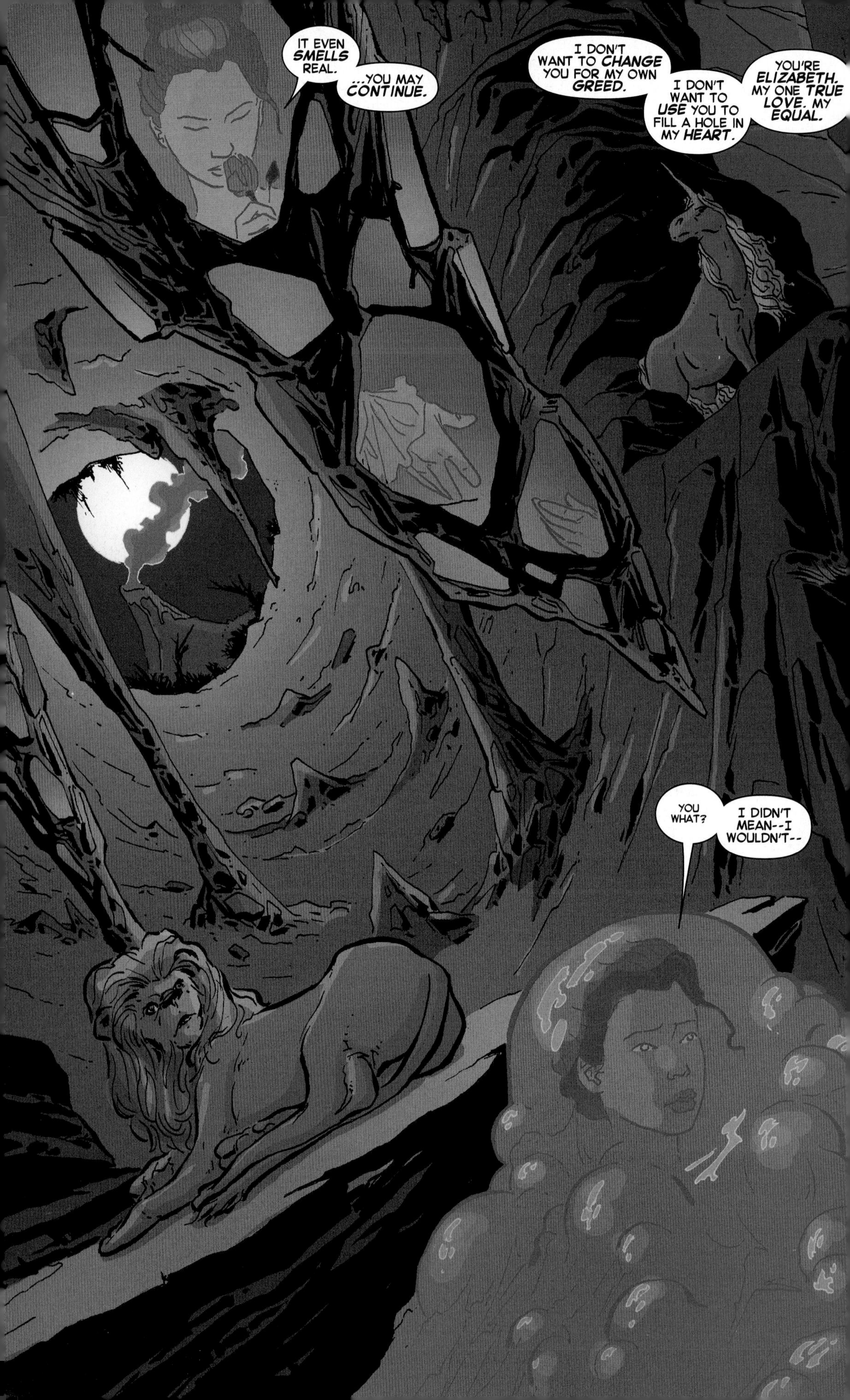
IT EVEN SMELLS REAL.
...YOU MAY CONTINUE.
I DON'T WANT TO CHANGE YOU FOR MY OWN GREED.
I DON'T WANT TO USE YOU TO FILL A HOLE IN MY HEART.
YOU'RE ELIZABETH. MY ONE TRUE LOVE. MY EQUAL.
YOU WHAT?
I DIDN'T MEAN--I WOULDN'T--

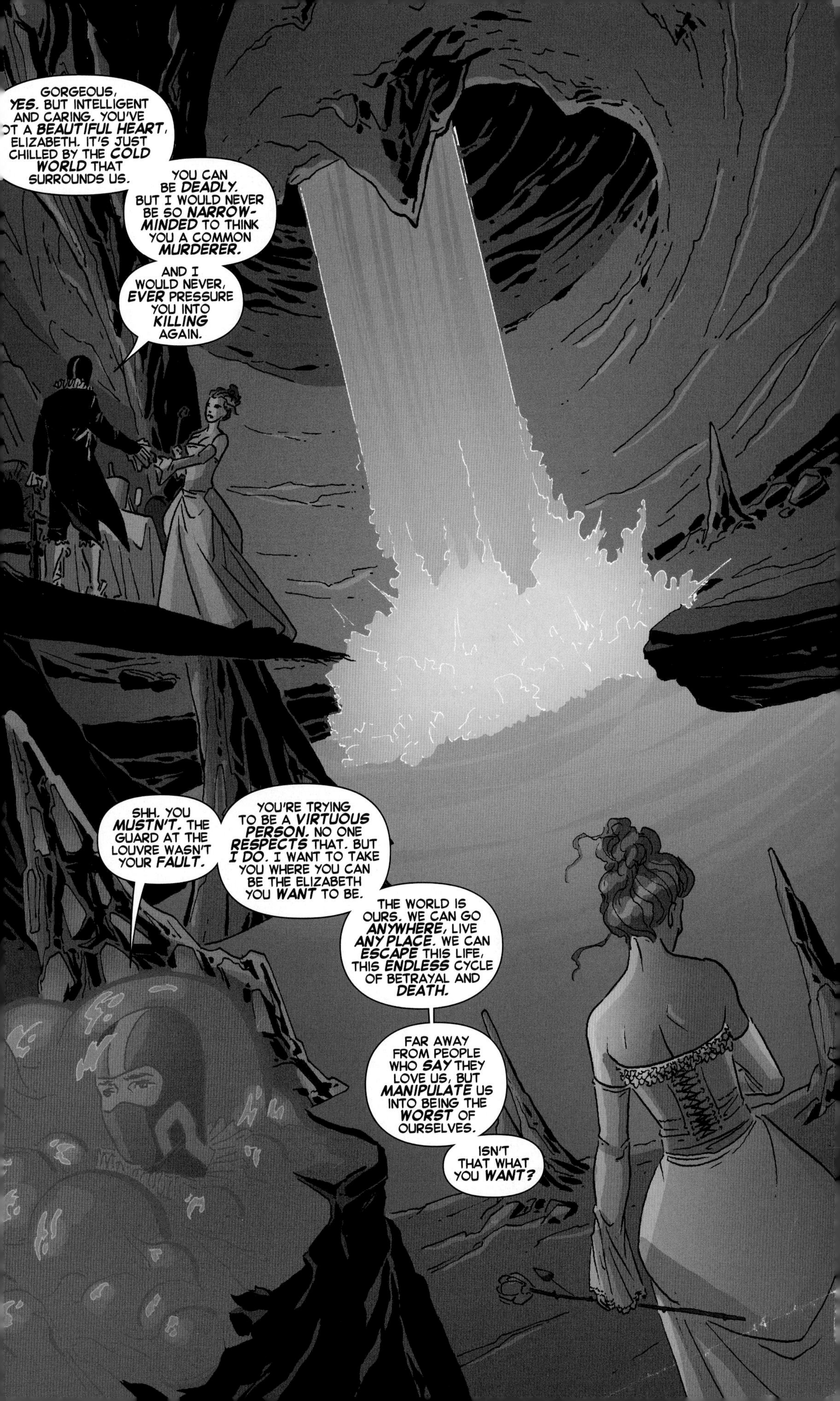
GORGEOUS, YES. BUT INTELLIGENT AND CARING. YOU'VE OT A BEAUTIFUL HEART, ELIZABETH. IT'S JUST CHILLED BY THE COLD WORLD THAT SURROUNDS US.
YOU CAN BE DEADLY. BUT I WOULD NEVER BE SO NARROW-MINDED TO THINK YOU A COMMON MURDERER.
AND I WOULD NEVER, EVER PRESSURE YOU INTO KILLING AGAIN.
SHH. YOU MUSTN'T. THE GUARD AT THE LOUVRE WASN'T YOUR FAULT.
YOU'RE TRYING TO BE A VIRTUOUS PERSON. NO ONE RESPECTS THAT. BUT I DO. I WANT TO TAKE YOU WHERE YOU CAN BE THE ELIZABETH YOU WANT TO BE.
THE WORLD IS OURS. WE CAN GO ANYWHERE, LIVE ANYPLACE. WE CAN ESCAPE THIS LIFE, THIS ENDLESS CYCLE OF BETRAYAL AND DEATH.
FAR AWAY FROM PEOPLE WHO SAY THEY LOVE US, BUT MANIPULATE US INTO BEING THE WORST OF OURSELVES.
ISN'T THAT WHAT YOU WANT?

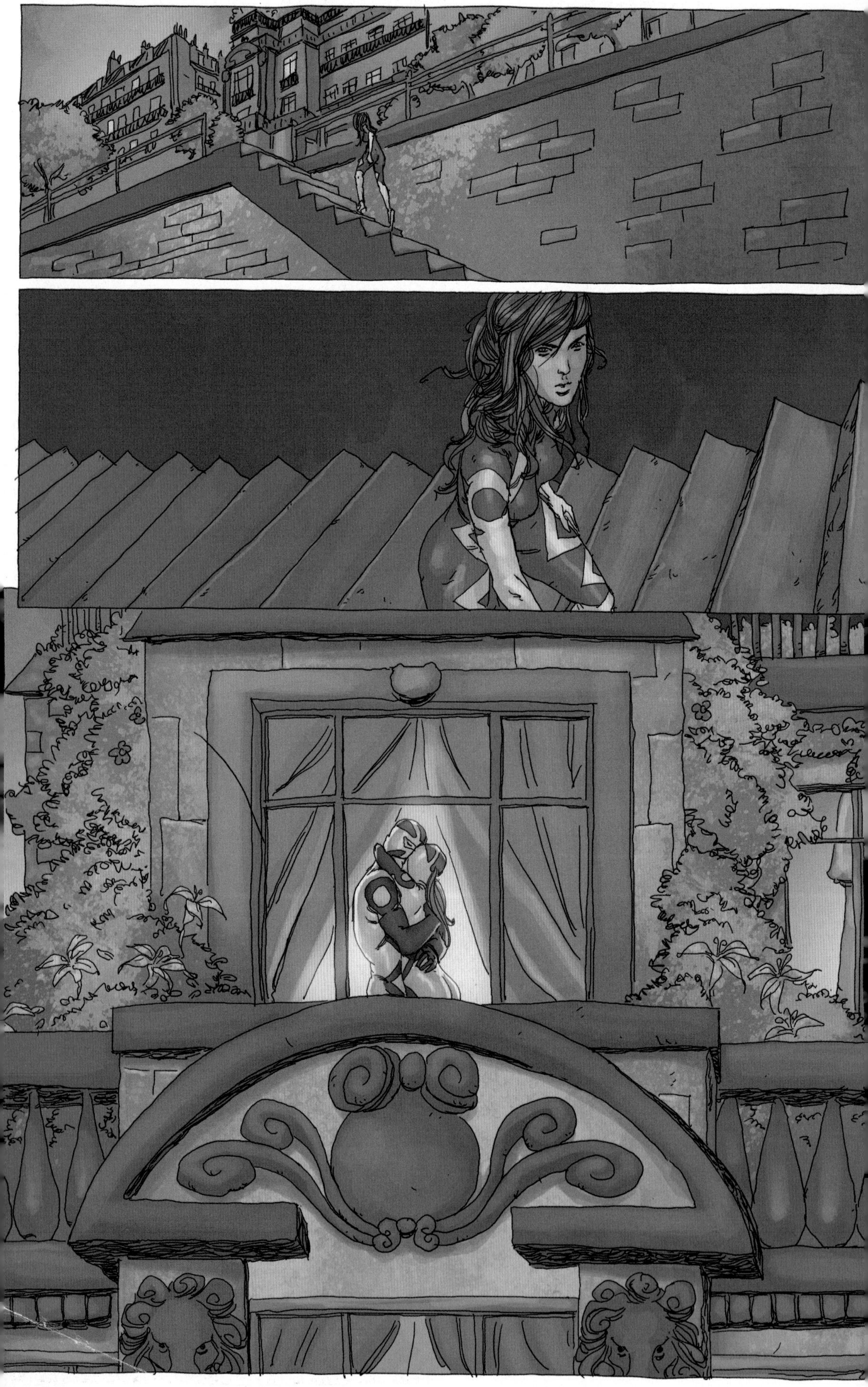

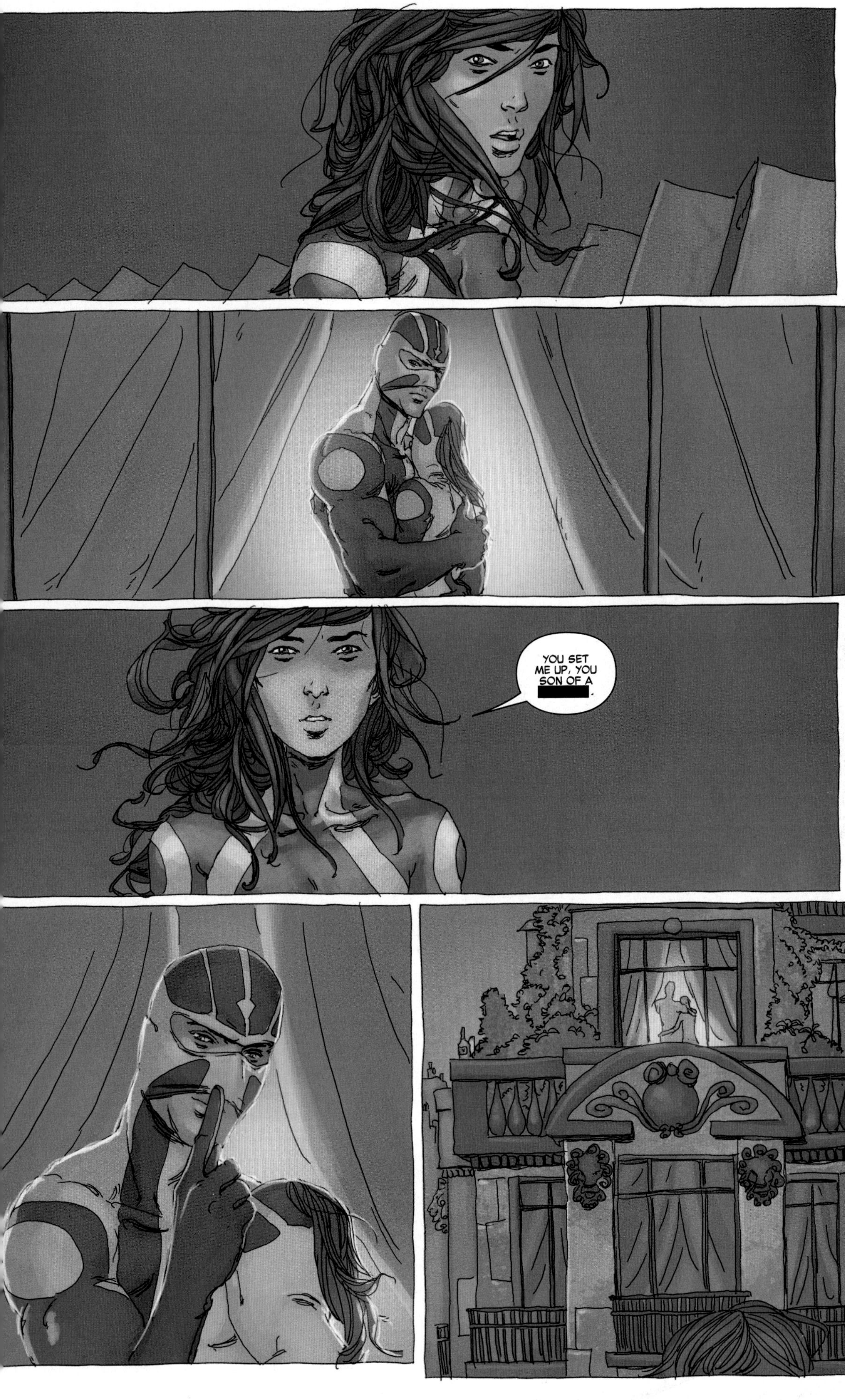
YOU SET ME UP, YOU SON OF A [redacted].

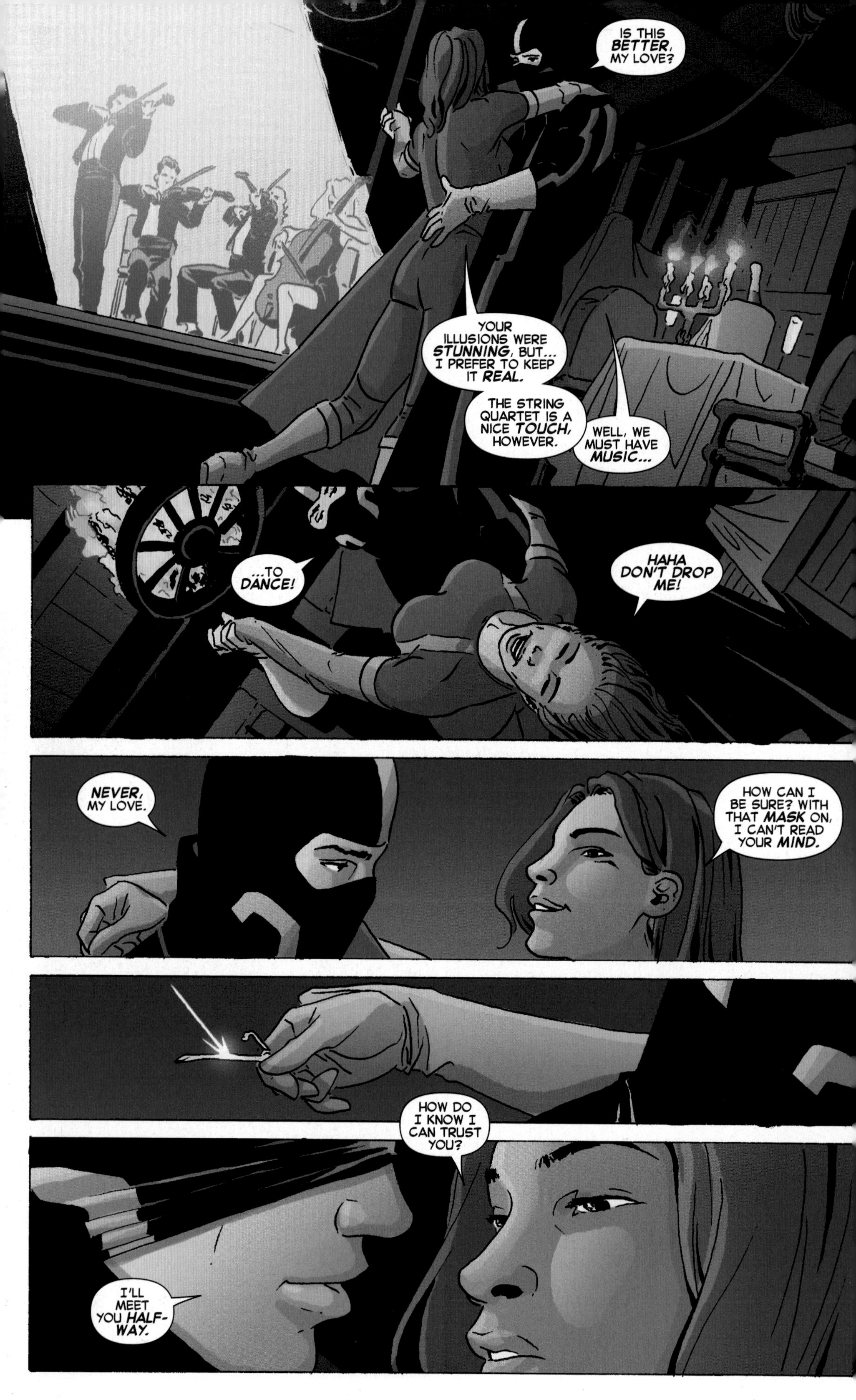
IS THIS BETTER, MY LOVE?
YOUR ILLUSIONS WERE STUNNING, BUT... I PREFER TO KEEP IT REAL.
THE STRING QUARTET IS A NICE TOUCH, HOWEVER.
WELL, WE MUST HAVE MUSIC...
...TO DANCE!
HAHA DON'T DROP ME!
NEVER, MY LOVE.
HOW CAN I BE SURE? WITH THAT MASK ON, I CAN'T READ YOUR MIND.
HOW DO I KNOW I CAN TRUST YOU?
I'LL MEET YOU HALF-WAY.

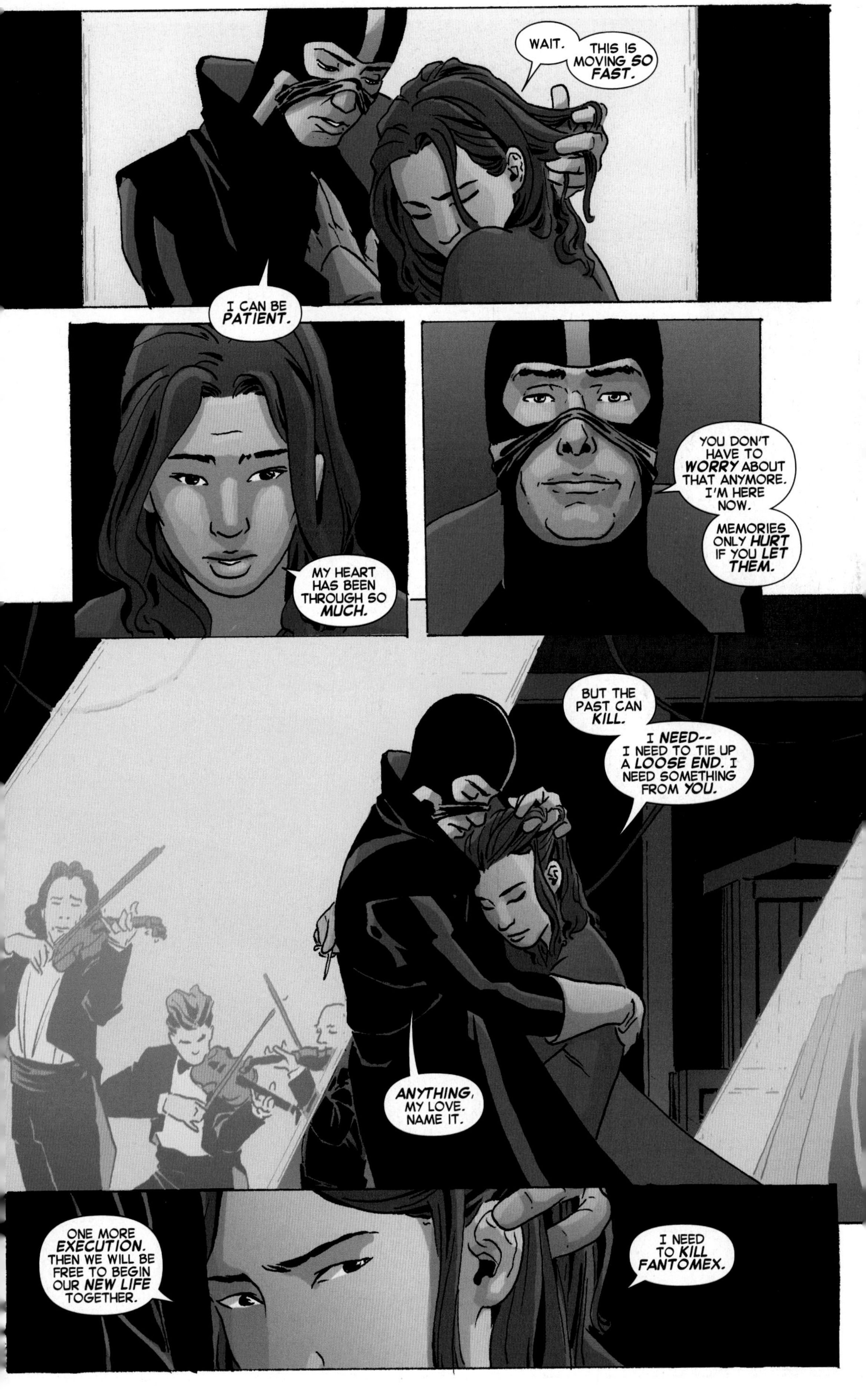
WAIT.
THIS IS MOVING SO FAST.
I CAN BE PATIENT.
MY HEART HAS BEEN THROUGH SO MUCH.
YOU DON'T HAVE TO WORRY ABOUT THAT ANYMORE. I'M HERE NOW.
MEMORIES ONLY HURT IF YOU LET THEM.
BUT THE PAST CAN KILL.
I NEED-- I NEED TO TIE UP A LOOSE END. I NEED SOMETHING FROM YOU.
ANYTHING, MY LOVE. NAME IT.
ONE MORE EXECUTION. THEN WE WILL BE FREE TO BEGIN OUR NEW LIFE TOGETHER.
I NEED TO KILL FANTOMEX.

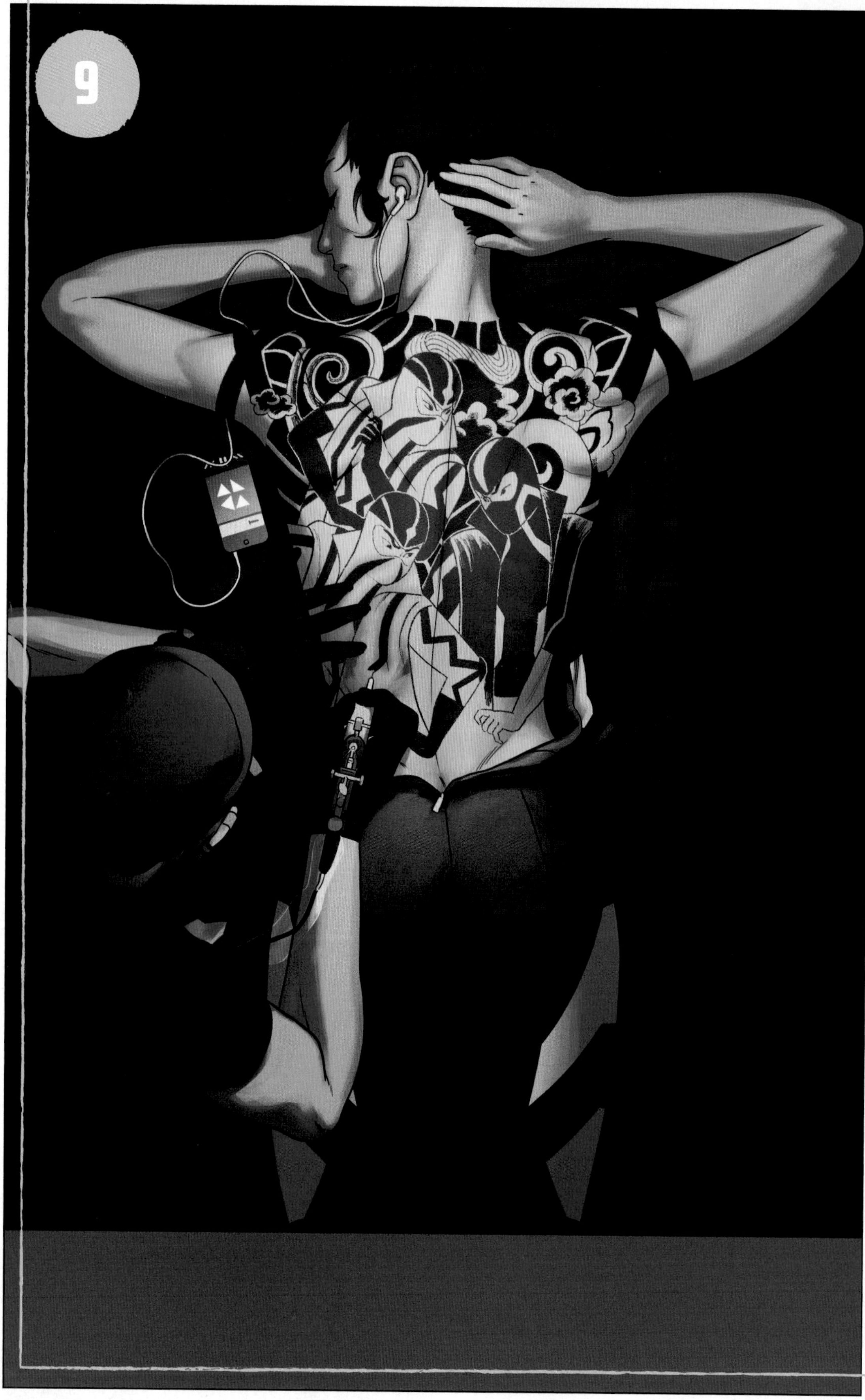
9

THE CHAIN

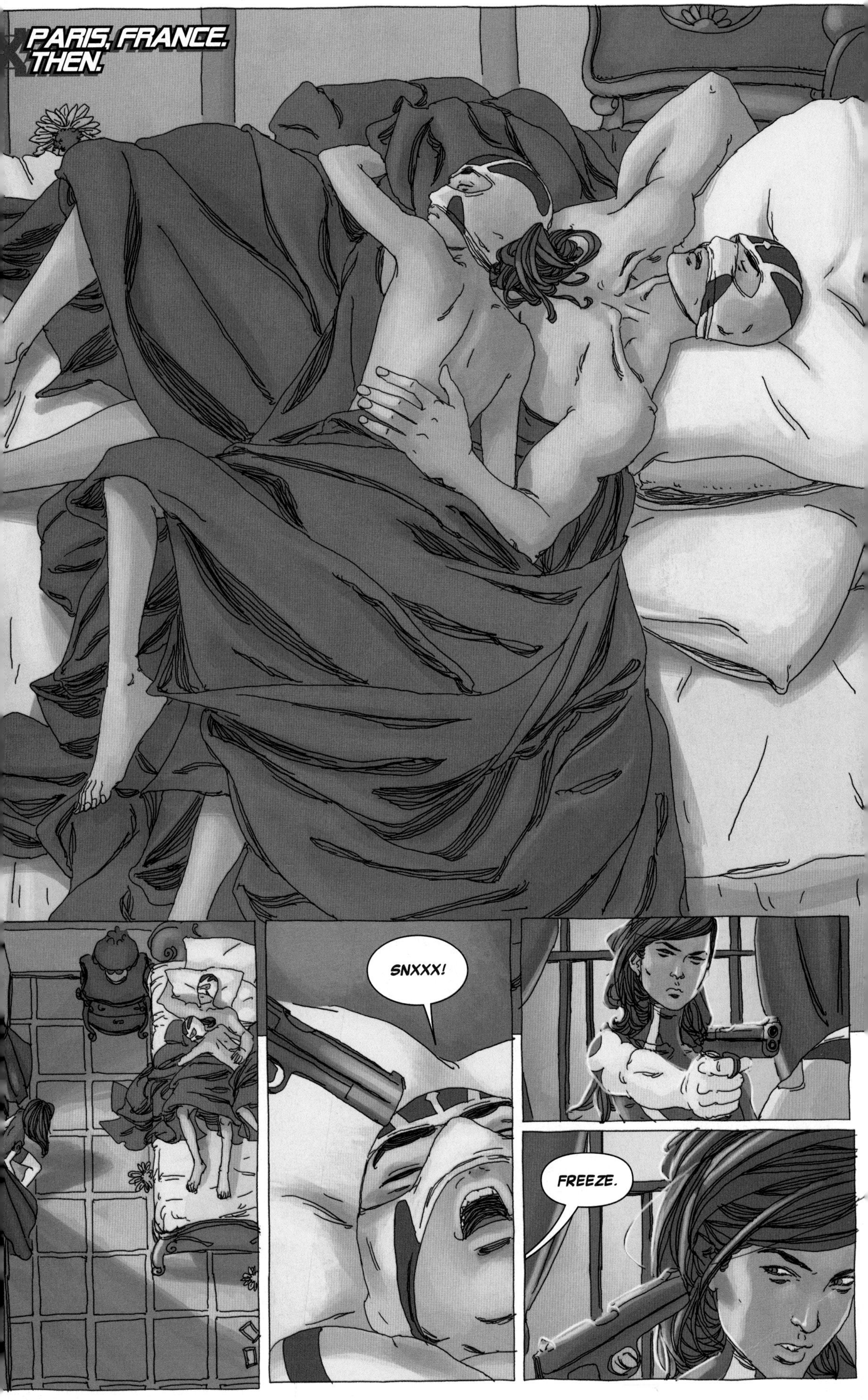
PARIS, FRANCE. THEN.
SNXXX!
FREEZE.

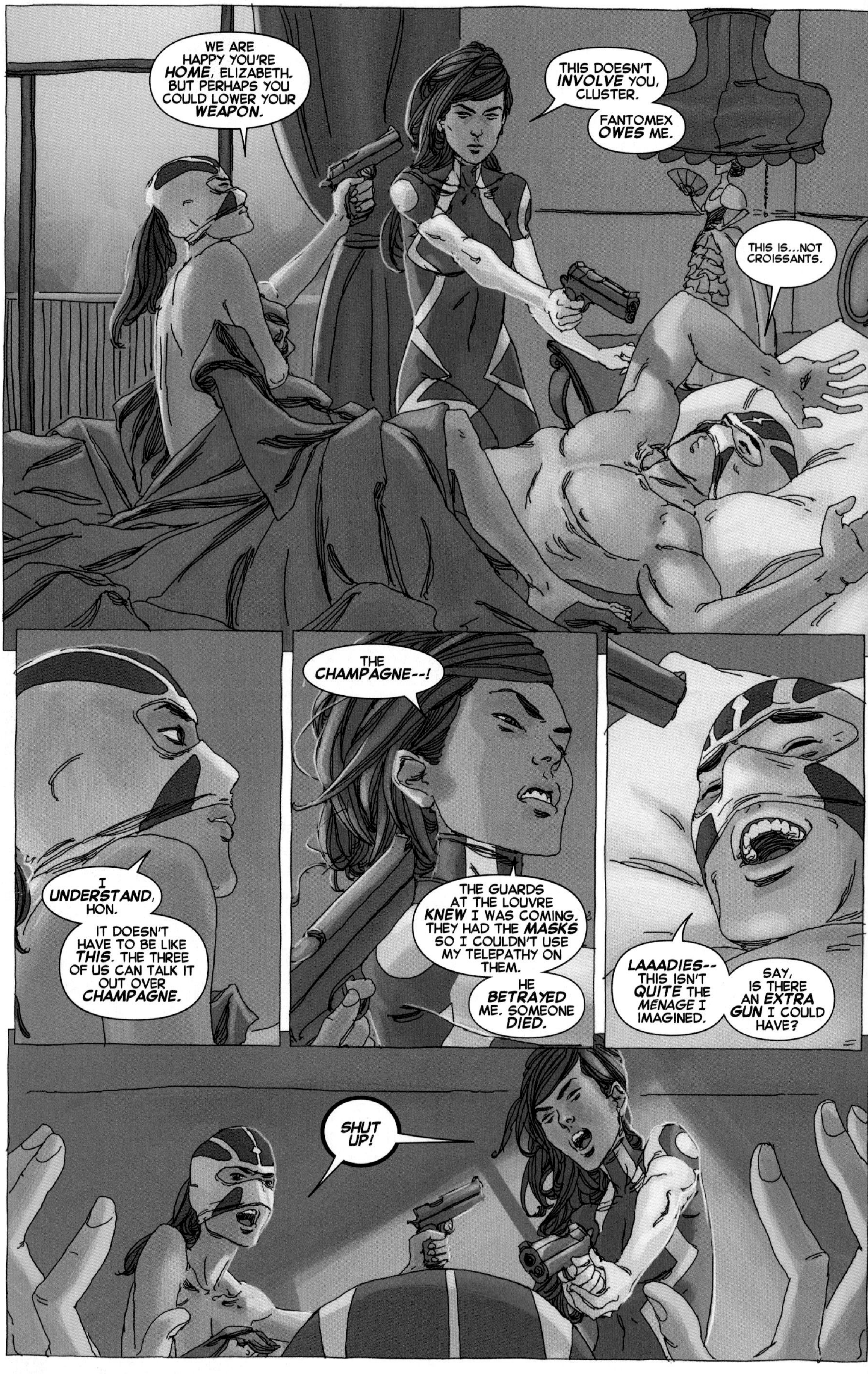
WE ARE HAPPY YOU'RE HOME, ELIZABETH. BUT PERHAPS YOU COULD LOWER YOUR WEAPON.
THIS DOESN'T INVOLVE YOU, CLUSTER.
FANTOMEX OWES ME.
THIS IS...NOT CROISSANTS.
I UNDERSTAND, HON.
IT DOESN'T HAVE TO BE LIKE THIS. THE THREE OF US CAN TALK IT OUT OVER CHAMPAGNE.
THE CHAMPAGNE--!
THE GUARDS AT THE LOUVRE KNEW I WAS COMING. THEY HAD THE MASKS SO I COULDN'T USE MY TELEPATHY ON THEM.
HE BETRAYED ME. SOMEONE DIED.
LAAADIES-- THIS ISN'T QUITE THE MENAGE I IMAGINED.
SAY, IS THERE AN EXTRA GUN I COULD HAVE?
SHUT UP!

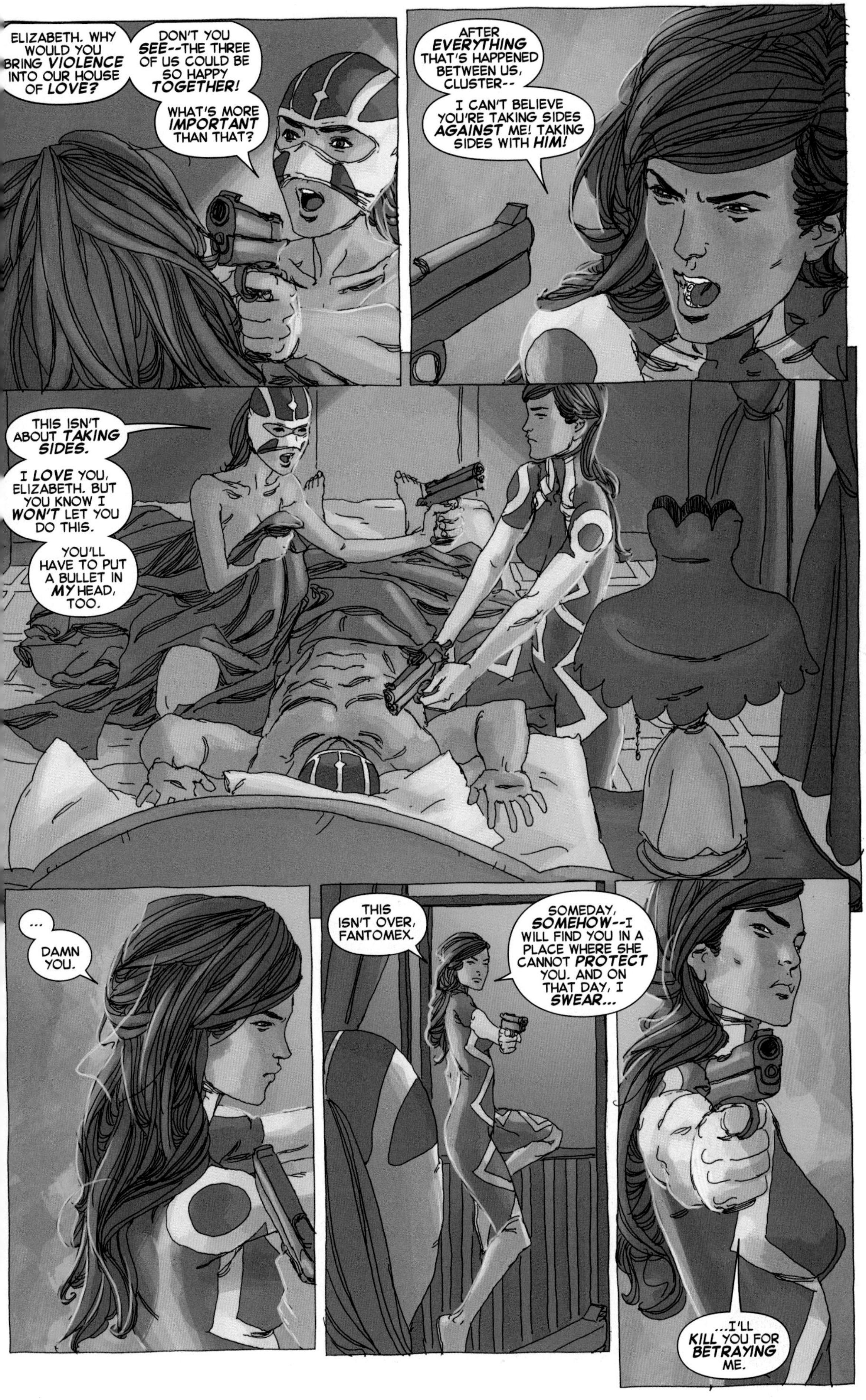
ELIZABETH. WHY WOULD YOU BRING VIOLENCE INTO OUR HOUSE OF LOVE?
DON'T YOU SEE--THE THREE OF US COULD BE SO HAPPY TOGETHER!
WHAT'S MORE IMPORTANT THAN THAT?
AFTER EVERYTHING THAT'S HAPPENED BETWEEN US, CLUSTER--
I CAN'T BELIEVE YOU'RE TAKING SIDES AGAINST ME! TAKING SIDES WITH HIM!
THIS ISN'T ABOUT TAKING SIDES.
I LOVE YOU, ELIZABETH. BUT YOU KNOW I WON'T LET YOU DO THIS.
YOU'LL HAVE TO PUT A BULLET IN MY HEAD, TOO.
...
DAMN YOU.
THIS ISN'T OVER, FANTOMEX.
SOMEDAY, SOMEHOW--I WILL FIND YOU IN A PLACE WHERE SHE CANNOT PROTECT YOU. AND ON THAT DAY, I SWEAR...
...I'LL KILL YOU FOR BETRAYING ME.

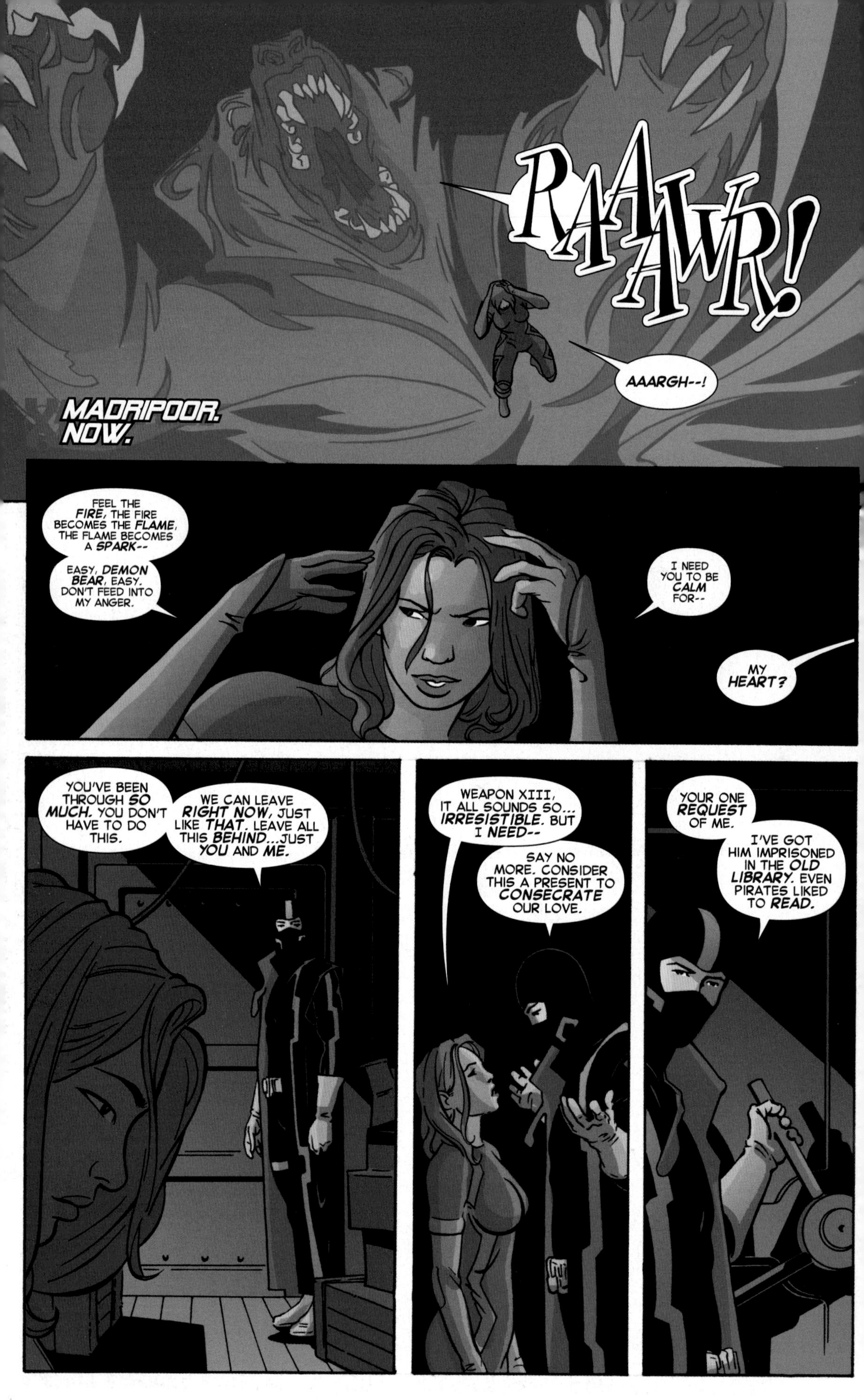
RAAAWR!
AAARGH--!
MADRIPOOR. NOW.
FEEL THE FIRE, THE FIRE BECOMES THE FLAME, THE FLAME BECOMES A SPARK--
EASY, DEMON BEAR, EASY. DON'T FEED INTO MY ANGER.
I NEED YOU TO BE CALM FOR--
MY HEART?
YOU'VE BEEN THROUGH SO MUCH. YOU DON'T HAVE TO DO THIS.
WE CAN LEAVE RIGHT NOW, JUST LIKE THAT. LEAVE ALL THIS BEHIND...JUST YOU AND ME.
WEAPON XIII, IT ALL SOUNDS SO... IRRESISTIBLE. BUT I NEED--
SAY NO MORE. CONSIDER THIS A PRESENT TO CONSECRATE OUR LOVE.
YOUR ONE REQUEST OF ME.
I'VE GOT HIM IMPRISONED IN THE OLD LIBRARY. EVEN PIRATES LIKED TO READ.

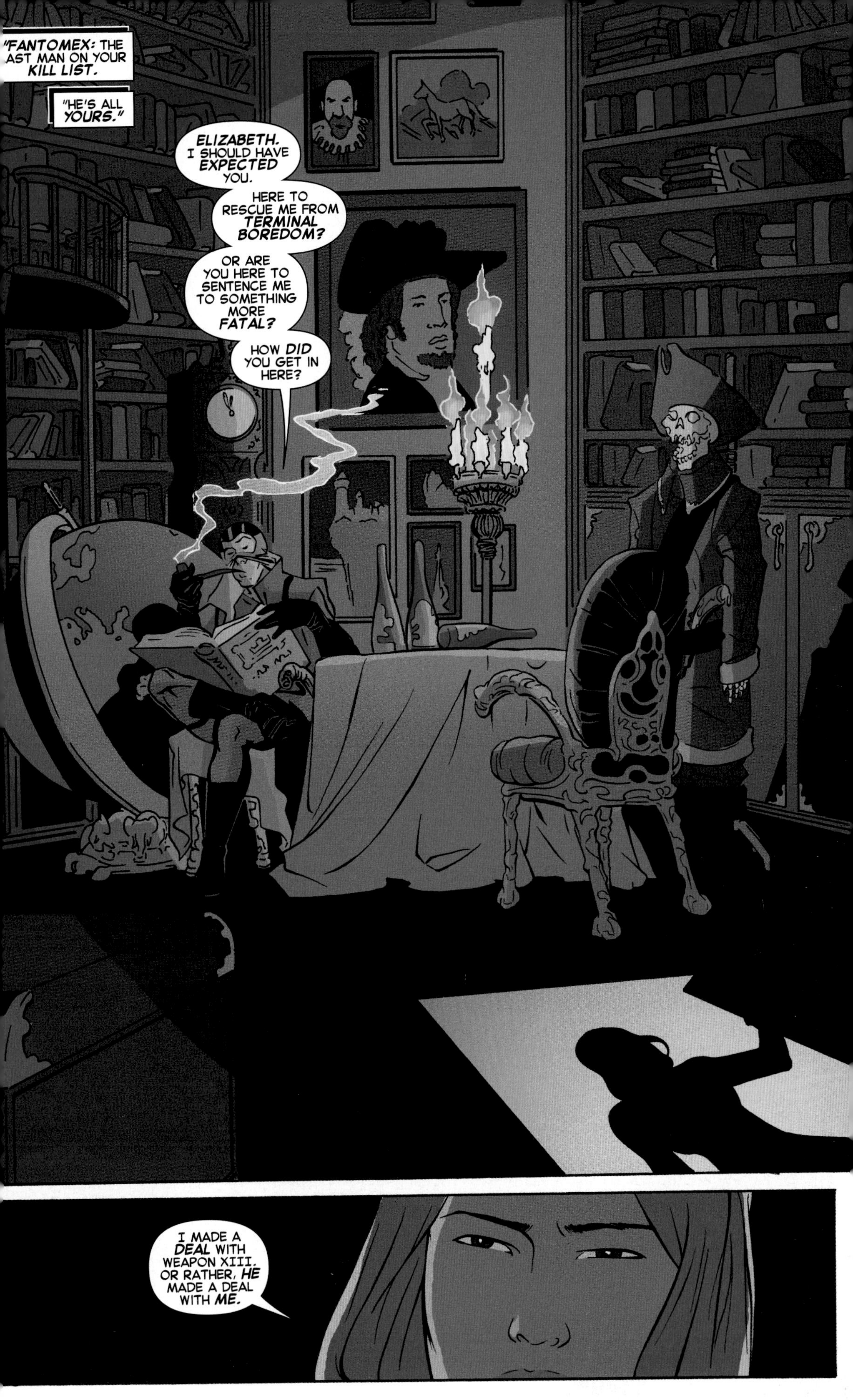
"FANTOMEX: THE AST MAN ON YOUR KILL LIST.
"HE'S ALL YOURS."
ELIZABETH. I SHOULD HAVE EXPECTED YOU.
HERE TO RESCUE ME FROM TERMINAL BOREDOM?
OR ARE YOU HERE TO SENTENCE ME TO SOMETHING MORE FATAL?
HOW DID YOU GET IN HERE?
I MADE A DEAL WITH WEAPON XIII. OR RATHER, HE MADE A DEAL WITH ME.

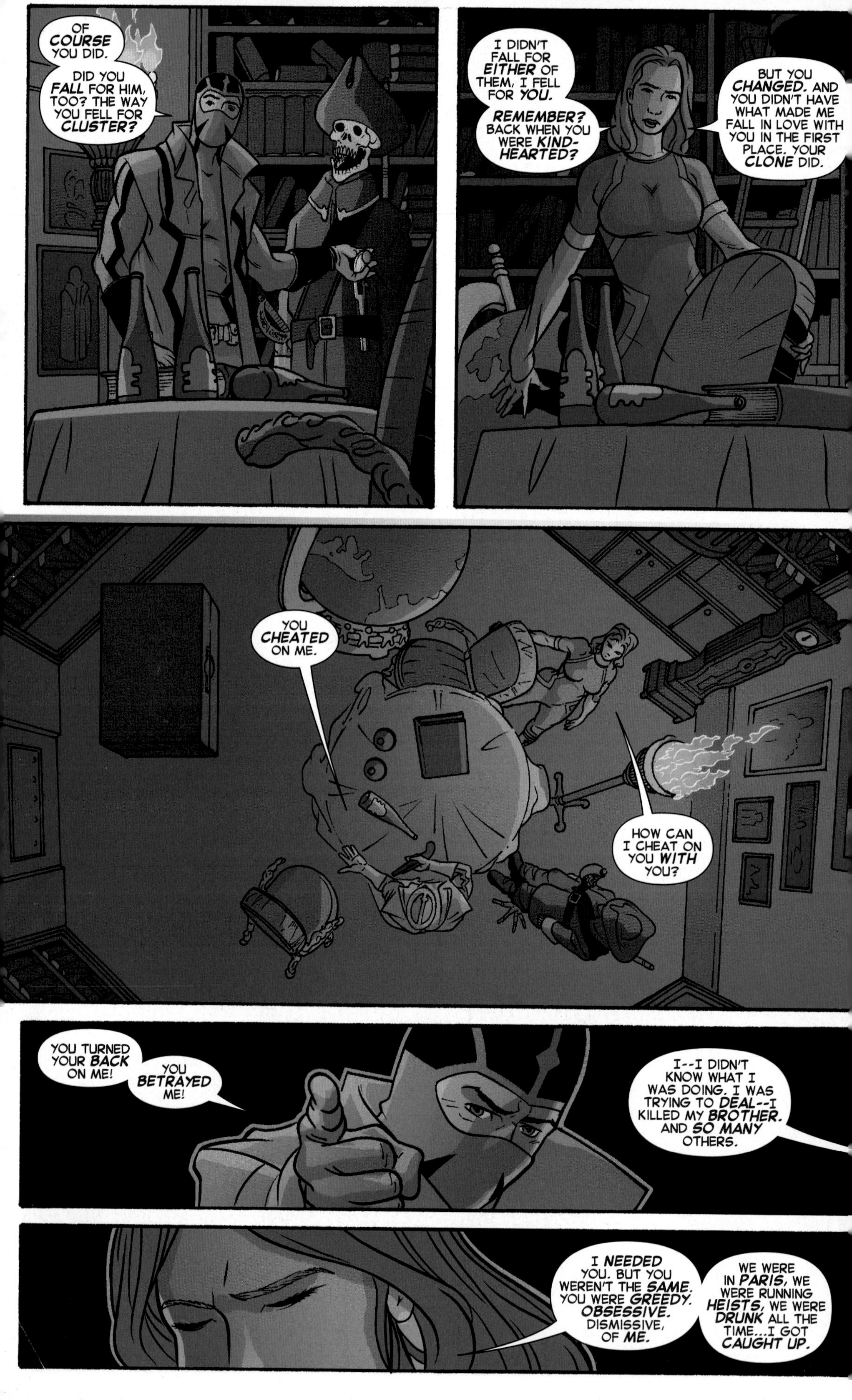
OF COURSE YOU DID.
DID YOU FALL FOR HIM, TOO? THE WAY YOU FELL FOR CLUSTER?
I DIDN'T FALL FOR EITHER OF THEM, I FELL FOR YOU.
REMEMBER? BACK WHEN YOU WERE KIND-HEARTED?
BUT YOU CHANGED. AND YOU DIDN'T HAVE WHAT MADE ME FALL IN LOVE WITH YOU IN THE FIRST PLACE. YOUR CLONE DID.
YOU CHEATED ON ME.
HOW CAN I CHEAT ON YOU WITH YOU?
YOU TURNED YOUR BACK ON ME!
YOU BETRAYED ME!
I--I DIDN'T KNOW WHAT I WAS DOING. I WAS TRYING TO DEAL--I KILLED MY BROTHER. AND SO MANY OTHERS.
I NEEDED YOU. BUT YOU WEREN'T THE SAME. YOU WERE GREEDY. OBSESSIVE. DISMISSIVE, OF ME.
WE WERE IN PARIS, WE WERE RUNNING HEISTS, WE WERE DRUNK ALL THE TIME...I GOT CAUGHT UP.

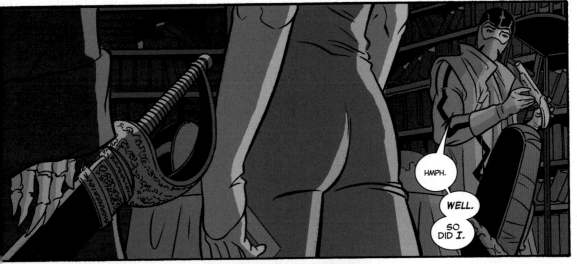

HMPH.

WELL.

SO DID *I*.

NO. NO. THAT DOES *NOT* COVER IT, FANTOMEX.

OF *ALL* THE PEOPLE WHO *COULD* SELL ME OUT TO THE COPS--*THE COPS*--I DID *NOT* THINK THE SO-CALLED "*WORLD'S GREATEST THIEF*" WOULD BE THE *ONE* TO DO IT.

YOU WERE *WRONG.*

I WAS "*WRONG*"?!

I VOWED ON MY *BROTHER'S* LIFE NEVER TO *MURDER* AGAIN. WHEN YOU SET ME UP, YOU SPIT IN MY *FACE!*

WHEN *EVERYONE ELSE* WROTE YOU OFF AS A *BASTARD,* I SAW THE *GOOD* IN YOU. WHY COULDN'T YOU DO THE SAME FOR *ME?*

DON'T PLAY SO *HIGH CLASS,* ELIZABETH. "*TEMET NOSCE.*"

YOU KEEP *TRYING* TO QUIT. BUT YOU KEEP *KILLING* ANYWAY. AND NOW YOU'RE HERE TO *KILL* ME.

KILL, KILL, KILL. WHAT DOES THAT MAKE *YOU?*

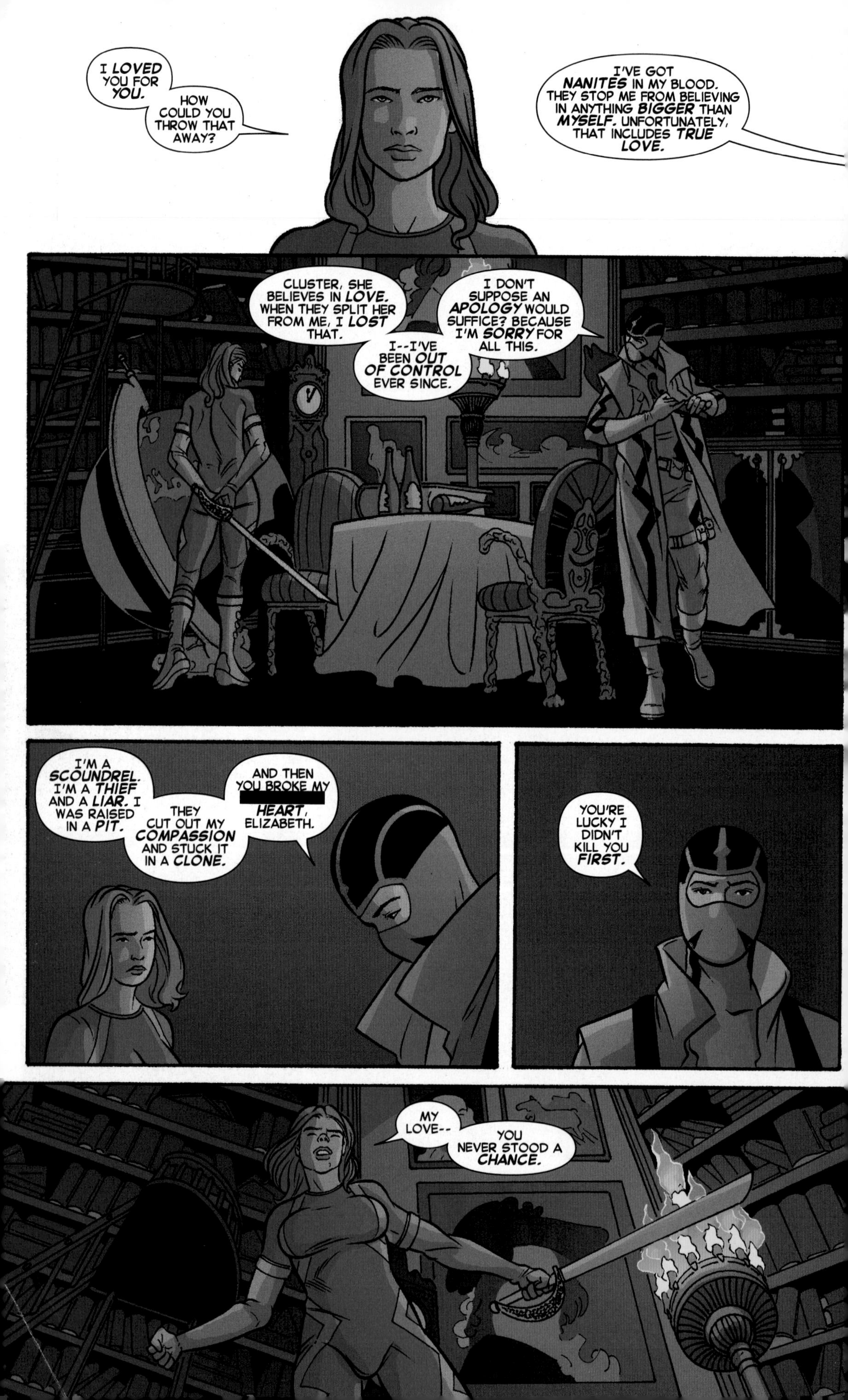
I LOVED YOU FOR YOU.
HOW COULD YOU THROW THAT AWAY?
I'VE GOT NANITES IN MY BLOOD. THEY STOP ME FROM BELIEVING IN ANYTHING BIGGER THAN MYSELF. UNFORTUNATELY, THAT INCLUDES TRUE LOVE.
CLUSTER, SHE BELIEVES IN LOVE. WHEN THEY SPLIT HER FROM ME, I LOST THAT.
I--I'VE BEEN OUT OF CONTROL EVER SINCE.
I DON'T SUPPOSE AN APOLOGY WOULD SUFFICE? BECAUSE I'M SORRY FOR ALL THIS.
I'M A SCOUNDREL. I'M A THIEF AND A LIAR. I WAS RAISED IN A PIT.
THEY CUT OUT MY COMPASSION AND STUCK IT IN A CLONE.
AND THEN YOU BROKE MY [redacted] HEART, ELIZABETH.
YOU'RE LUCKY I DIDN'T KILL YOU FIRST.
MY LOVE--
YOU NEVER STOOD A CHANCE.

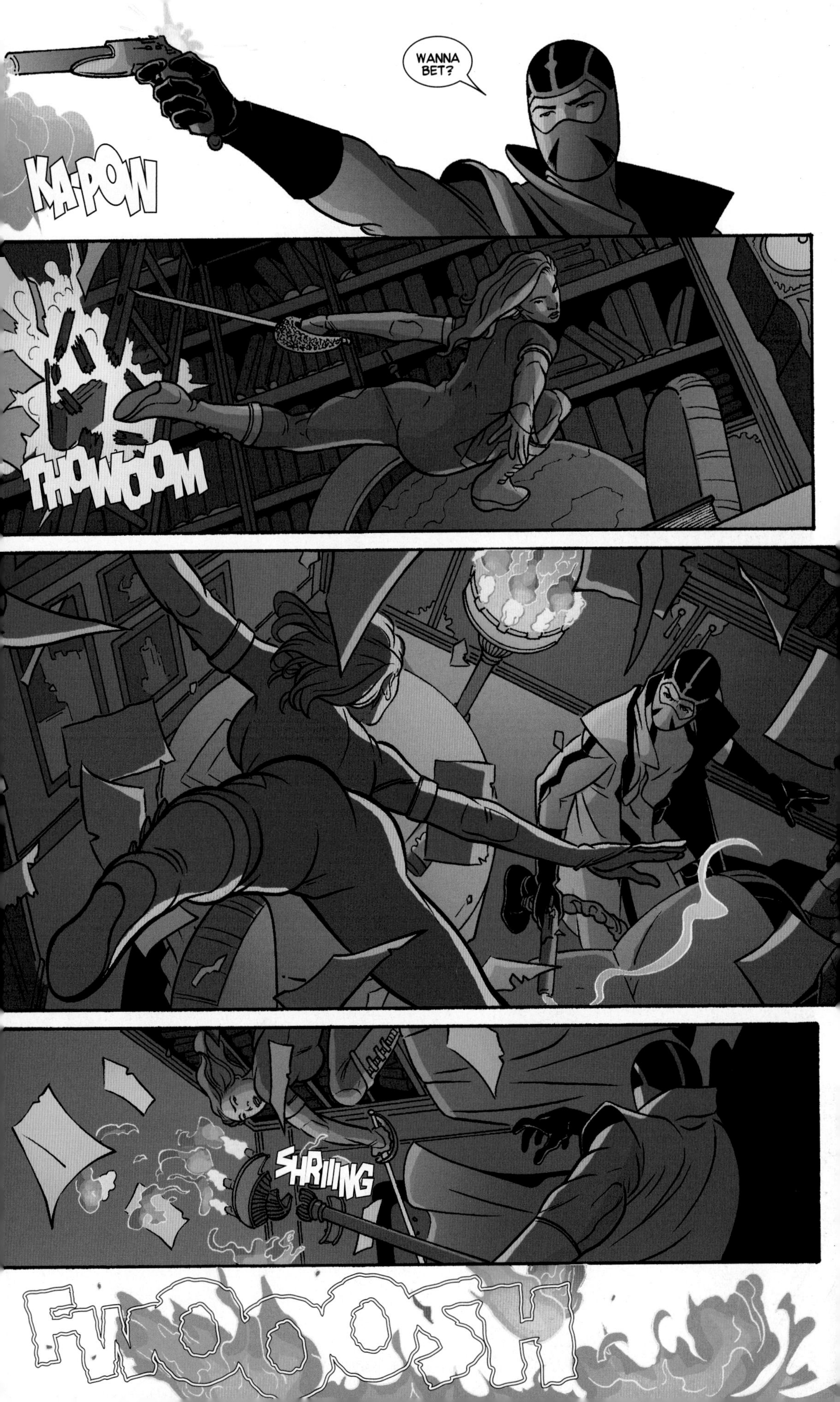
WANNA BET?
KA-POW
THOWOOM
SHRIIIING
FWOOOOSH

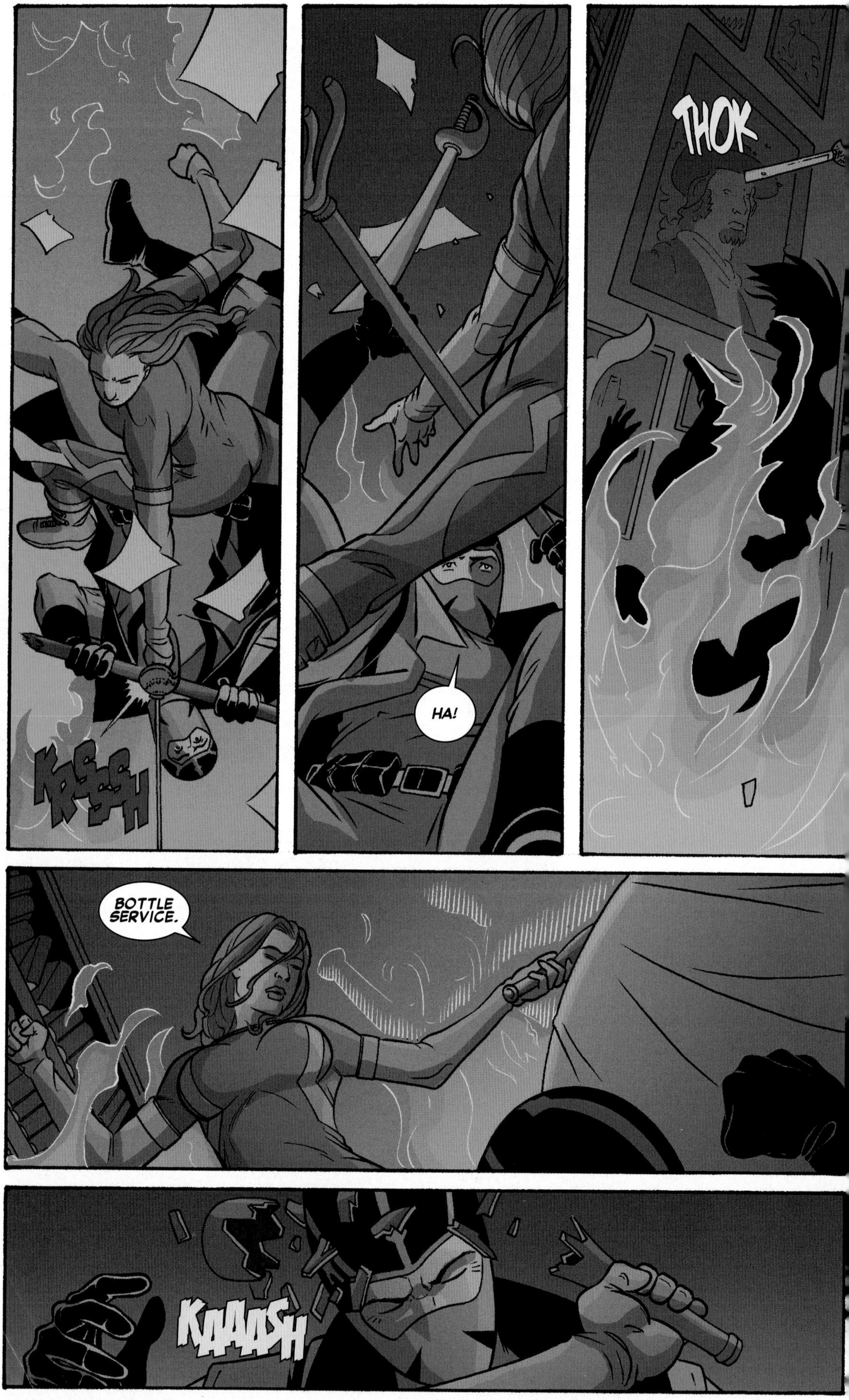
KRSSSH
HA!
THOK
BOTTLE SERVICE.
KAAASH

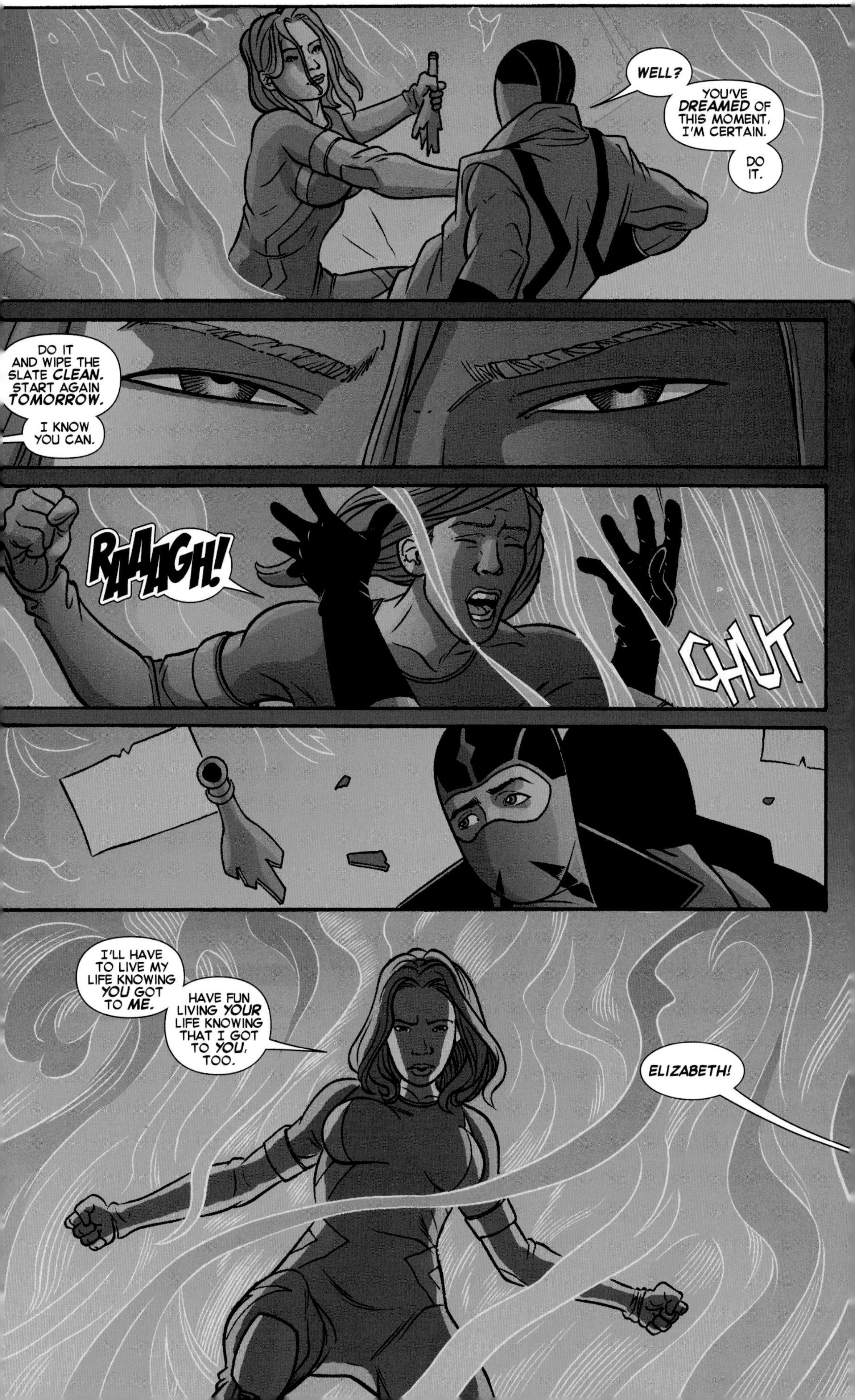
WELL?
YOU'VE DREAMED OF THIS MOMENT, I'M CERTAIN.
DO IT.
DO IT AND WIPE THE SLATE CLEAN. START AGAIN TOMORROW.
I KNOW YOU CAN.
RAAAAGH!
CHUT
I'LL HAVE TO LIVE MY LIFE KNOWING YOU GOT TO ME.
HAVE FUN LIVING YOUR LIFE KNOWING THAT I GOT TO YOU, TOO.
ELIZABETH!

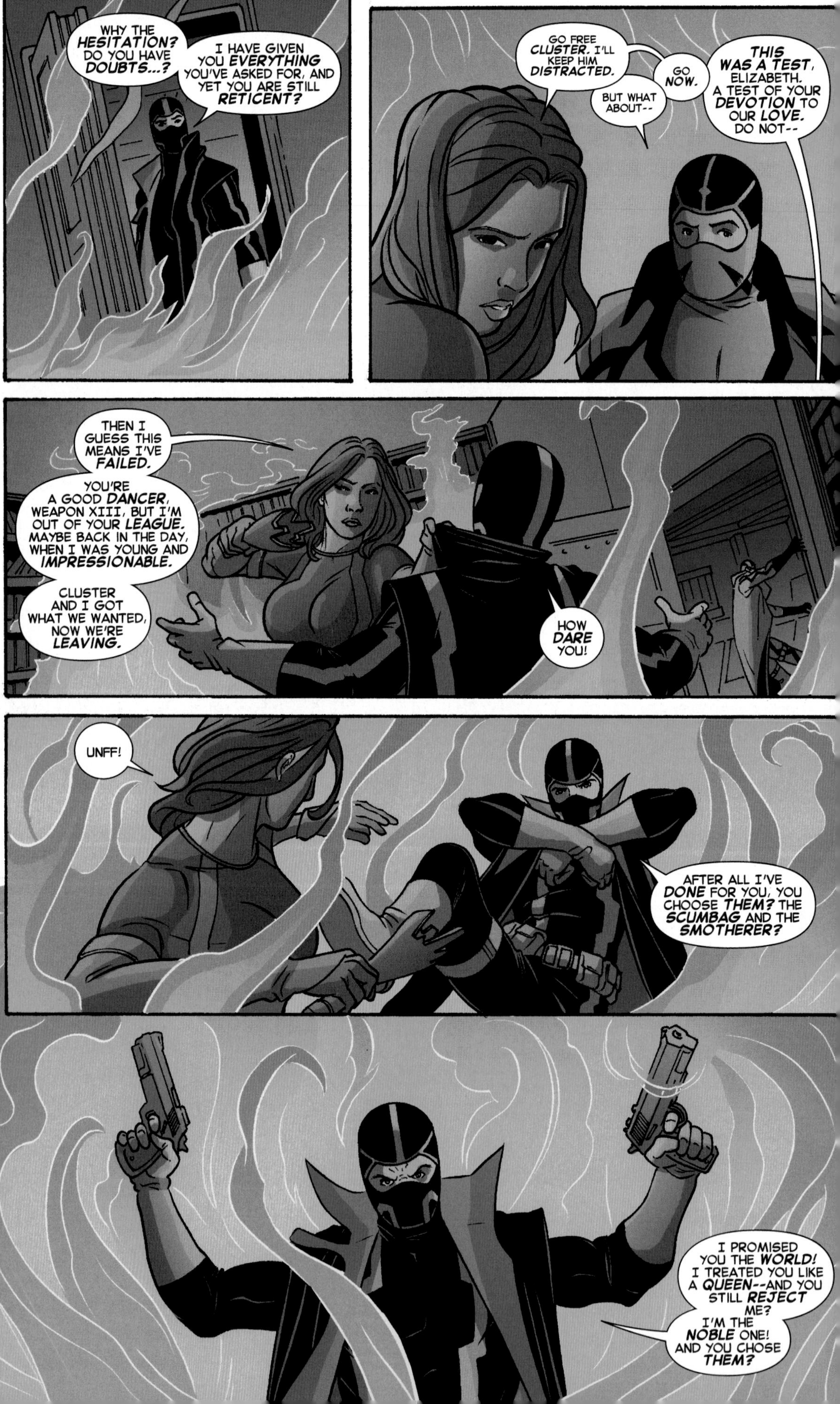

WHY THE HESITATION? DO YOU HAVE DOUBTS...?
I HAVE GIVEN YOU EVERYTHING YOU'VE ASKED FOR, AND YET YOU ARE STILL RETICENT?
GO FREE CLUSTER. I'LL KEEP HIM DISTRACTED.
BUT WHAT ABOUT--
GO NOW.
THIS WAS A TEST, ELIZABETH. A TEST OF YOUR DEVOTION TO OUR LOVE. DO NOT--
THEN I GUESS THIS MEANS I'VE FAILED.
YOU'RE A GOOD DANCER, WEAPON XIII, BUT I'M OUT OF YOUR LEAGUE. MAYBE BACK IN THE DAY, WHEN I WAS YOUNG AND IMPRESSIONABLE.
CLUSTER AND I GOT WHAT WE WANTED, NOW WE'RE LEAVING.
HOW DARE YOU!
UNFF!
AFTER ALL I'VE DONE FOR YOU, YOU CHOOSE THEM? THE SCUMBAG AND THE SMOTHERER?
I PROMISED YOU THE WORLD! I TREATED YOU LIKE A QUEEN--AND YOU STILL REJECT ME?
I'M THE NOBLE ONE! AND YOU CHOSE THEM?

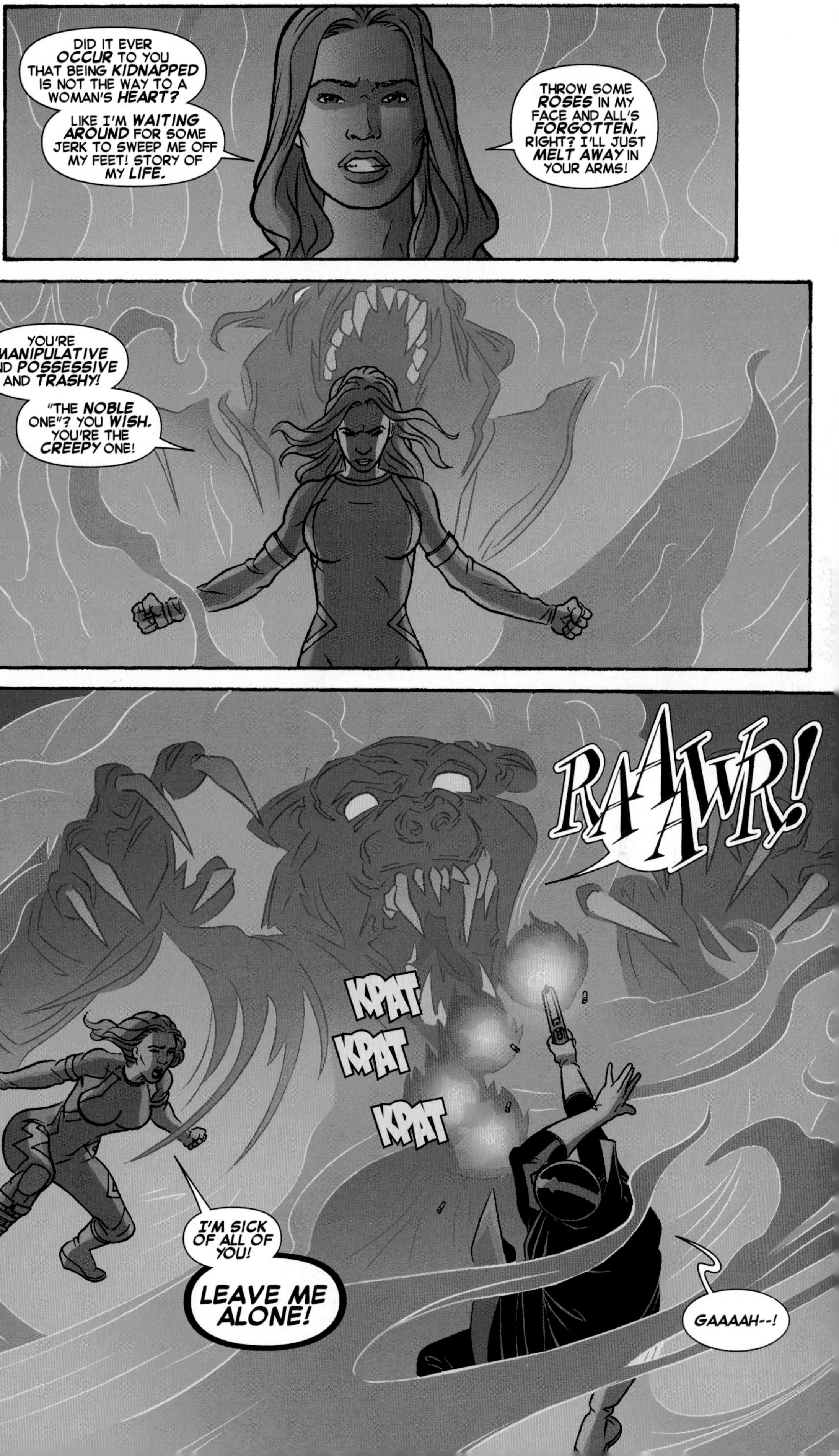
DID IT EVER OCCUR TO YOU THAT BEING KIDNAPPED IS NOT THE WAY TO A WOMAN'S HEART?
LIKE I'M WAITING AROUND FOR SOME JERK TO SWEEP ME OFF MY FEET! STORY OF MY LIFE.
THROW SOME ROSES IN MY FACE AND ALL'S FORGOTTEN, RIGHT? I'LL JUST MELT AWAY IN YOUR ARMS!
YOU'RE MANIPULATIVE AND POSSESSIVE AND TRASHY!
"THE NOBLE ONE"? YOU WISH. YOU'RE THE CREEPY ONE!
RAAAWR!
KPAT
KPAT
KPAT
I'M SICK OF ALL OF YOU!
LEAVE ME ALONE!
GAAAAH--!

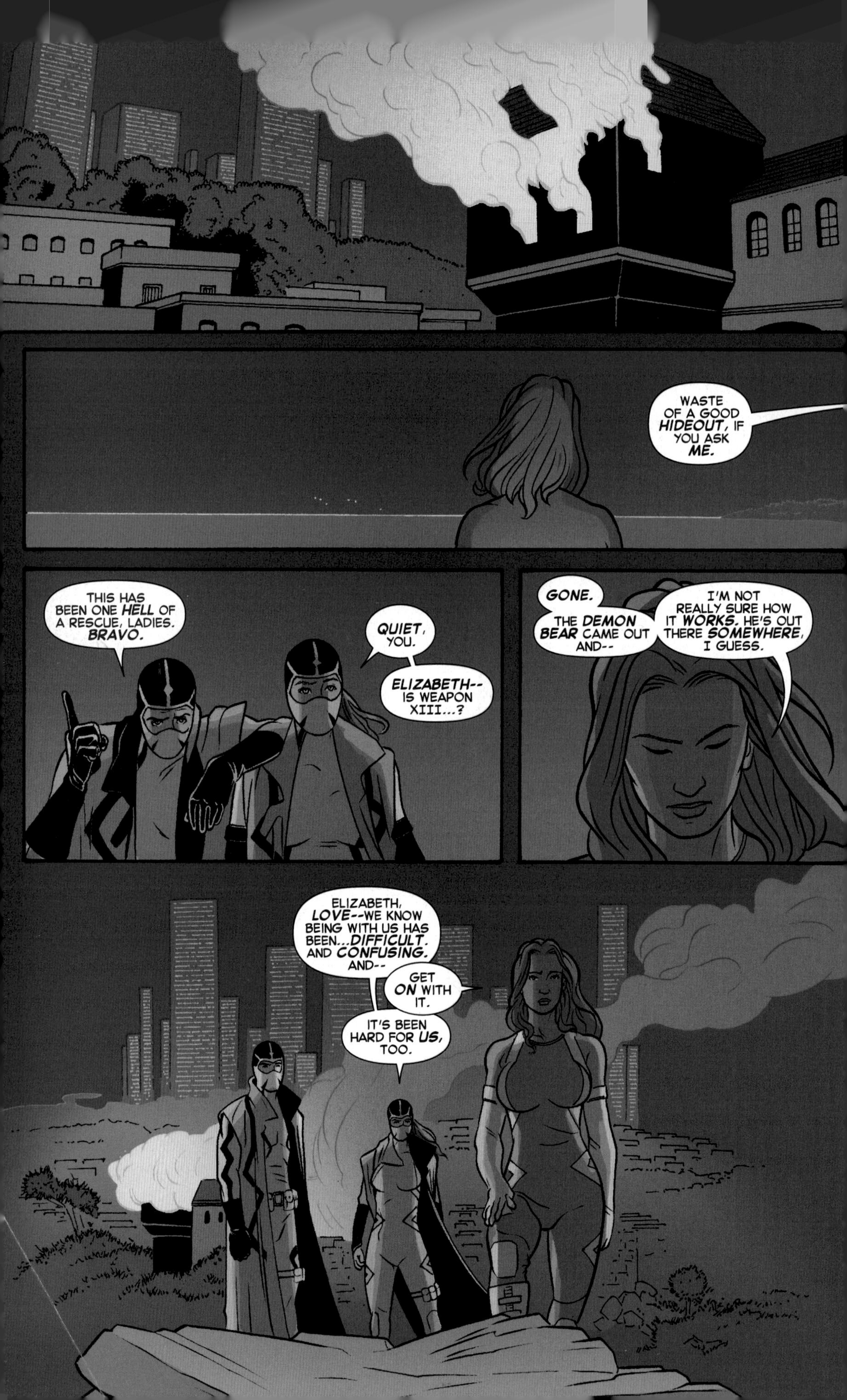
WASTE OF A GOOD HIDEOUT, IF YOU ASK ME.
THIS HAS BEEN ONE HELL OF A RESCUE, LADIES. BRAVO.
QUIET, YOU.
ELIZABETH-- IS WEAPON XIII...?
GONE.
THE DEMON BEAR CAME OUT AND--
I'M NOT REALLY SURE HOW IT WORKS. HE'S OUT THERE SOMEWHERE, I GUESS.
ELIZABETH, LOVE--WE KNOW BEING WITH US HAS BEEN...DIFFICULT. AND CONFUSING. AND--
GET ON WITH IT.
IT'S BEEN HARD FOR US, TOO.

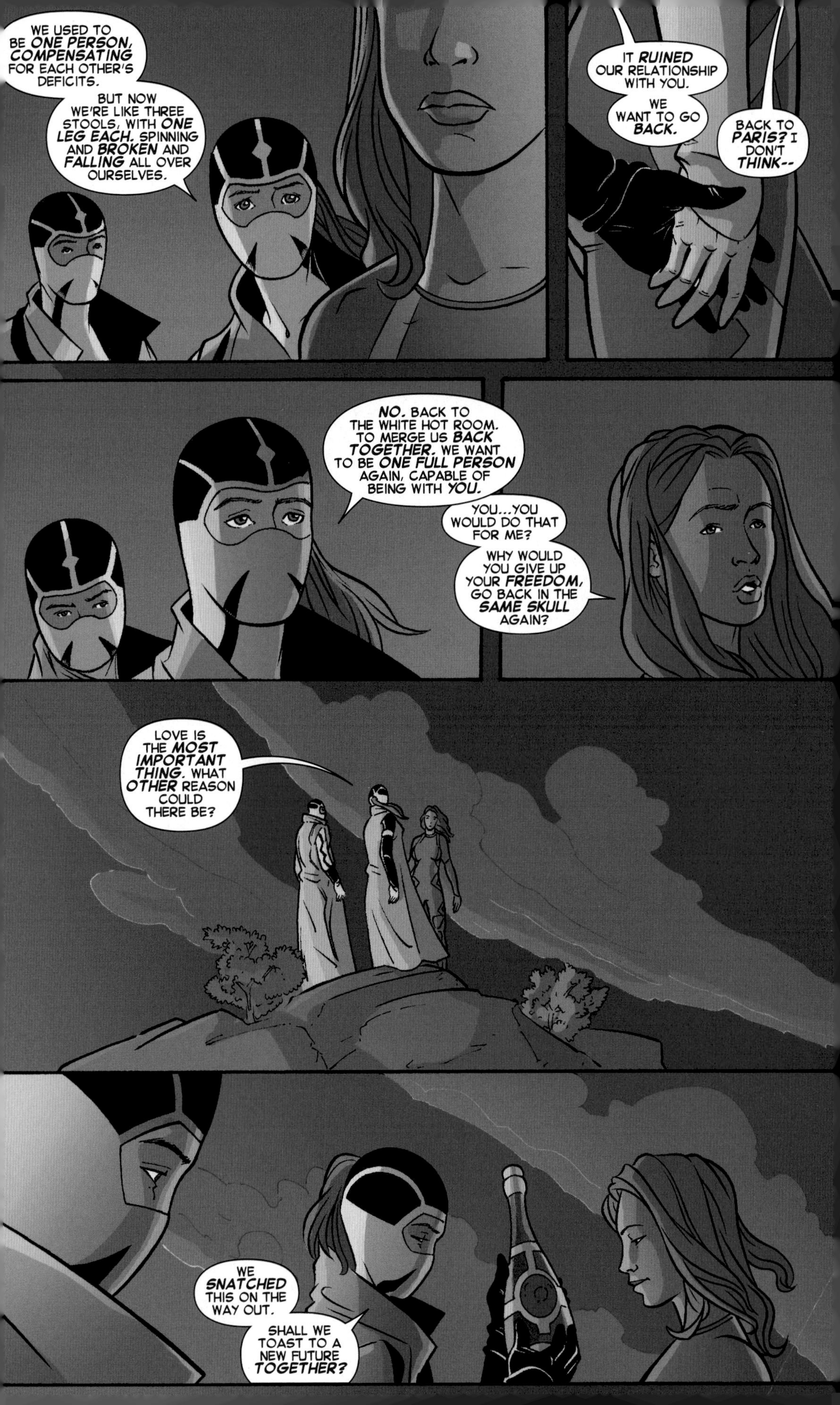
WE USED TO BE ONE PERSON, COMPENSATING FOR EACH OTHER'S DEFICITS.
BUT NOW WE'RE LIKE THREE STOOLS, WITH ONE LEG EACH. SPINNING AND BROKEN AND FALLING ALL OVER OURSELVES.
IT RUINED OUR RELATIONSHIP WITH YOU.
WE WANT TO GO BACK.
BACK TO PARIS? I DON'T THINK--
NO. BACK TO THE WHITE HOT ROOM. TO MERGE US BACK TOGETHER. WE WANT TO BE ONE FULL PERSON AGAIN, CAPABLE OF BEING WITH YOU.
YOU...YOU WOULD DO THAT FOR ME?
WHY WOULD YOU GIVE UP YOUR FREEDOM, GO BACK IN THE SAME SKULL AGAIN?
LOVE IS THE MOST IMPORTANT THING. WHAT OTHER REASON COULD THERE BE?
WE SNATCHED THIS ON THE WAY OUT.
SHALL WE TOAST TO A NEW FUTURE TOGETHER?

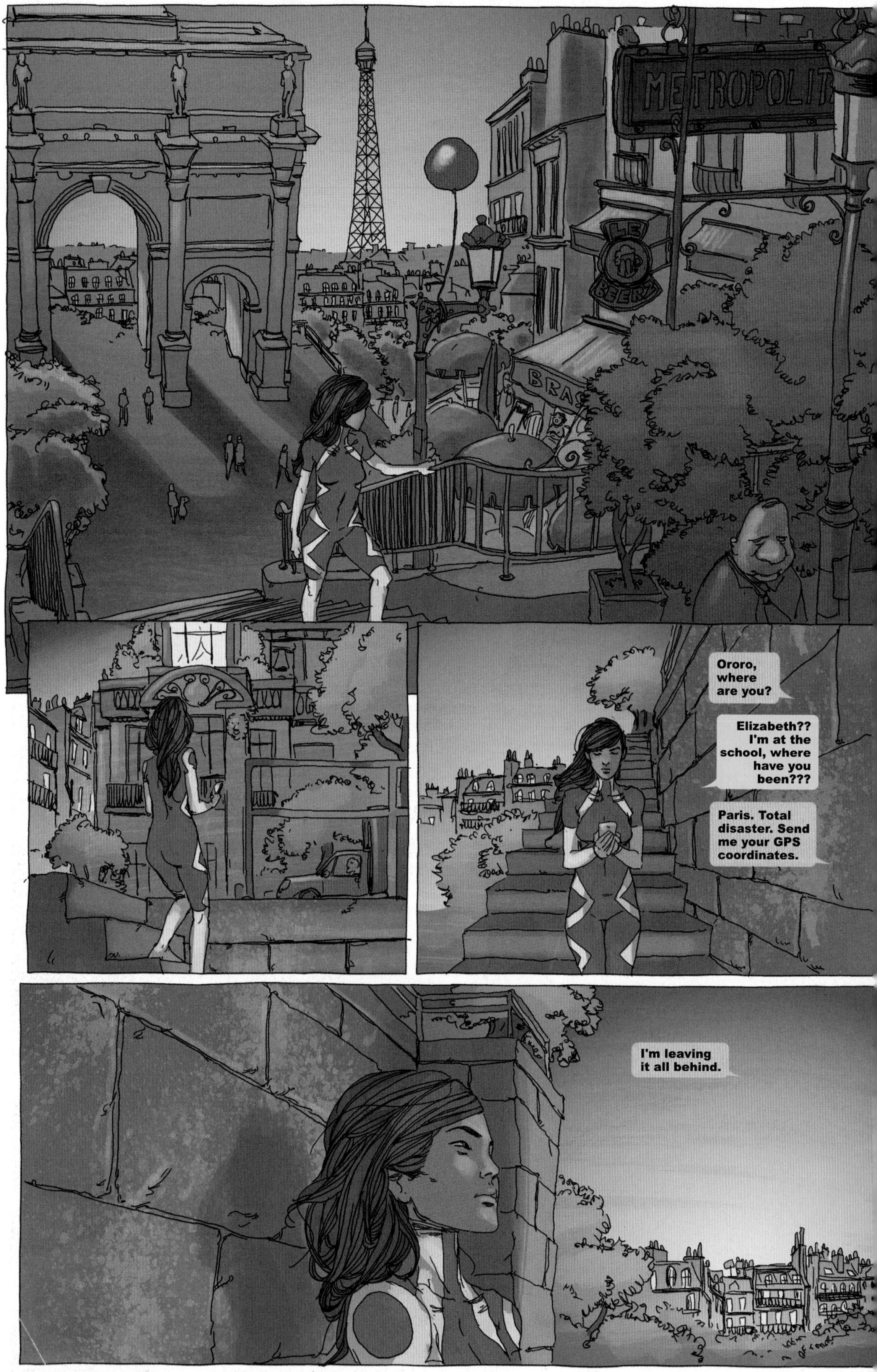
METROPOLIT
BRAS
Ororo, where are you?
Elizabeth?? I'm at the school, where have you been???
Paris. Total disaster. Send me your GPS coordinates.
I'm leaving it all behind.

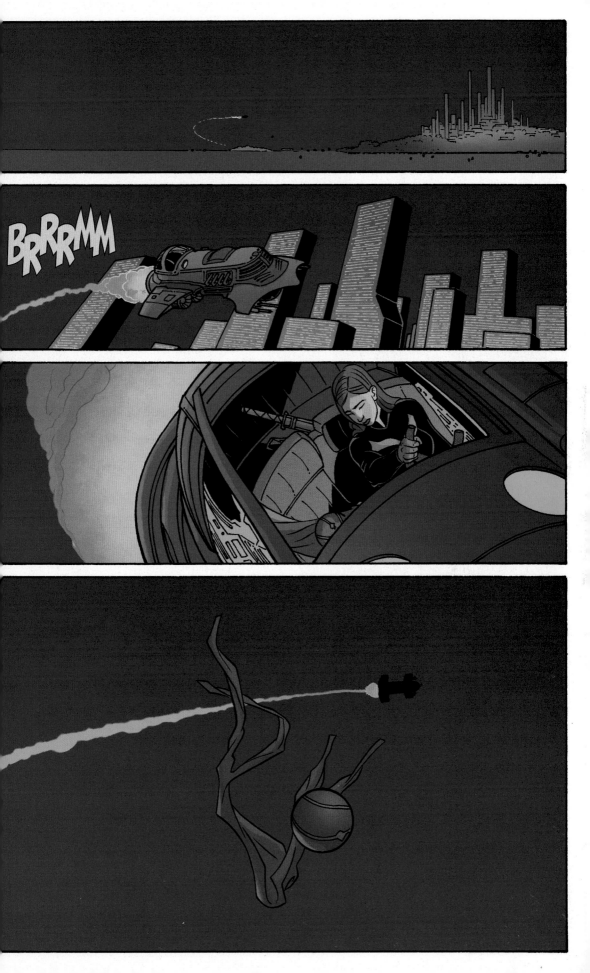

BRRRMM

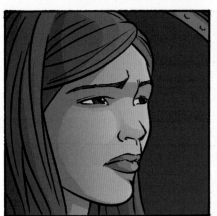

"DRINK IT WITH SOMEONE AND FALL IN LOVE FOREVER..."

A BILLION DOLLAR BOTTLE, HUH?

BROK

IT, I DESERVE IT.

AUTOPILOT.

YES, ELIZABETH?

SET A COURSE FOR LOS ANGELES.

I'M GOING TO GET ROYALLY PLASTERED.

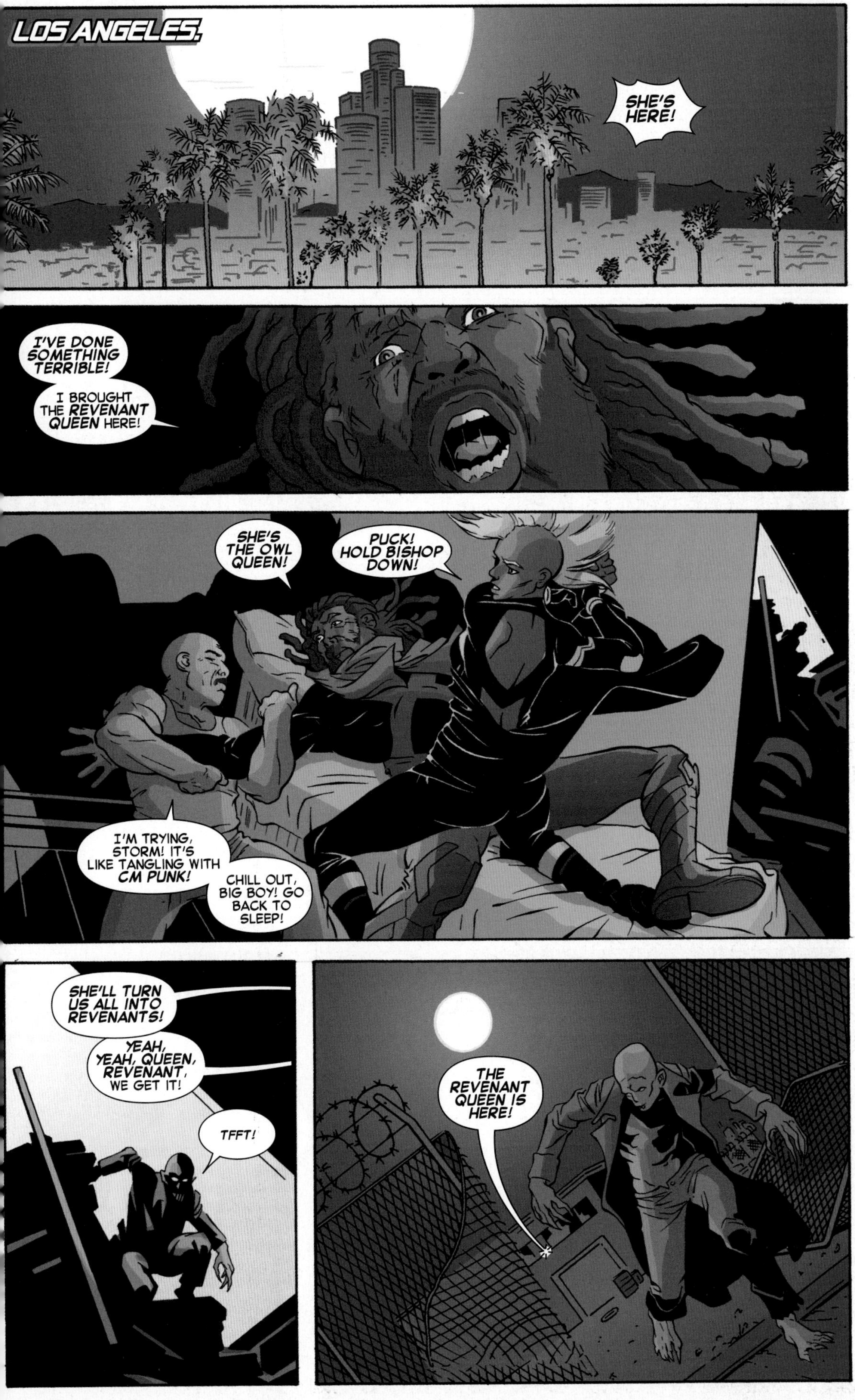
LOS ANGELES.
SHE'S HERE!
I'VE DONE SOMETHING TERRIBLE!
I BROUGHT THE REVENANT QUEEN HERE!
SHE'S THE OWL QUEEN!
PUCK! HOLD BISHOP DOWN!
I'M TRYING, STORM! IT'S LIKE TANGLING WITH CM PUNK!
CHILL OUT, BIG BOY! GO BACK TO SLEEP!
SHE'LL TURN US ALL INTO REVENANTS!
YEAH, YEAH, QUEEN, REVENANT, WE GET IT!
TFFT!
THE REVENANT QUEEN IS HERE!

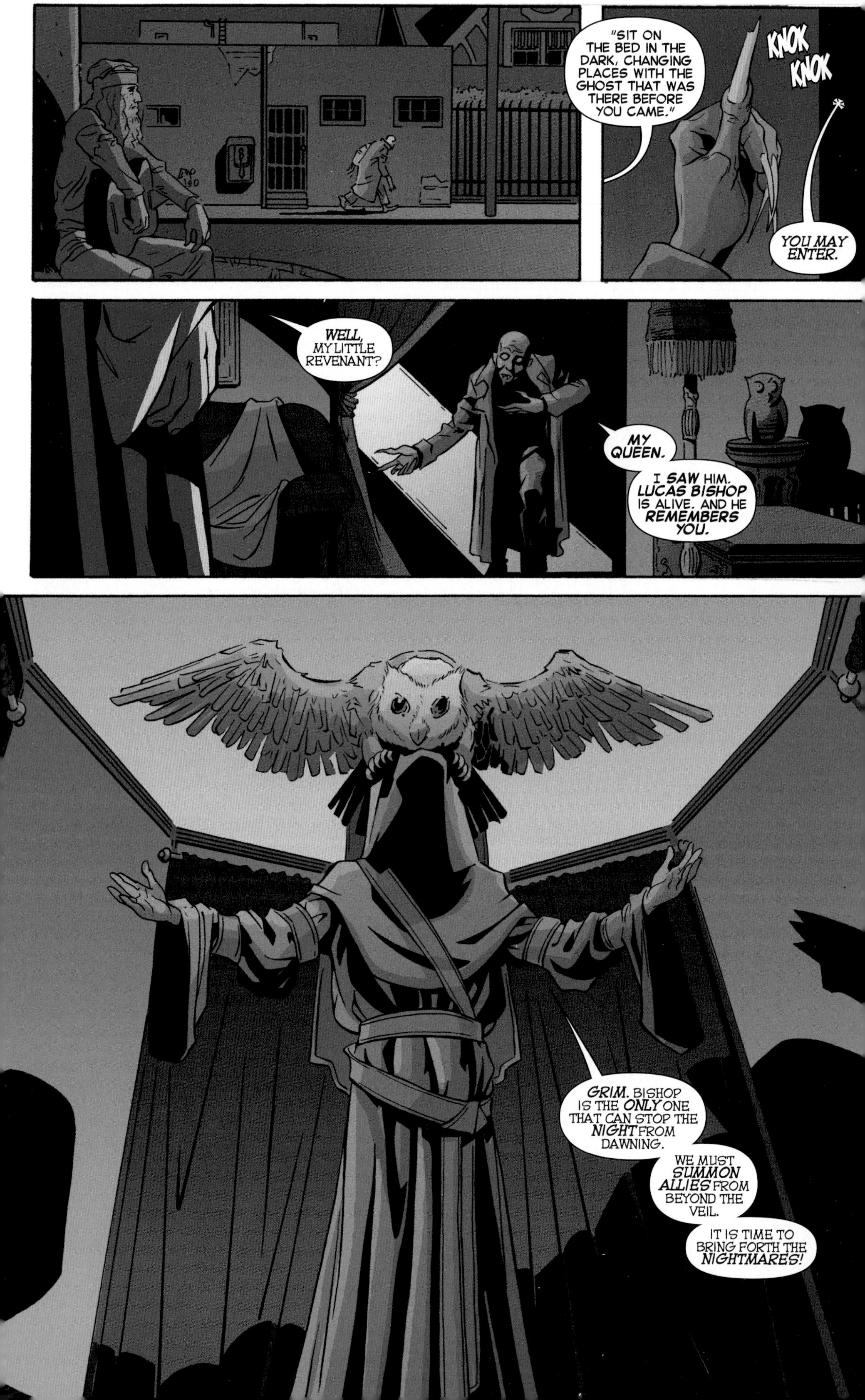
"SIT ON THE BED IN THE DARK, CHANGING PLACES WITH THE GHOST THAT WAS THERE BEFORE YOU CAME."
KNOK KNOK
YOU MAY ENTER.
WELL, MY LITTLE REVENANT?
MY QUEEN.
I SAW HIM. LUCAS BISHOP IS ALIVE. AND HE REMEMBERS YOU.
GRIM. BISHOP IS THE ONLY ONE THAT CAN STOP THE NIGHT FROM DAWNING.
WE MUST SUMMON ALLIES FROM BEYOND THE VEIL.
IT IS TIME TO BRING FORTH THE NIGHTMARES!

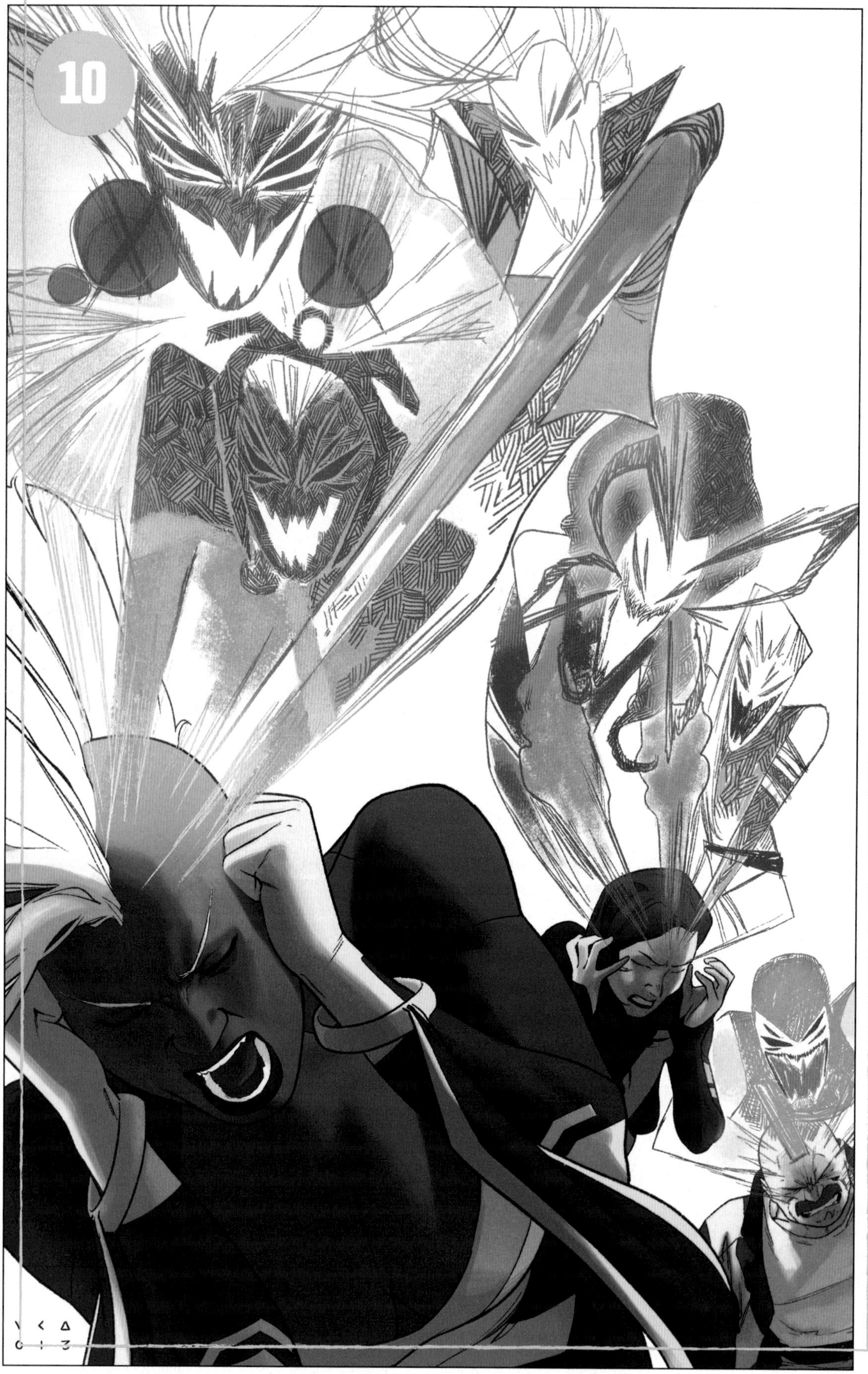
10

TORN AND FRAYED

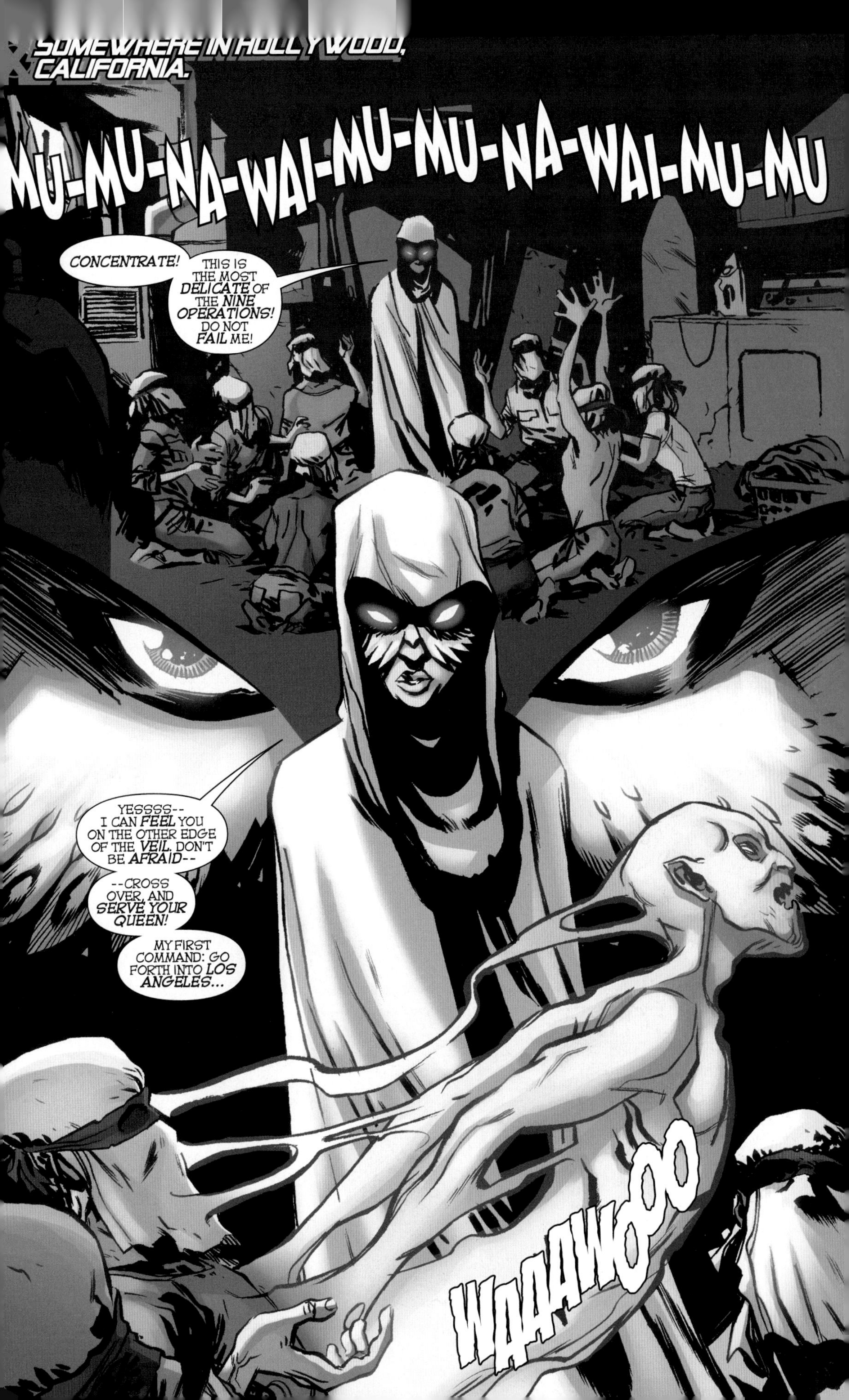
SOMEWHERE IN HOLLYWOOD, CALIFORNIA.
MU-MU-NA-WAI-MU-MU-NA-WAI-MU-MU
CONCENTRATE!
THIS IS THE MOST DELICATE OF THE NINE OPERATIONS! DO NOT FAIL ME!
YESSSS-- I CAN FEEL YOU ON THE OTHER EDGE OF THE VEIL. DON'T BE AFRAID--
--CROSS OVER, AND SERVE YOUR QUEEN!
MY FIRST COMMAND: GO FORTH INTO LOS ANGELES...
WAAAWOOO

"...AND BRING ME THE HEAD OF *LUCAS BISHOP*."

DOWNTOWN LOS ANGELES.

THE *REVENANT QUEEN*...

SHE IS *HERE*.

YOU *SAID* THAT ALREADY.

A *MOMENT*, PUCK.

WHEN ELIZABETH AND I WERE INSIDE BISHOP'S MIND, WE SAW--

WE SAW A *NIGHTMARE*.

A *NIGHTMARE* I'D RATHER NOT *RELIVE*, THANK YOU.

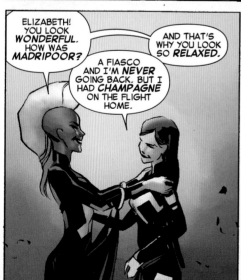

ELIZABETH! YOU LOOK *WONDERFUL*. HOW WAS *MADRIPOOR*?

AND THAT'S WHY YOU LOOK SO *RELAXED*.

A *FIASCO* AND I'M *NEVER* GOING BACK. BUT I HAD *CHAMPAGNE* ON THE FLIGHT HOME.

HULLO, LUCAS.

HI, BETSY.

MAY I...?

OKAY.

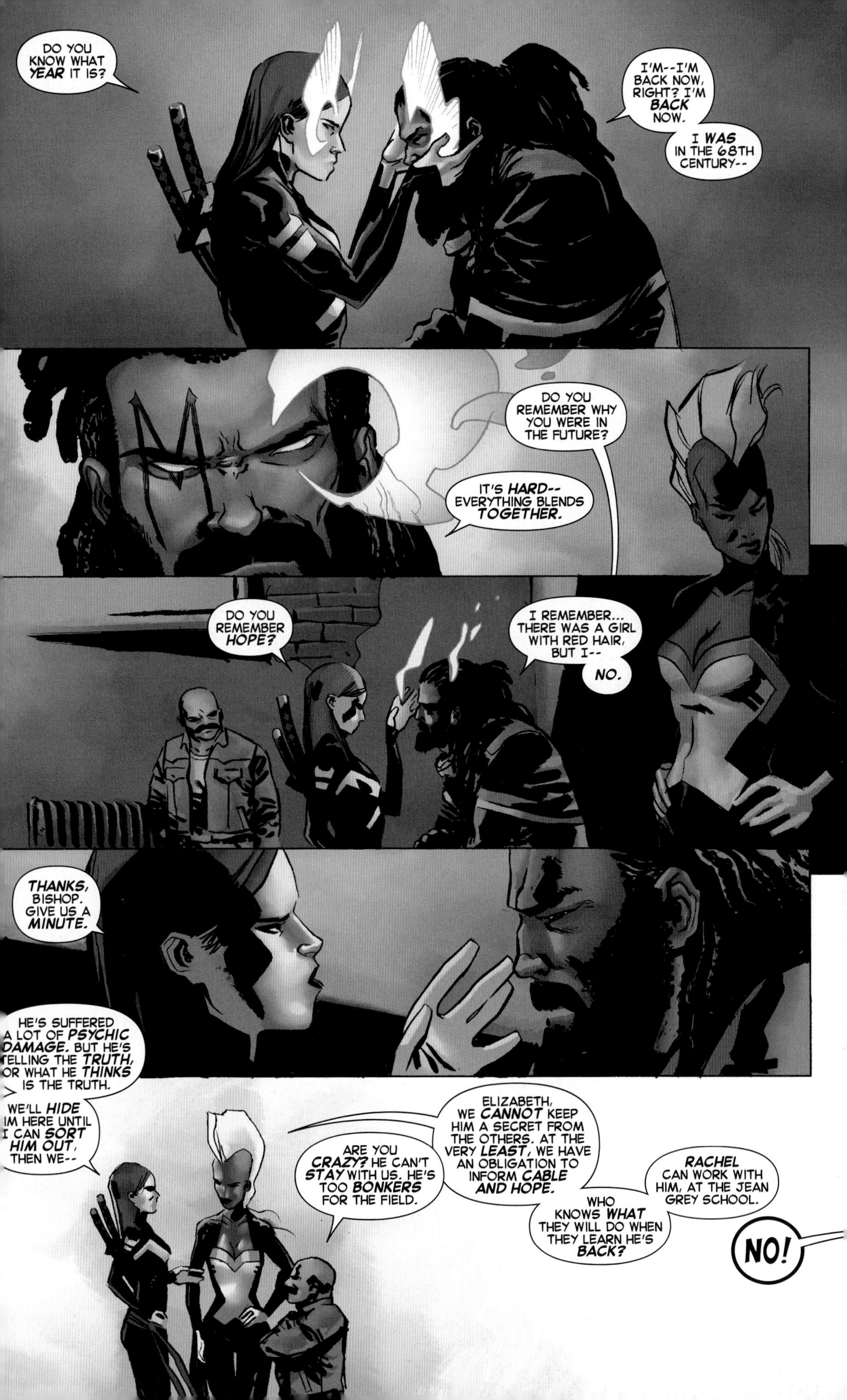

DO YOU KNOW WHAT YEAR IT IS?
I'M--I'M BACK NOW, RIGHT? I'M BACK NOW.
I WAS IN THE 68TH CENTURY--
DO YOU REMEMBER WHY YOU WERE IN THE FUTURE?
IT'S HARD-- EVERYTHING BLENDS TOGETHER.
DO YOU REMEMBER HOPE?
I REMEMBER... THERE WAS A GIRL WITH RED HAIR, BUT I--
NO.
THANKS, BISHOP. GIVE US A MINUTE.
HE'S SUFFERED A LOT OF PSYCHIC DAMAGE. BUT HE'S TELLING THE TRUTH, OR WHAT HE THINKS IS THE TRUTH.
WE'LL HIDE IM HERE UNTIL I CAN SORT HIM OUT, THEN WE--
ARE YOU CRAZY? HE CAN'T STAY WITH US. HE'S TOO BONKERS FOR THE FIELD.
ELIZABETH, WE CANNOT KEEP HIM A SECRET FROM THE OTHERS. AT THE VERY LEAST, WE HAVE AN OBLIGATION TO INFORM CABLE AND HOPE.
WHO KNOWS WHAT THEY WILL DO WHEN THEY LEARN HE'S BACK?
RACHEL CAN WORK WITH HIM, AT THE JEAN GREY SCHOOL.
NO!

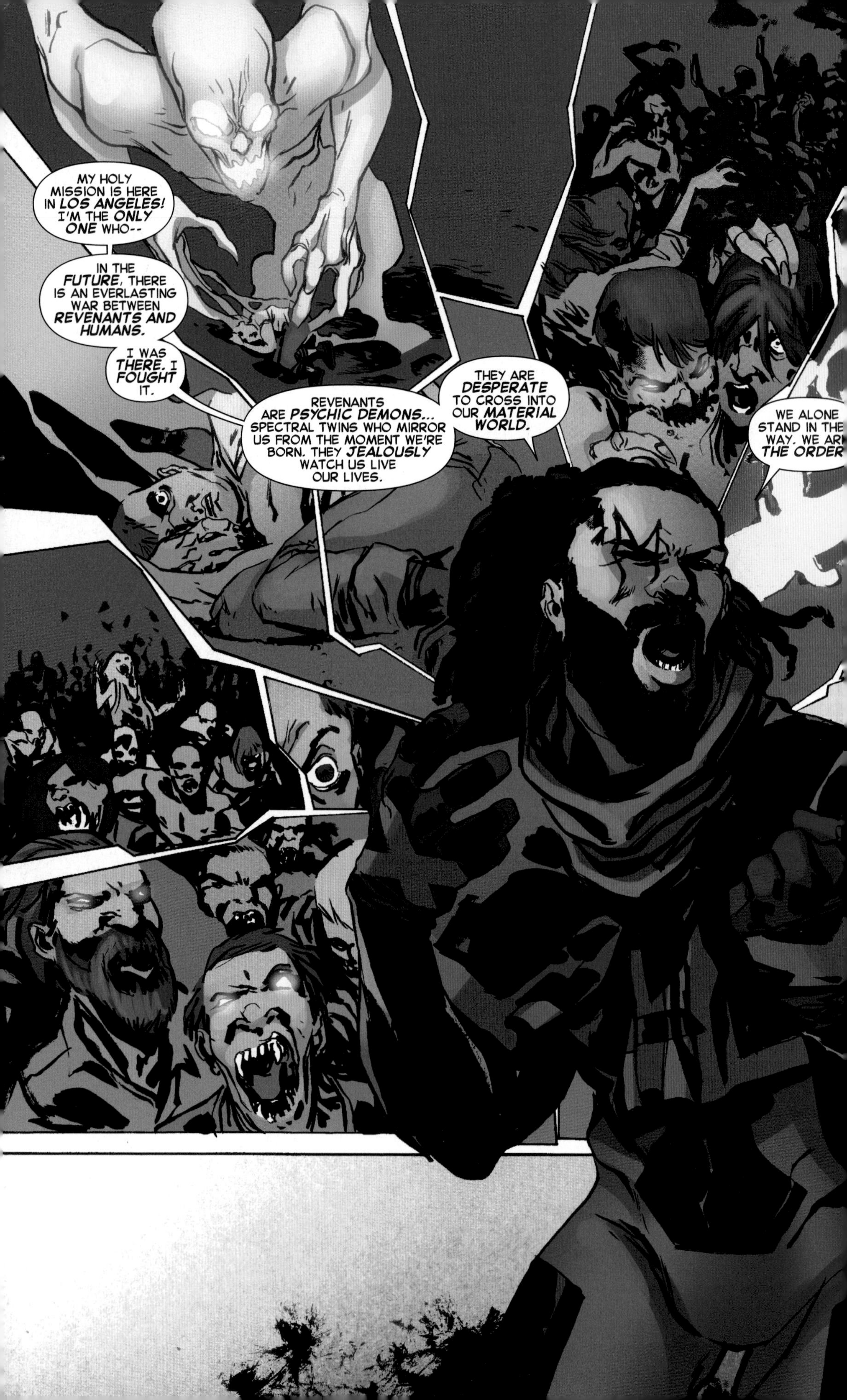
MY HOLY MISSION IS HERE IN LOS ANGELES! I'M THE ONLY ONE WHO--
IN THE FUTURE, THERE IS AN EVERLASTING WAR BETWEEN REVENANTS AND HUMANS.
I WAS THERE. I FOUGHT IT.
REVENANTS ARE PSYCHIC DEMONS... SPECTRAL TWINS WHO MIRROR US FROM THE MOMENT WE'RE BORN. THEY JEALOUSLY WATCH US LIVE OUR LIVES.
THEY ARE DESPERATE TO CROSS INTO OUR MATERIAL WORLD.
WE ALONE STAND IN THE WAY. WE AR THE ORDER

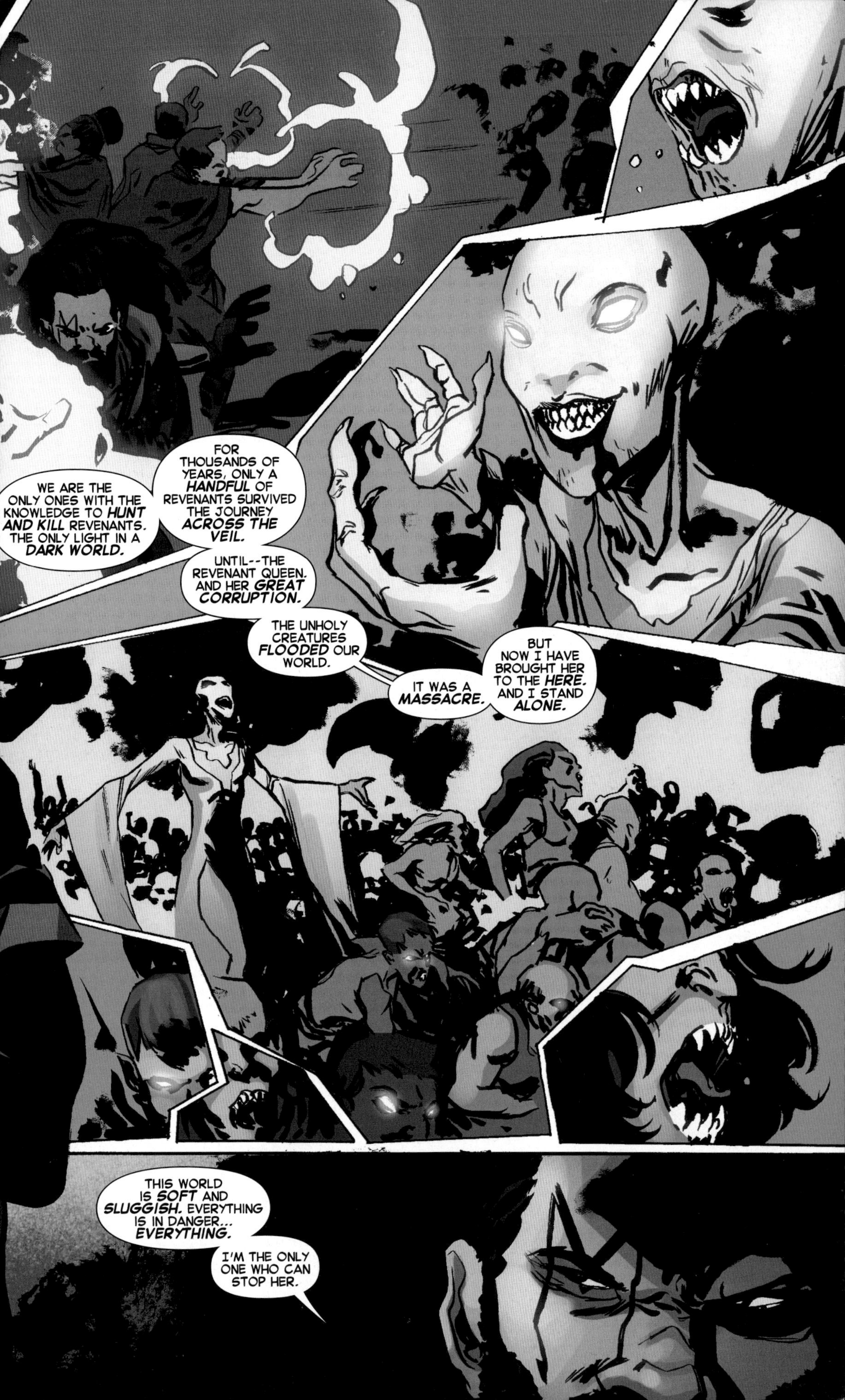

WE ARE THE ONLY ONES WITH THE KNOWLEDGE TO HUNT AND KILL REVENANTS. THE ONLY LIGHT IN A DARK WORLD.
FOR THOUSANDS OF YEARS, ONLY A HANDFUL OF REVENANTS SURVIVED THE JOURNEY ACROSS THE VEIL.
UNTIL--THE REVENANT QUEEN. AND HER GREAT CORRUPTION.
THE UNHOLY CREATURES FLOODED OUR WORLD.
IT WAS A MASSACRE.
BUT NOW I HAVE BROUGHT HER TO THE HERE. AND I STAND ALONE.
THIS WORLD IS SOFT AND SLUGGISH. EVERYTHING IS IN DANGER... EVERYTHING.
I'M THE ONLY ONE WHO CAN STOP HER.

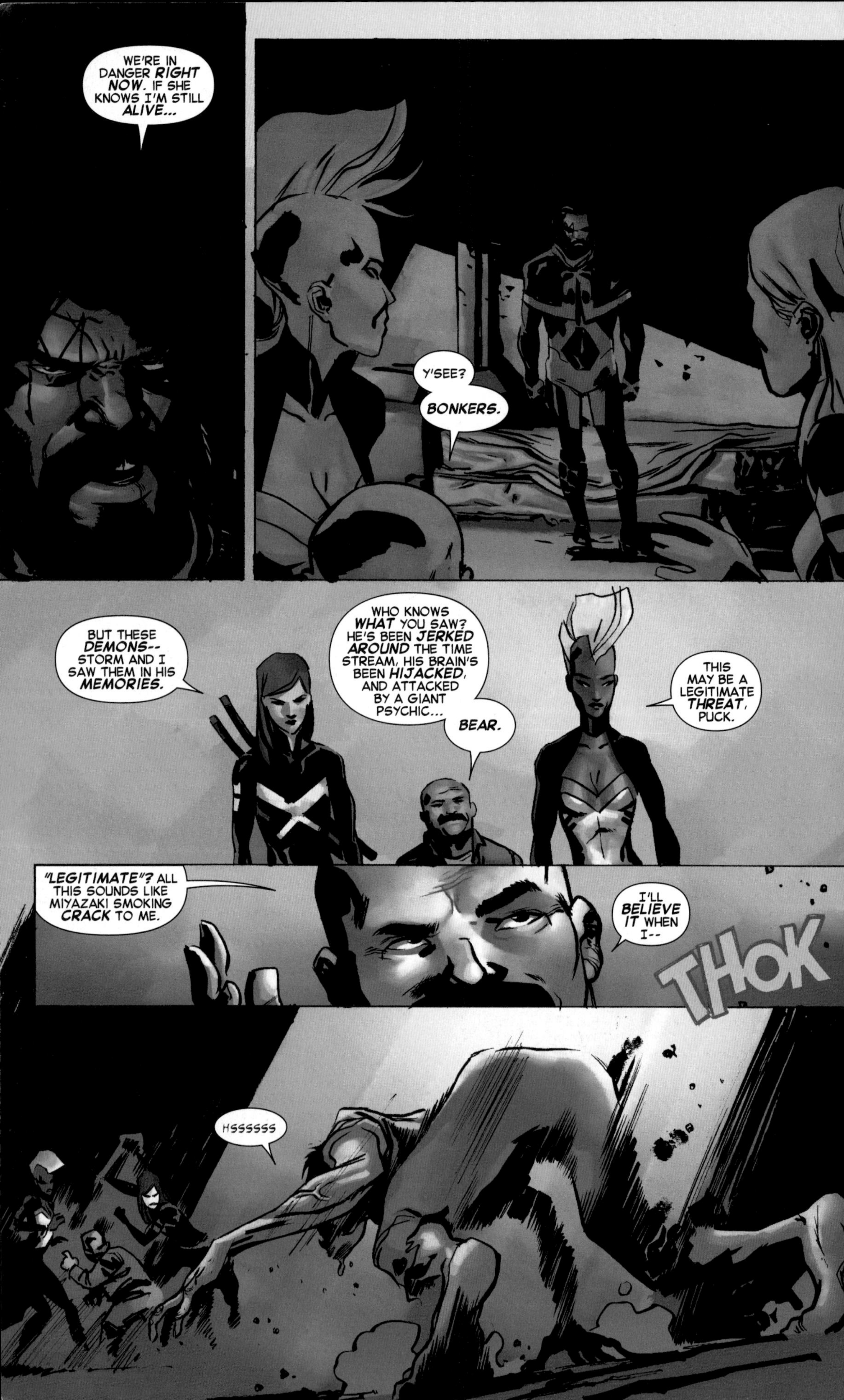
WE'RE IN DANGER RIGHT NOW. IF SHE KNOWS I'M STILL ALIVE...
Y'SEE?
BONKERS.
BUT THESE DEMONS-- STORM AND I SAW THEM IN HIS MEMORIES.
WHO KNOWS WHAT YOU SAW? HE'S BEEN JERKED AROUND THE TIME STREAM, HIS BRAIN'S BEEN HIJACKED, AND ATTACKED BY A GIANT PSYCHIC...
BEAR.
THIS MAY BE A LEGITIMATE THREAT, PUCK.
"LEGITIMATE"? ALL THIS SOUNDS LIKE MIYAZAKI SMOKING CRACK TO ME.
I'LL BELIEVE IT WHEN I--
THOK
HSSSSSS

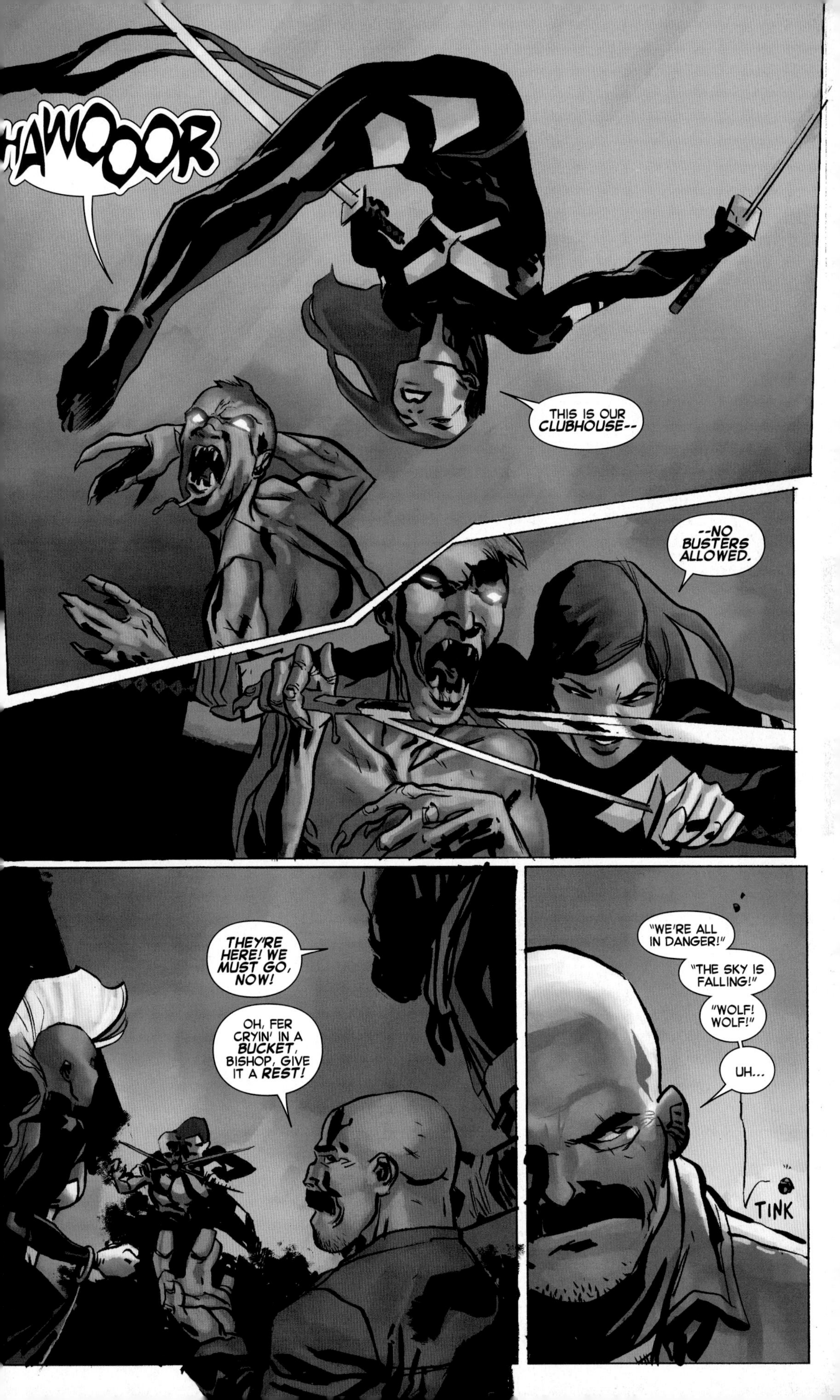

HAWOOOR
THIS IS OUR CLUBHOUSE--
--NO BUSTERS ALLOWED.
THEY'RE HERE! WE MUST GO, NOW!
OH, FER CRYIN' IN A BUCKET, BISHOP, GIVE IT A REST!
"WE'RE ALL IN DANGER!"
"THE SKY IS FALLING!"
"WOLF! WOLF!"
UH...
TINK

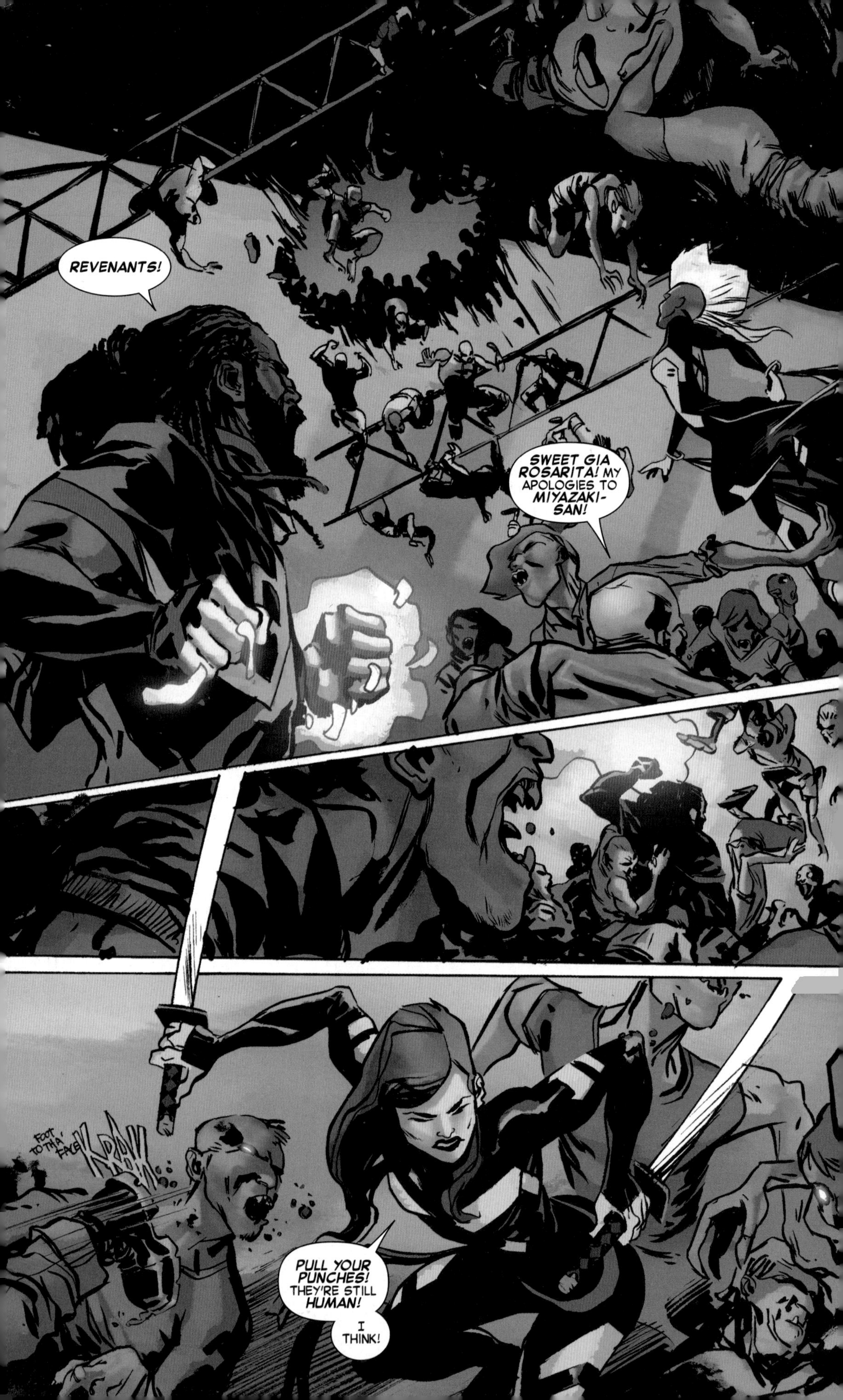
REVENANTS!
SWEET GIA ROSARITA! MY APOLOGIES TO MIYAZAKI-SAN!
FOOT TO THA' FACE
PULL YOUR PUNCHES! THEY'RE STILL HUMAN!
I THINK!

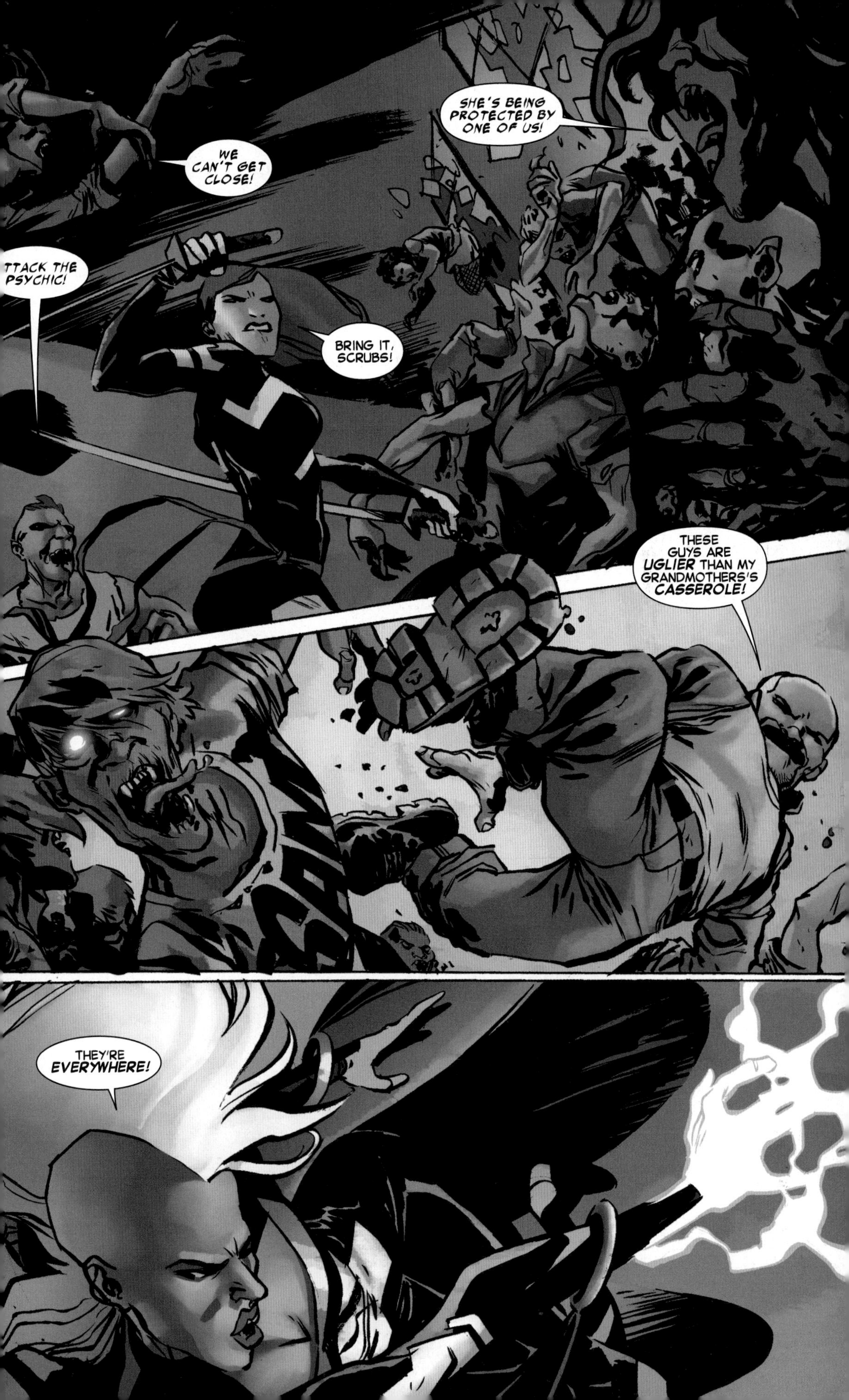
WE CAN'T GET CLOSE!
SHE'S BEING PROTECTED BY ONE OF US!
TTACK THE PSYCHIC!
BRING IT, SCRUBS!
THESE GUYS ARE UGLIER THAN MY GRANDMOTHERS'S CASSEROLE!
THEY'RE EVERYWHERE!

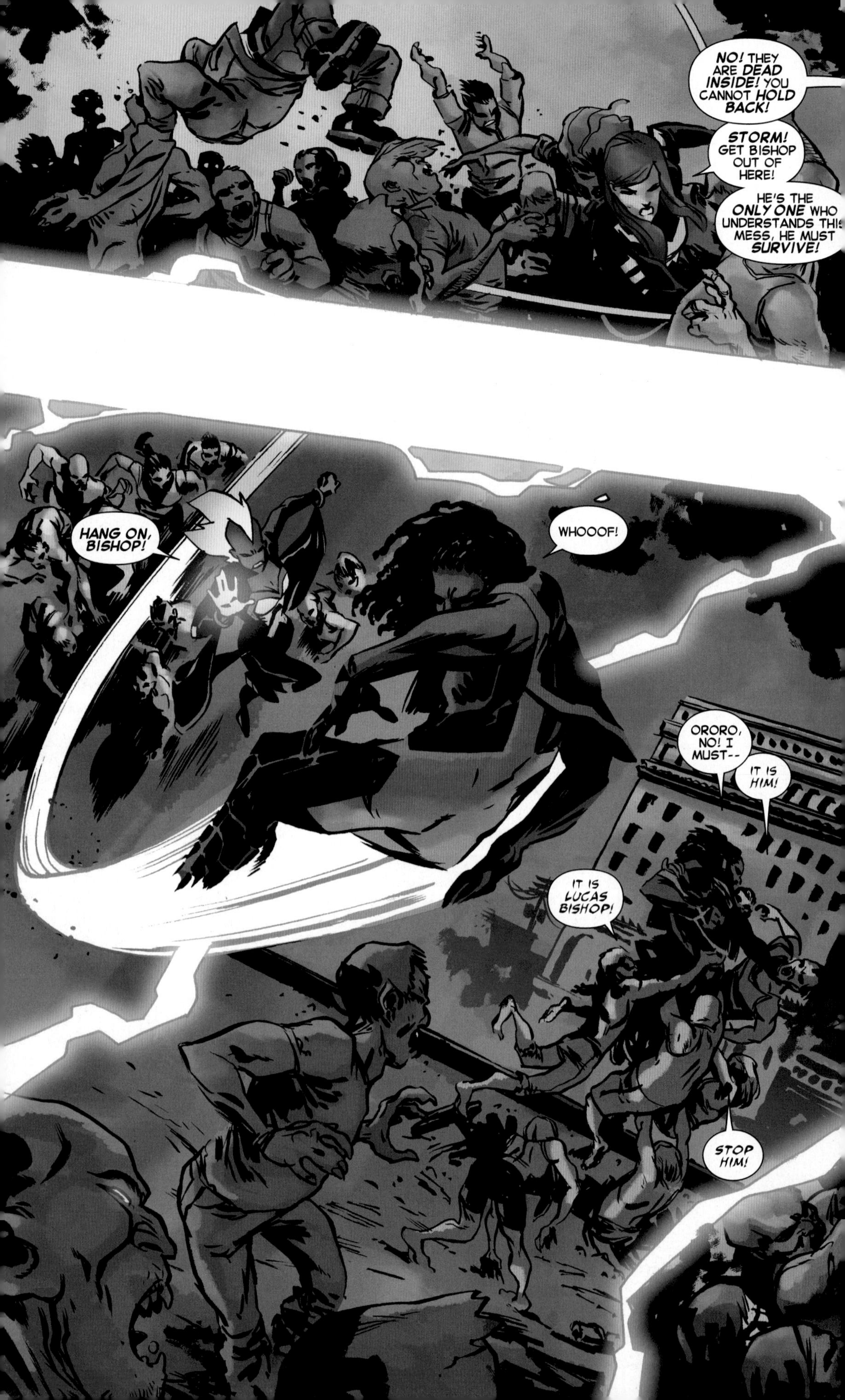
NO! THEY ARE DEAD INSIDE! YOU CANNOT HOLD BACK!
STORM! GET BISHOP OUT OF HERE!
HE'S THE ONLY ONE WHO UNDERSTANDS THIS MESS, HE MUST SURVIVE!
HANG ON, BISHOP!
WHOOOF!
ORORO, NO! I MUST--
IT IS HIM!
IT IS LUCAS BISHOP!
STOP HIM!

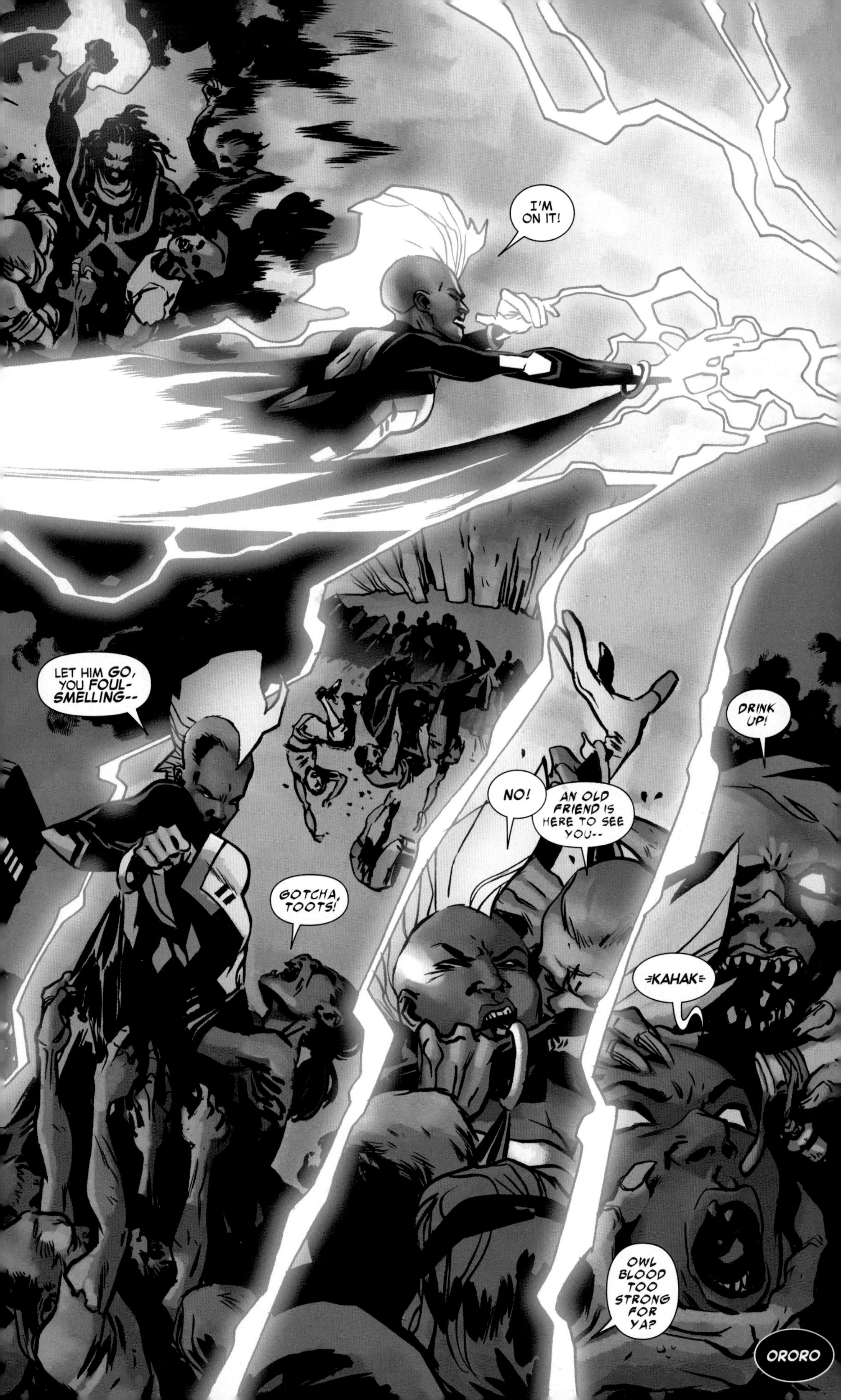
I'M ON IT!
LET HIM GO, YOU FOUL-SMELLING--
GOTCHA, TOOTS!
NO!
AN OLD FRIEND IS HERE TO SEE YOU--
DRINK UP!
KAHAK
OWL BLOOD TOO STRONG FOR YA?
ORORO

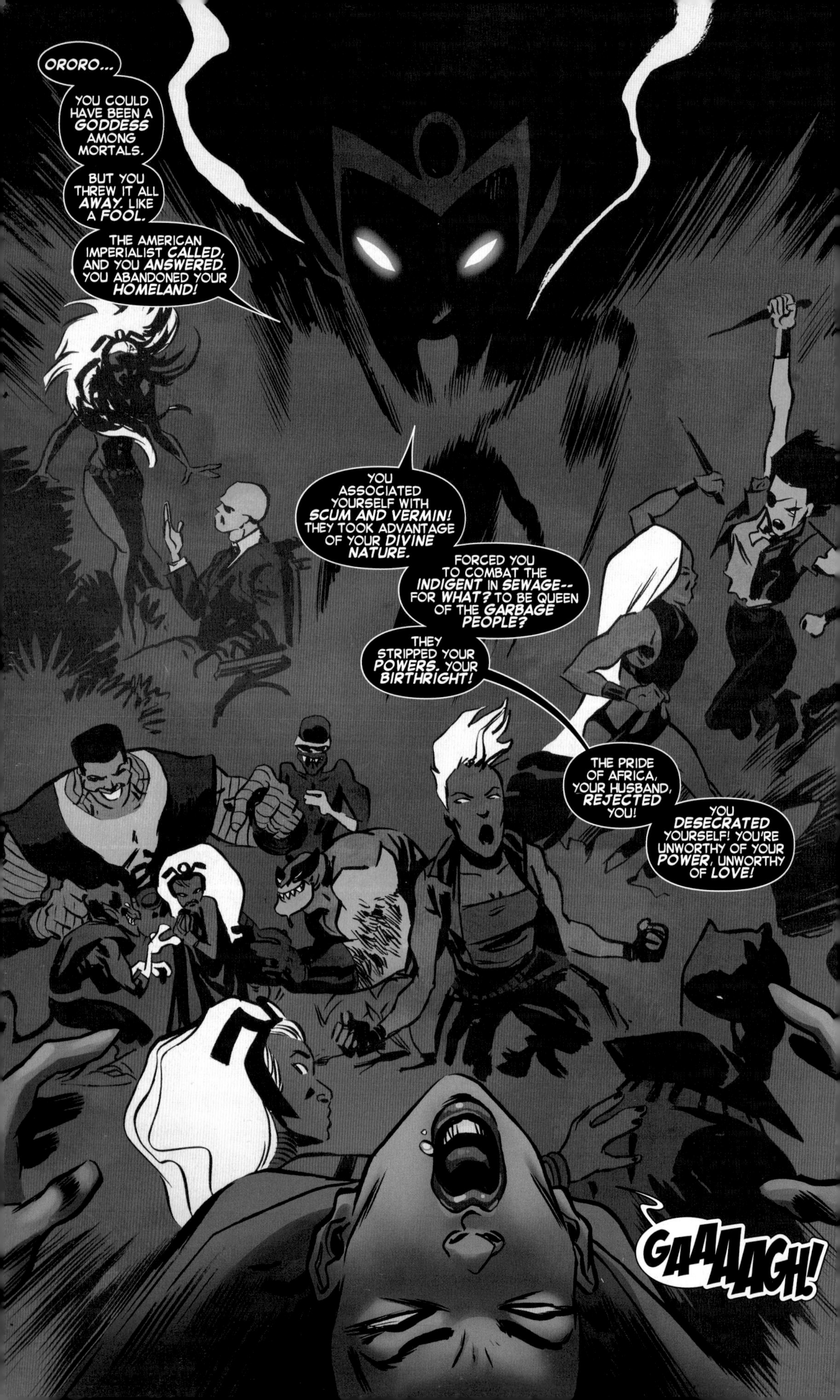

ORORO...
YOU COULD HAVE BEEN A GODDESS AMONG MORTALS.
BUT YOU THREW IT ALL AWAY. LIKE A FOOL.
THE AMERICAN IMPERIALIST CALLED, AND YOU ANSWERED. YOU ABANDONED YOUR HOMELAND!
YOU ASSOCIATED YOURSELF WITH SCUM AND VERMIN! THEY TOOK ADVANTAGE OF YOUR DIVINE NATURE.
FORCED YOU TO COMBAT THE INDIGENT IN SEWAGE-- FOR WHAT? TO BE QUEEN OF THE GARBAGE PEOPLE?
THEY STRIPPED YOUR POWERS. YOUR BIRTHRIGHT!
THE PRIDE OF AFRICA, YOUR HUSBAND, REJECTED YOU!
YOU DESECRATED YOURSELF! YOU'RE UNWORTHY OF YOUR POWER, UNWORTHY OF LOVE!
GAAAAAGH!

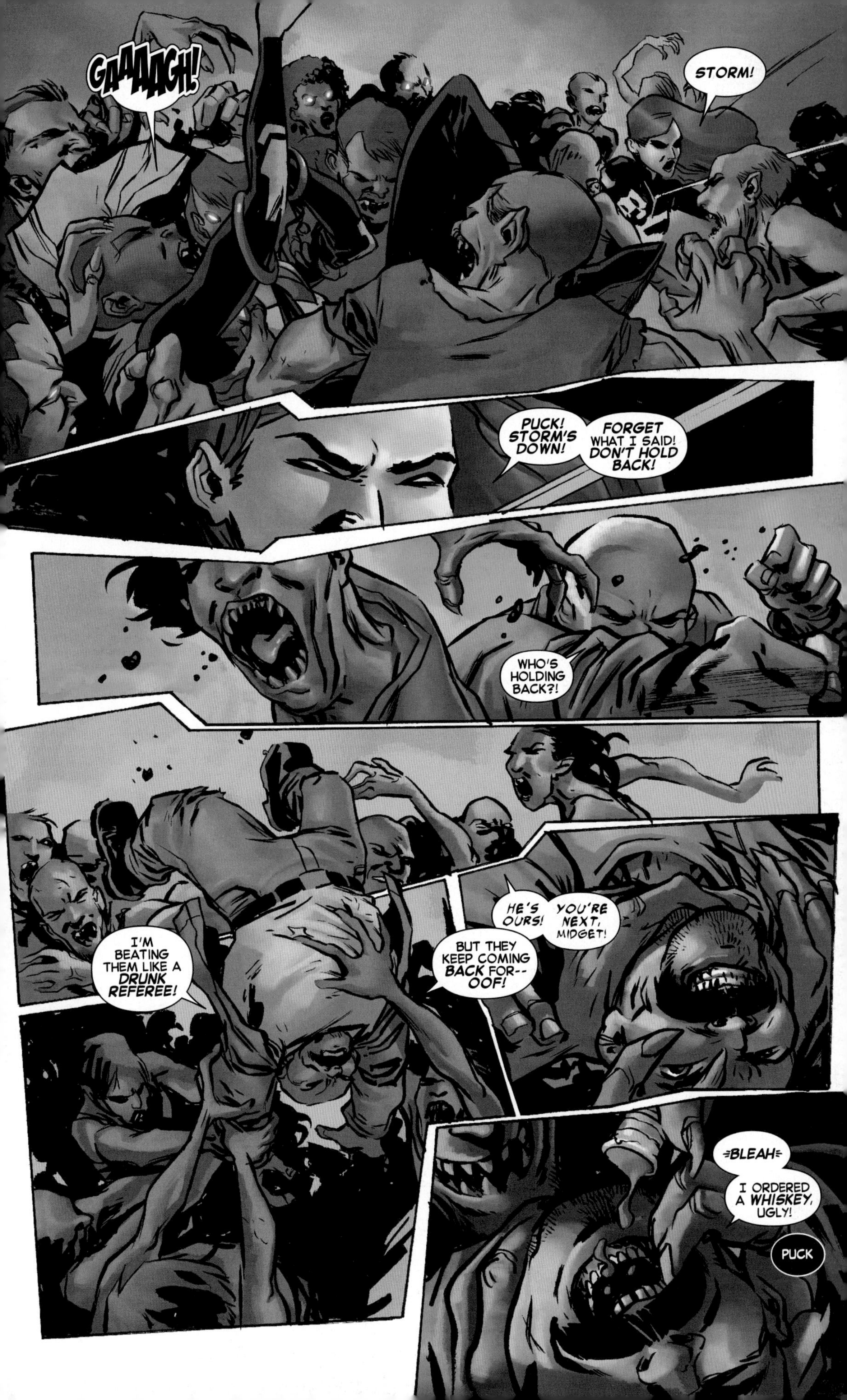
GAAAAGH!
STORM!
PUCK! STORM'S DOWN!
FORGET WHAT I SAID! DON'T HOLD BACK!
WHO'S HOLDING BACK?!
I'M BEATING THEM LIKE A DRUNK REFEREE!
BUT THEY KEEP COMING BACK FOR-- OOF!
HE'S OURS!
YOU'RE NEXT, MIDGET!
BLEAH
I ORDERED A WHISKEY, UGLY!
PUCK

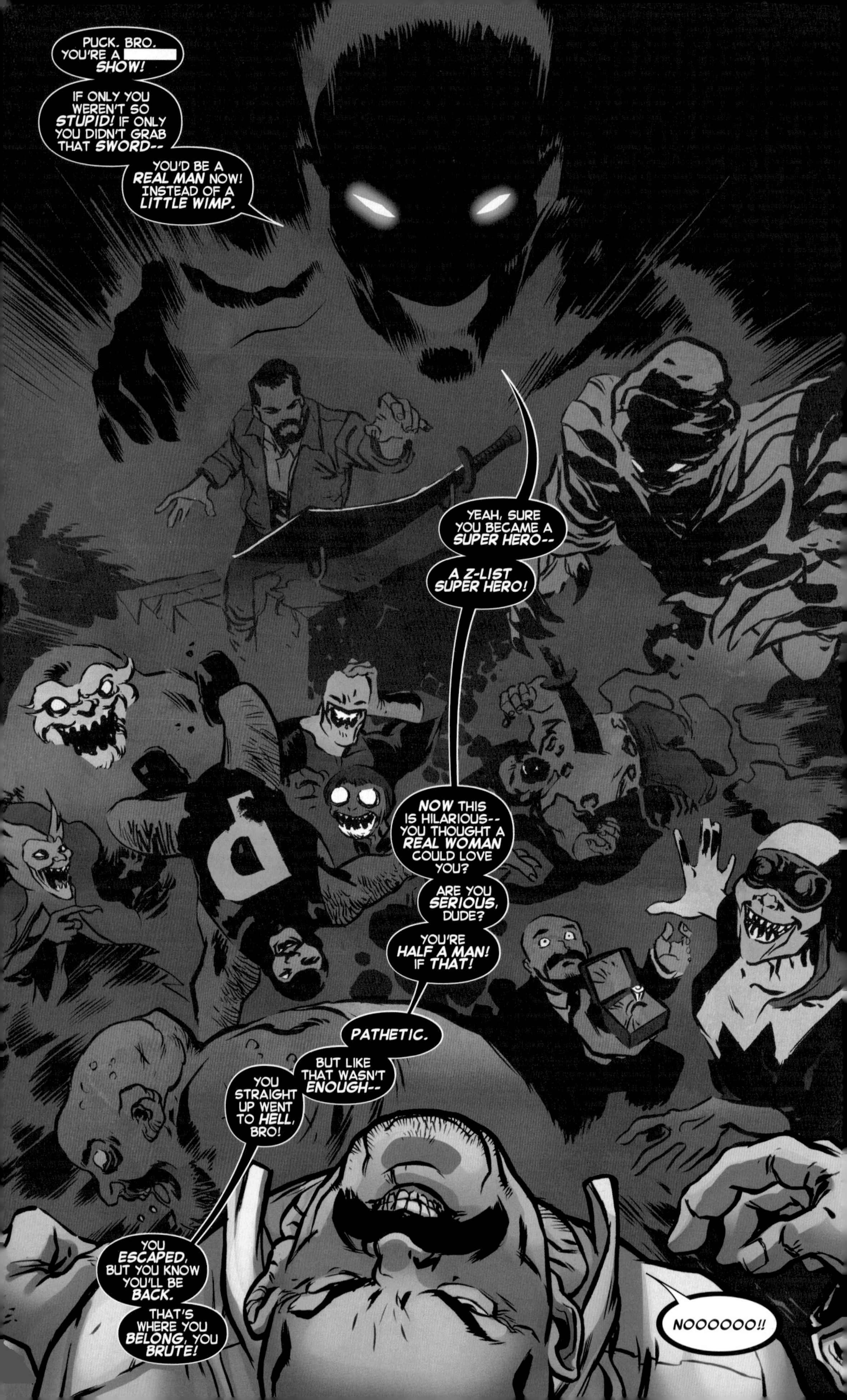
PUCK. BRO. YOU'RE A SHOW!
IF ONLY YOU WEREN'T SO STUPID! IF ONLY YOU DIDN'T GRAB THAT SWORD--
YOU'D BE A REAL MAN NOW! INSTEAD OF A LITTLE WIMP.
YEAH, SURE YOU BECAME A SUPER HERO--
A Z-LIST SUPER HERO!
NOW THIS IS HILARIOUS-- YOU THOUGHT A REAL WOMAN COULD LOVE YOU?
ARE YOU SERIOUS, DUDE?
YOU'RE HALF A MAN! IF THAT!
PATHETIC.
BUT LIKE THAT WASN'T ENOUGH--
YOU STRAIGHT UP WENT TO HELL, BRO!
YOU ESCAPED, BUT YOU KNOW YOU'LL BE BACK.
THAT'S WHERE YOU BELONG, YOU BRUTE!
NOOOOOO!!

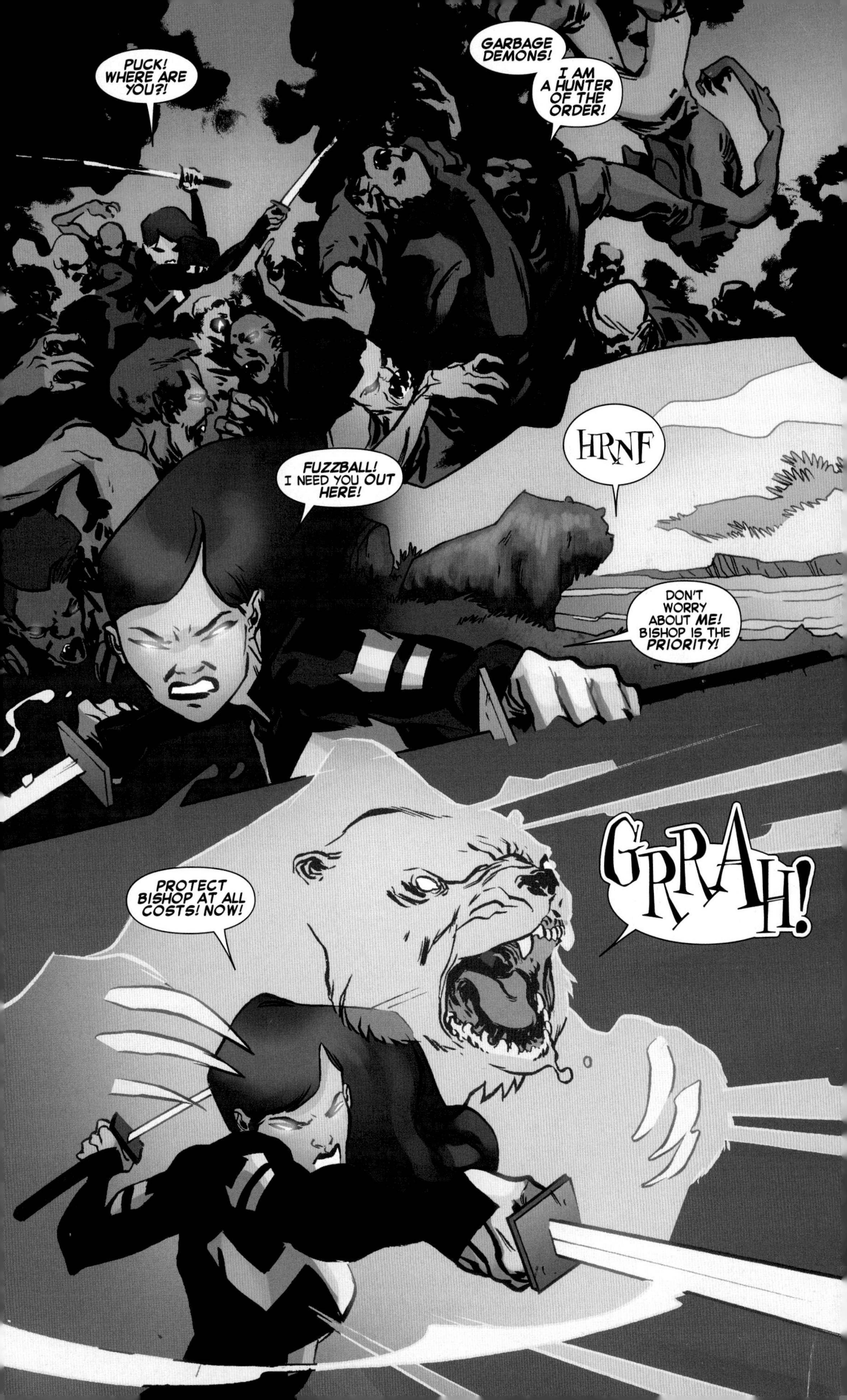
PUCK! WHERE ARE YOU?!
GARBAGE DEMONS!
I AM A HUNTER OF THE ORDER!
FUZZBALL! I NEED YOU OUT HERE!
HRNF
DON'T WORRY ABOUT ME! BISHOP IS THE PRIORITY!
PROTECT BISHOP AT ALL COSTS! NOW!
GRRAH!

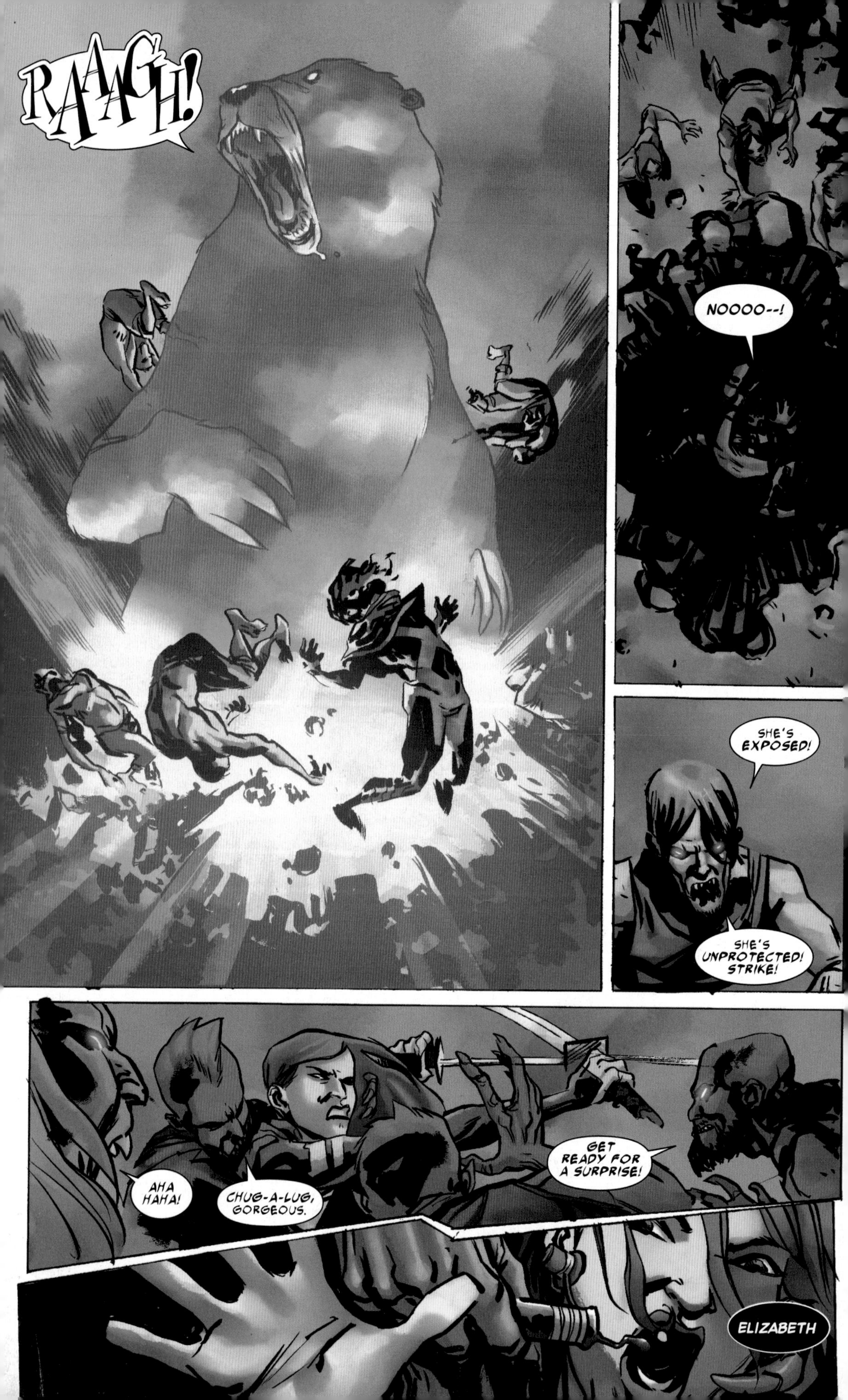

RAAAGH!
NOOOO--!
SHE'S EXPOSED!
SHE'S UNPROTECTED! STRIKE!
AHA HAHA!
CHUG-A-LUG, GORGEOUS.
GET READY FOR A SURPRISE!
ELIZABETH

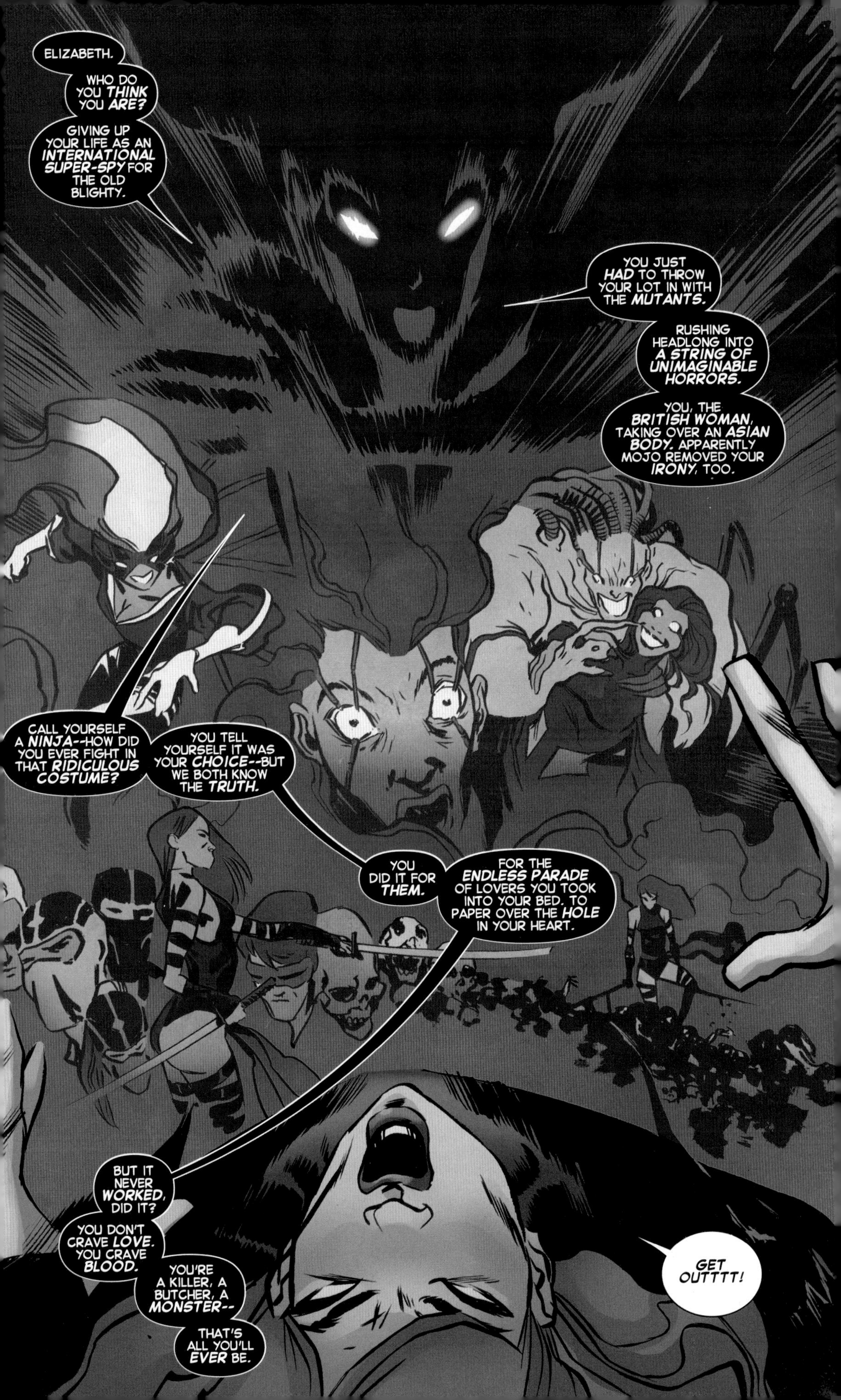
ELIZABETH.
WHO DO YOU THINK YOU ARE?
GIVING UP YOUR LIFE AS AN INTERNATIONAL SUPER-SPY FOR THE OLD BLIGHTY.
YOU JUST HAD TO THROW YOUR LOT IN WITH THE MUTANTS.
RUSHING HEADLONG INTO A STRING OF UNIMAGINABLE HORRORS.
YOU, THE BRITISH WOMAN, TAKING OVER AN ASIAN BODY. APPARENTLY MOJO REMOVED YOUR IRONY, TOO.
CALL YOURSELF A NINJA--HOW DID YOU EVER FIGHT IN THAT RIDICULOUS COSTUME?
YOU TELL YOURSELF IT WAS YOUR CHOICE--BUT WE BOTH KNOW THE TRUTH.
YOU DID IT FOR THEM.
FOR THE ENDLESS PARADE OF LOVERS YOU TOOK INTO YOUR BED. TO PAPER OVER THE HOLE IN YOUR HEART.
BUT IT NEVER WORKED, DID IT?
YOU DON'T CRAVE LOVE. YOU CRAVE BLOOD.
YOU'RE A KILLER, A BUTCHER, A MONSTER--
THAT'S ALL YOU'LL EVER BE.
GET OUTTTT!

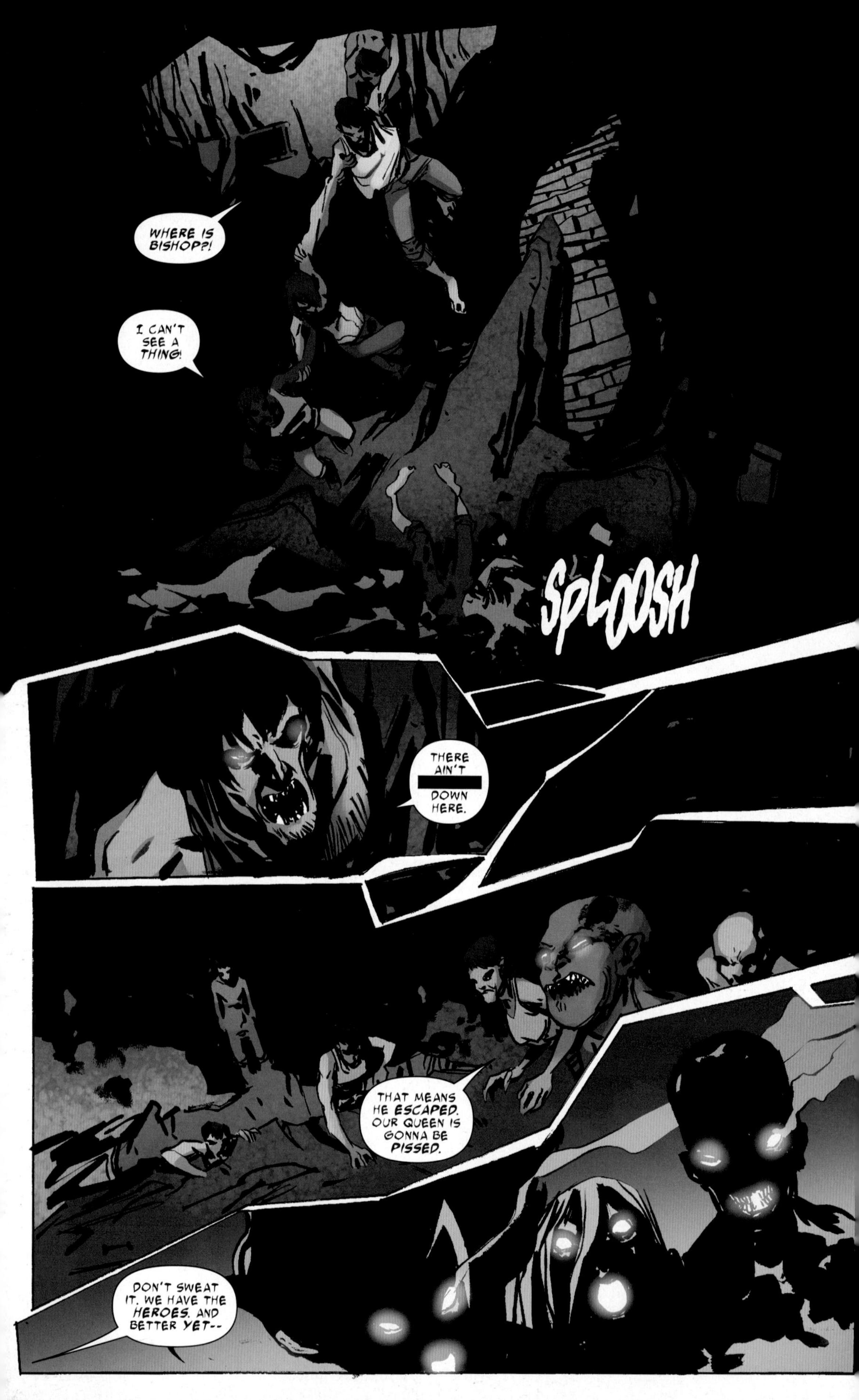
WHERE IS BISHOP?!
I CAN'T SEE A THING!
SPLOOSH
THERE AIN'T [redacted] DOWN HERE.
THAT MEANS HE ESCAPED. OUR QUEEN IS GONNA BE PISSED.
DON'T SWEAT IT. WE HAVE THE HEROES. AND BETTER YET--

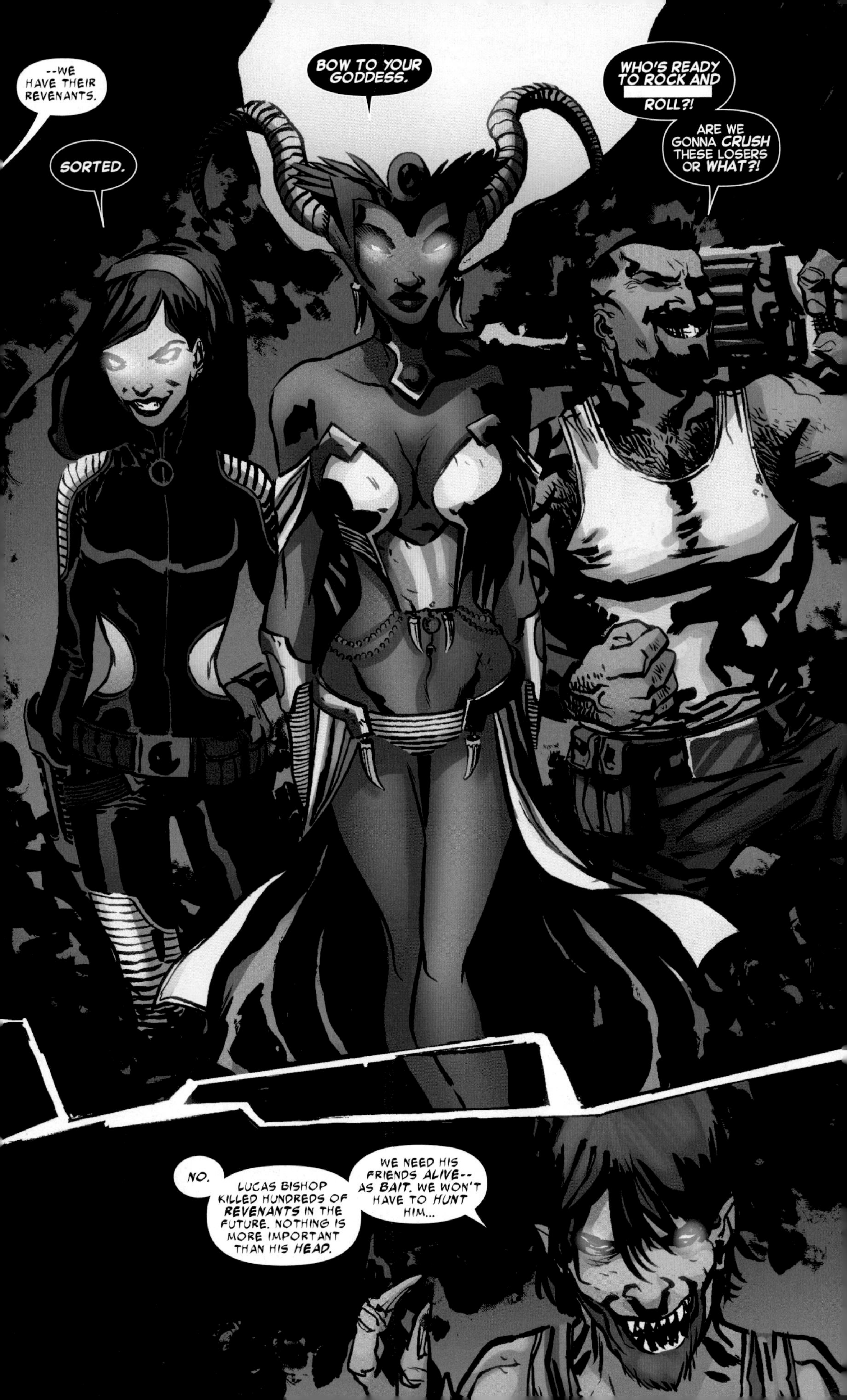

--WE HAVE THEIR REVENANTS.
SORTED.
BOW TO YOUR GODDESS.
WHO'S READY TO ROCK AND ROLL?!
ARE WE GONNA CRUSH THESE LOSERS OR WHAT?!
NO.
LUCAS BISHOP KILLED HUNDREDS OF REVENANTS IN THE FUTURE. NOTHING IS MORE IMPORTANT THAN HIS HEAD.
WE NEED HIS FRIENDS ALIVE--AS BAIT. WE WON'T HAVE TO HUNT HIM...

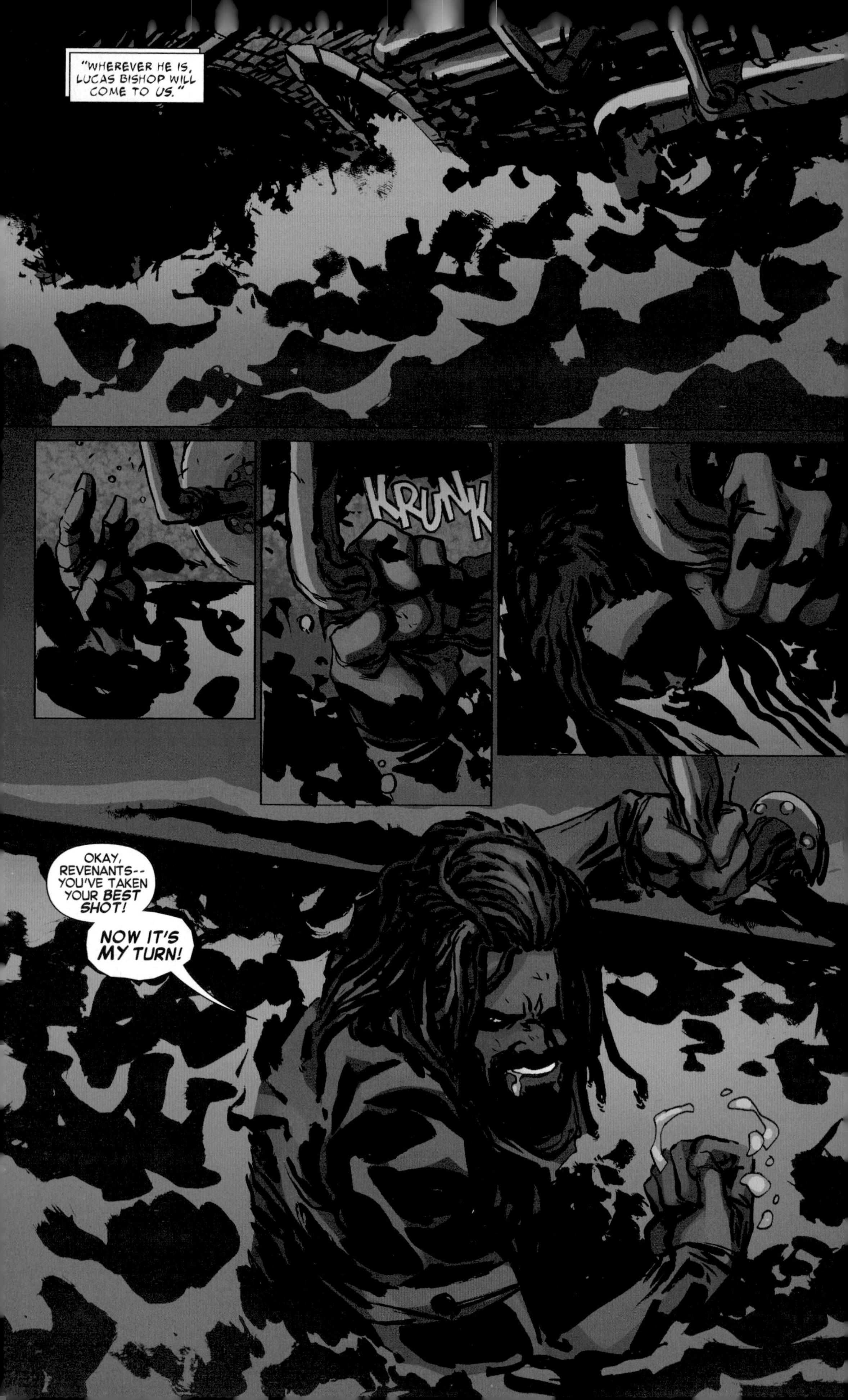
"WHEREVER HE IS, LUCAS BISHOP WILL COME TO US."
KRUNK
OKAY, REVENANTS-- YOU'VE TAKEN YOUR BEST SHOT!
NOW IT'S MY TURN!

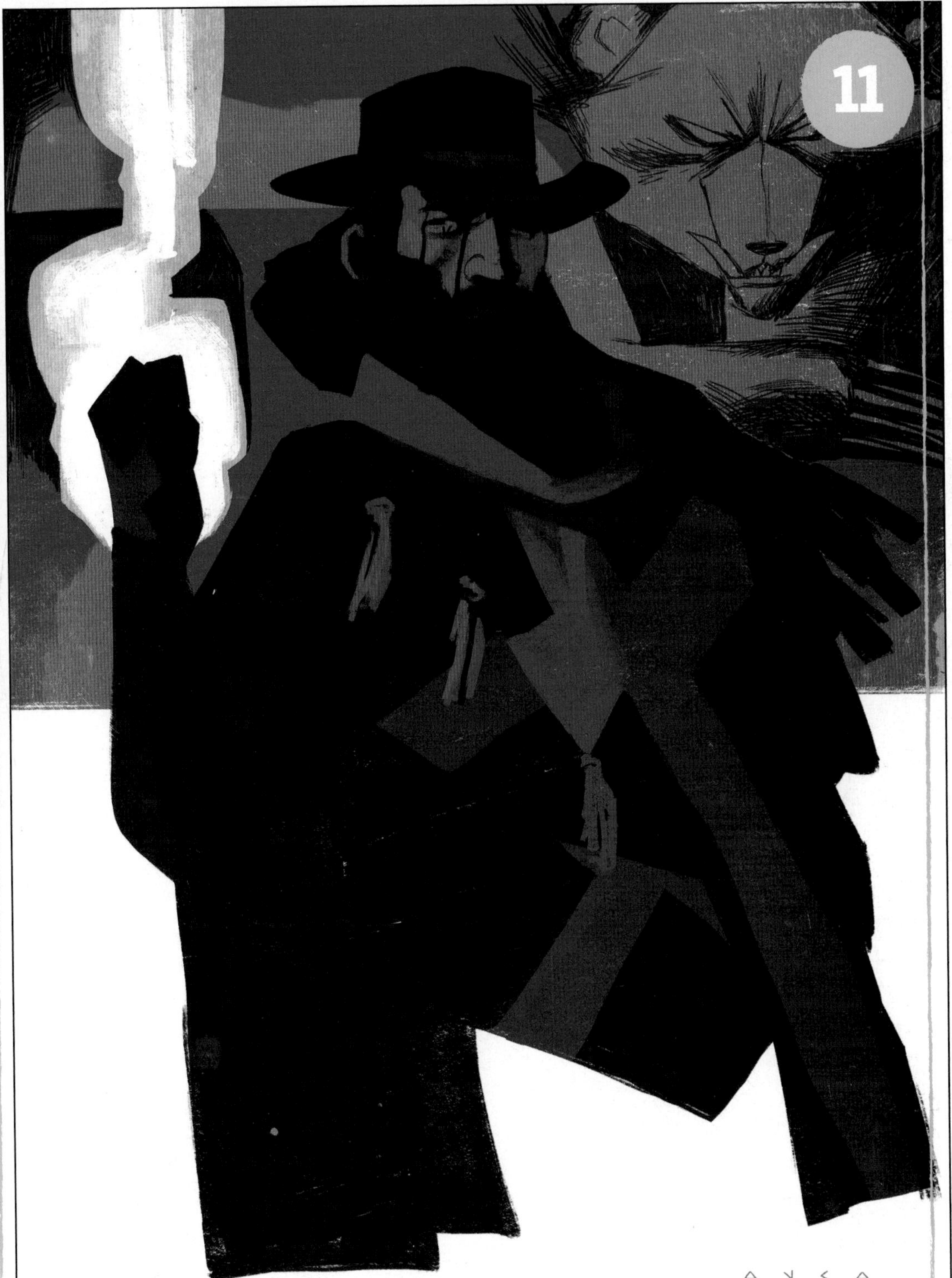
11
AVCA
2013

MIDNIGHT RAMBLER

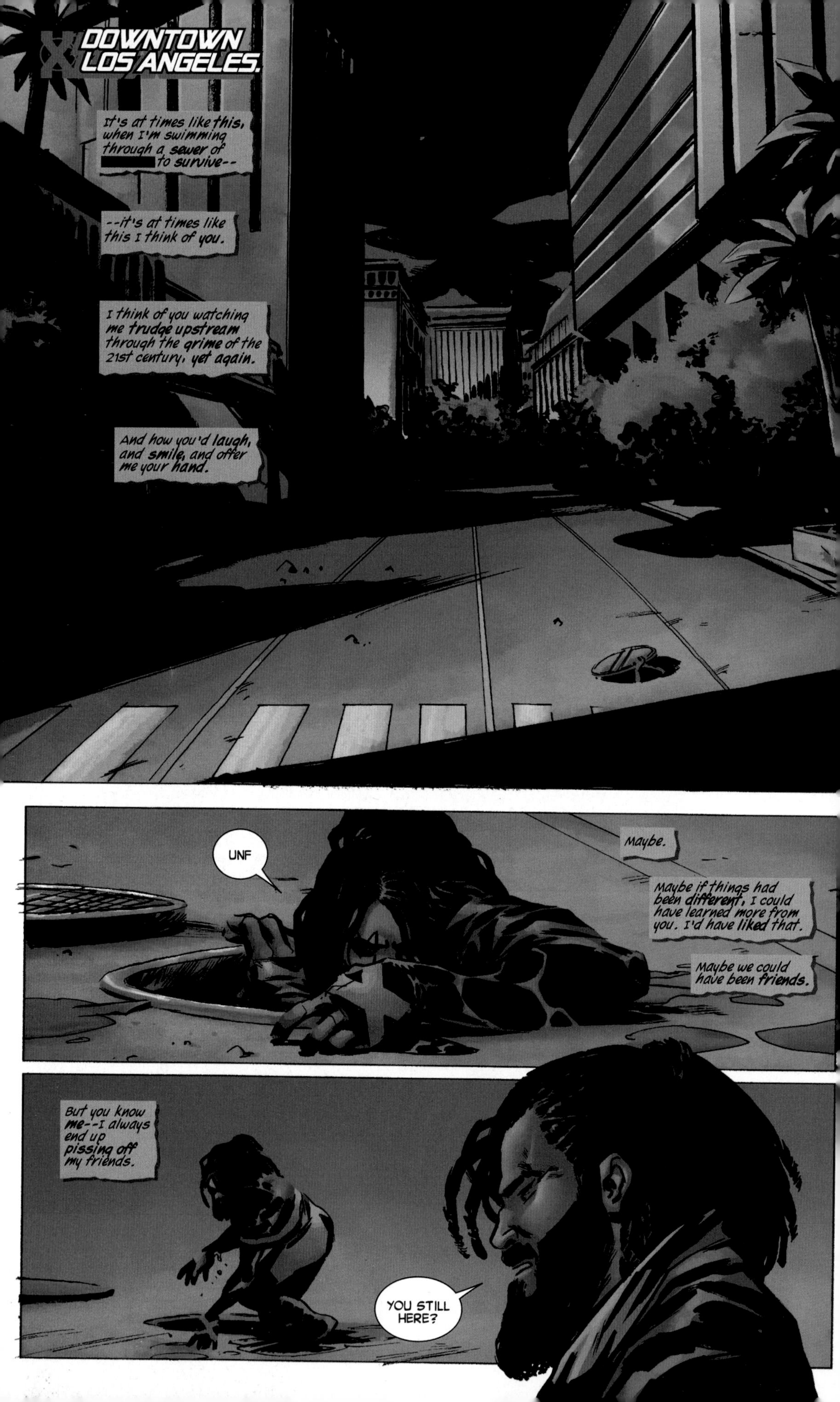

DOWNTOWN LOS ANGELES.
It's at times like this, when I'm swimming through a sewer of [redacted] to survive--
--it's at times like this I think of you.
I think of you watching me trudge upstream through the grime of the 21st century, yet again.
And how you'd laugh, and smile, and offer me your hand.
UNF
Maybe.
Maybe if things had been different, I could have learned more from you. I'd have liked that.
Maybe we could have been friends.
But you know me--I always end up pissing off my friends.
YOU STILL HERE?

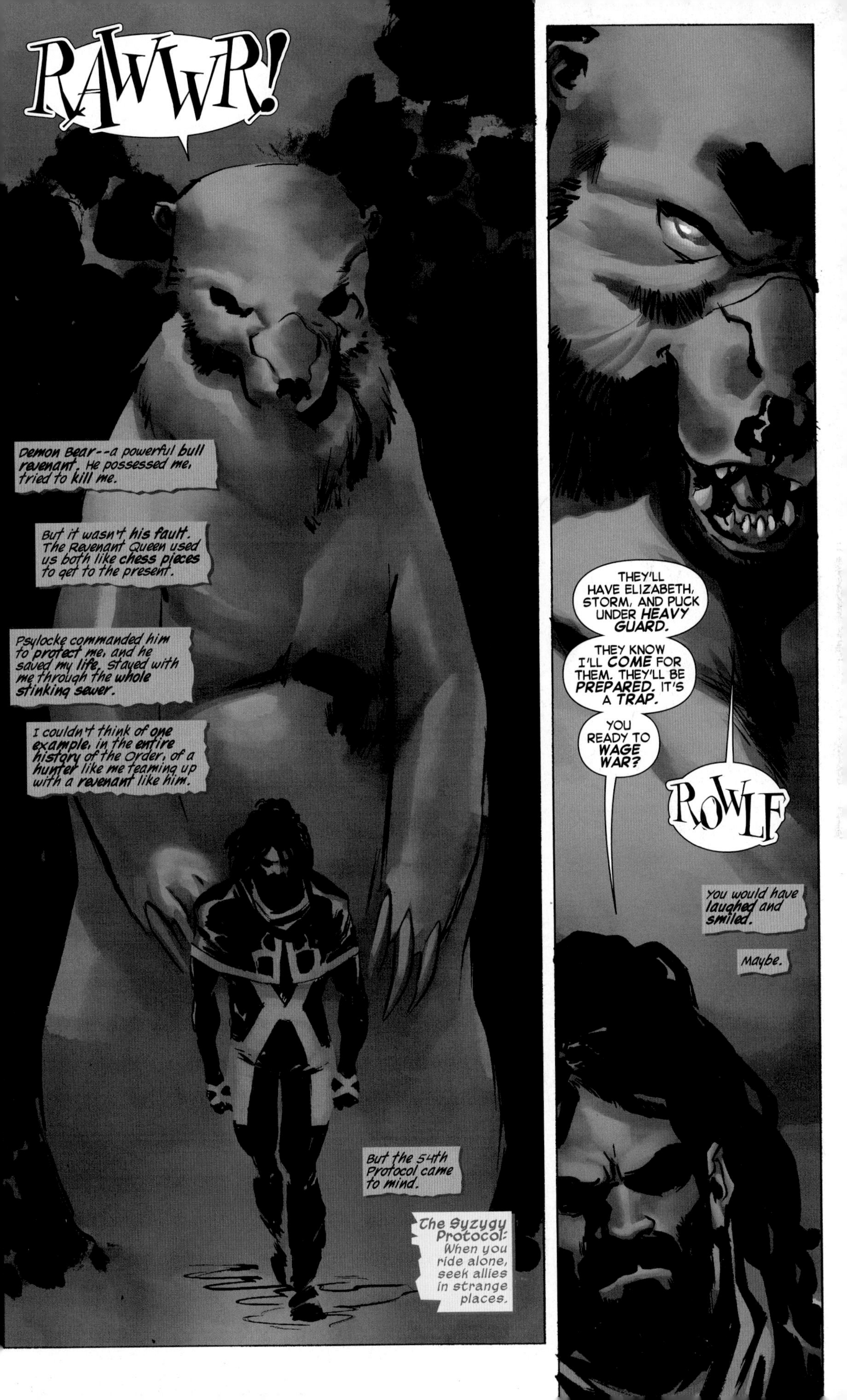
RAWWR!
Demon Bear--a powerful bull revenant. He possessed me, tried to kill me.
But it wasn't his fault. The Revenant Queen used us both like chess pieces to get to the present.
Psylocke commanded him to protect me, and he saved my life, stayed with me through the whole stinking sewer.
I couldn't think of one example, in the entire history of the Order, of a hunter like me teaming up with a revenant like him.
But the 54th Protocol came to mind.
The Syzygy Protocol: When you ride alone, seek allies in strange places.
THEY'LL HAVE ELIZABETH, STORM, AND PUCK UNDER HEAVY GUARD.
THEY KNOW I'LL COME FOR THEM. THEY'LL BE PREPARED. IT'S A TRAP.
YOU READY TO WAGE WAR?
ROWLF
You would have laughed and smiled.
Maybe.

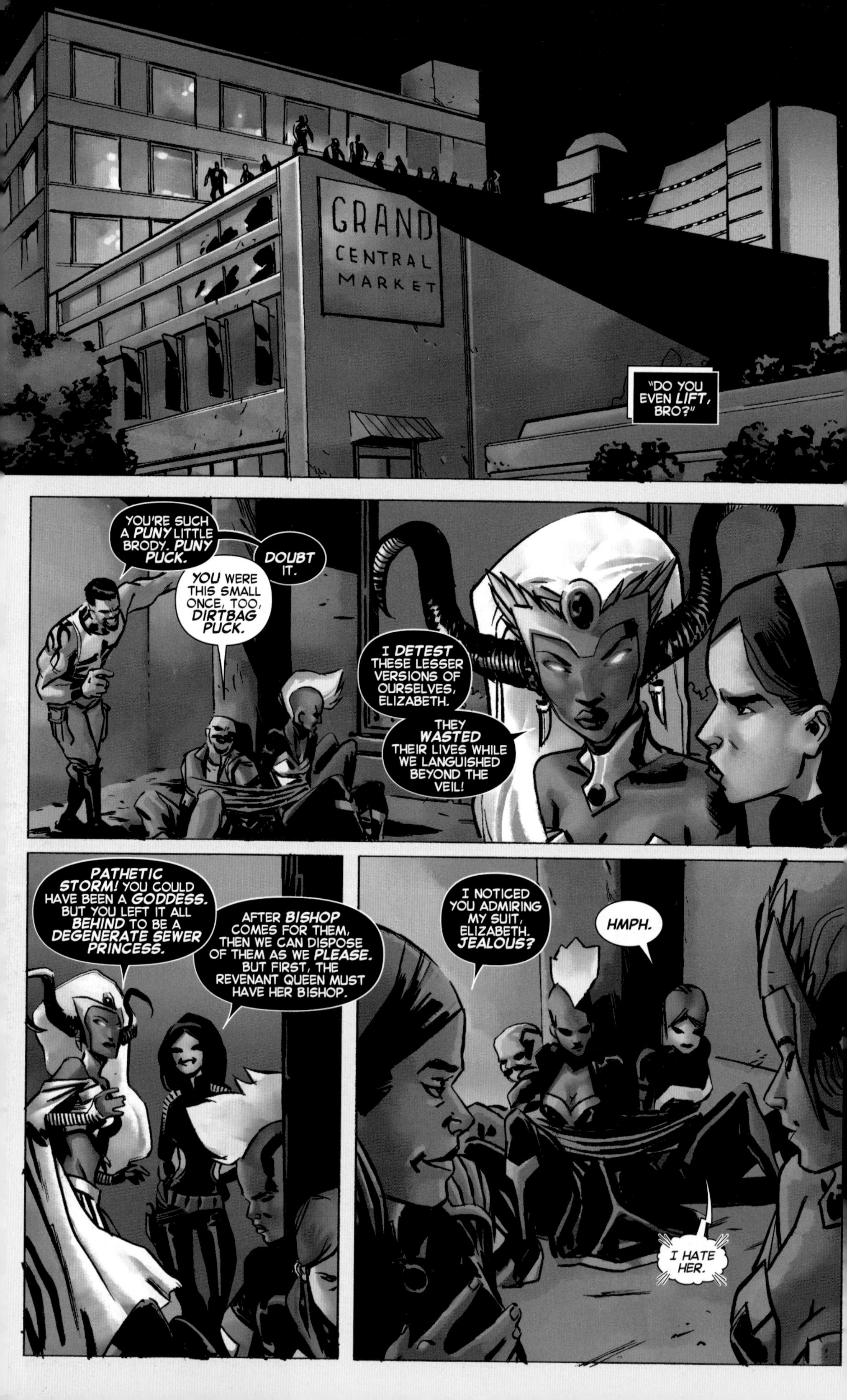
GRAND CENTRAL MARKET
"DO YOU EVEN LIFT, BRO?"
YOU'RE SUCH A PUNY LITTLE BRODY. PUNY PUCK.
YOU WERE THIS SMALL ONCE, TOO, DIRTBAG PUCK.
DOUBT IT.
I DETEST THESE LESSER VERSIONS OF OURSELVES, ELIZABETH.
THEY WASTED THEIR LIVES WHILE WE LANGUISHED BEYOND THE VEIL!
PATHETIC STORM! YOU COULD HAVE BEEN A GODDESS. BUT YOU LEFT IT ALL BEHIND TO BE A DEGENERATE SEWER PRINCESS.
AFTER BISHOP COMES FOR THEM, THEN WE CAN DISPOSE OF THEM AS WE PLEASE. BUT FIRST, THE REVENANT QUEEN MUST HAVE HER BISHOP.
I NOTICED YOU ADMIRING MY SUIT, ELIZABETH. JEALOUS?
HMPH.
I HATE HER.

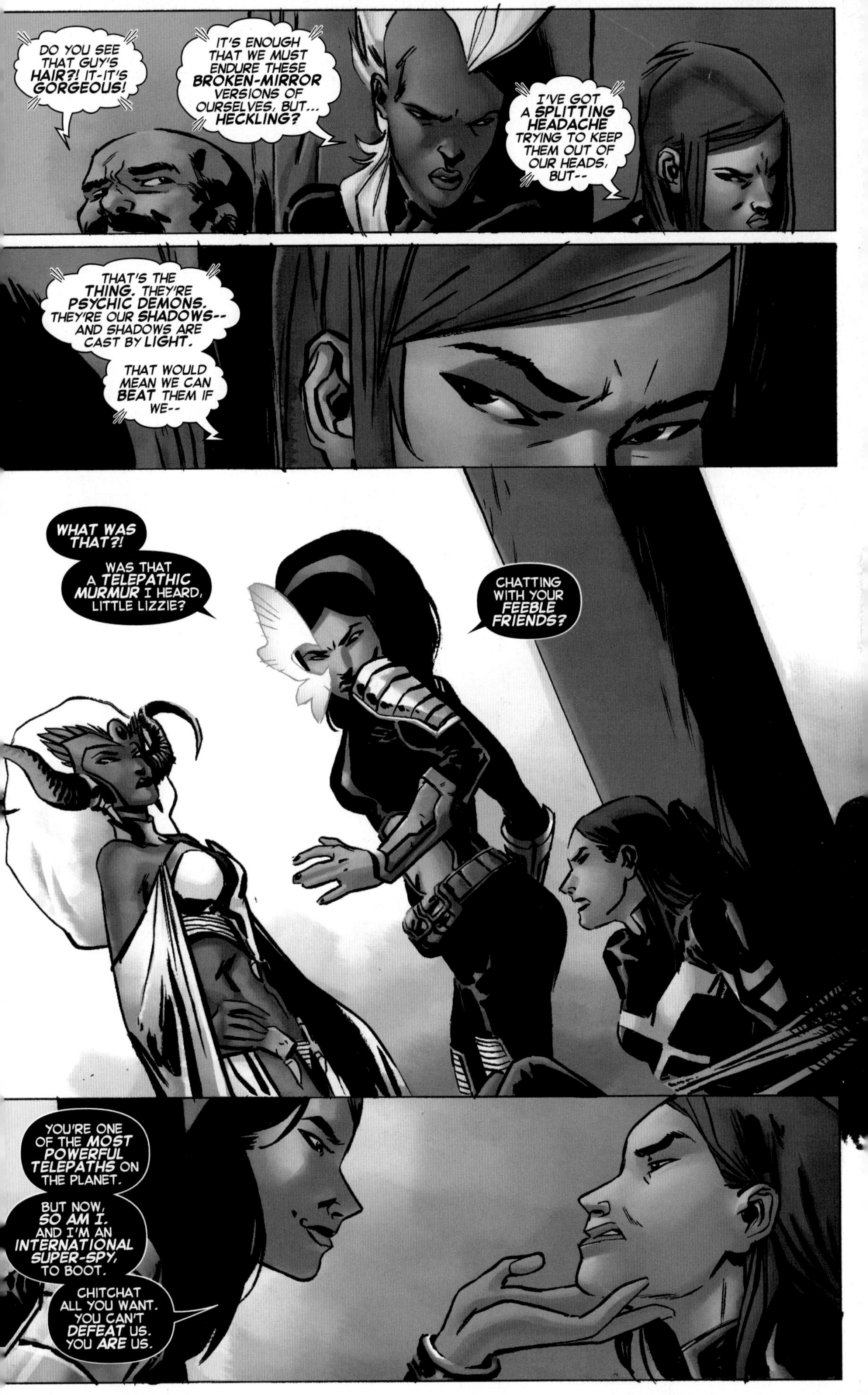
DO YOU SEE THAT GUY'S HAIR?! IT-IT'S GORGEOUS!
IT'S ENOUGH THAT WE MUST ENDURE THESE BROKEN-MIRROR VERSIONS OF OURSELVES, BUT... HECKLING?
I'VE GOT A SPLITTING HEADACHE TRYING TO KEEP THEM OUT OF OUR HEADS, BUT--
THAT'S THE THING. THEY'RE PSYCHIC DEMONS. THEY'RE OUR SHADOWS-- AND SHADOWS ARE CAST BY LIGHT.
THAT WOULD MEAN WE CAN BEAT THEM IF WE--
WHAT WAS THAT?!
WAS THAT A TELEPATHIC MURMUR I HEARD, LITTLE LIZZIE?
CHATTING WITH YOUR FEEBLE FRIENDS?
YOU'RE ONE OF THE MOST POWERFUL TELEPATHS ON THE PLANET.
BUT NOW, SO AM I. AND I'M AN INTERNATIONAL SUPER-SPY, TO BOOT.
CHITCHAT ALL YOU WANT. YOU CAN'T DEFEAT US. YOU ARE US.

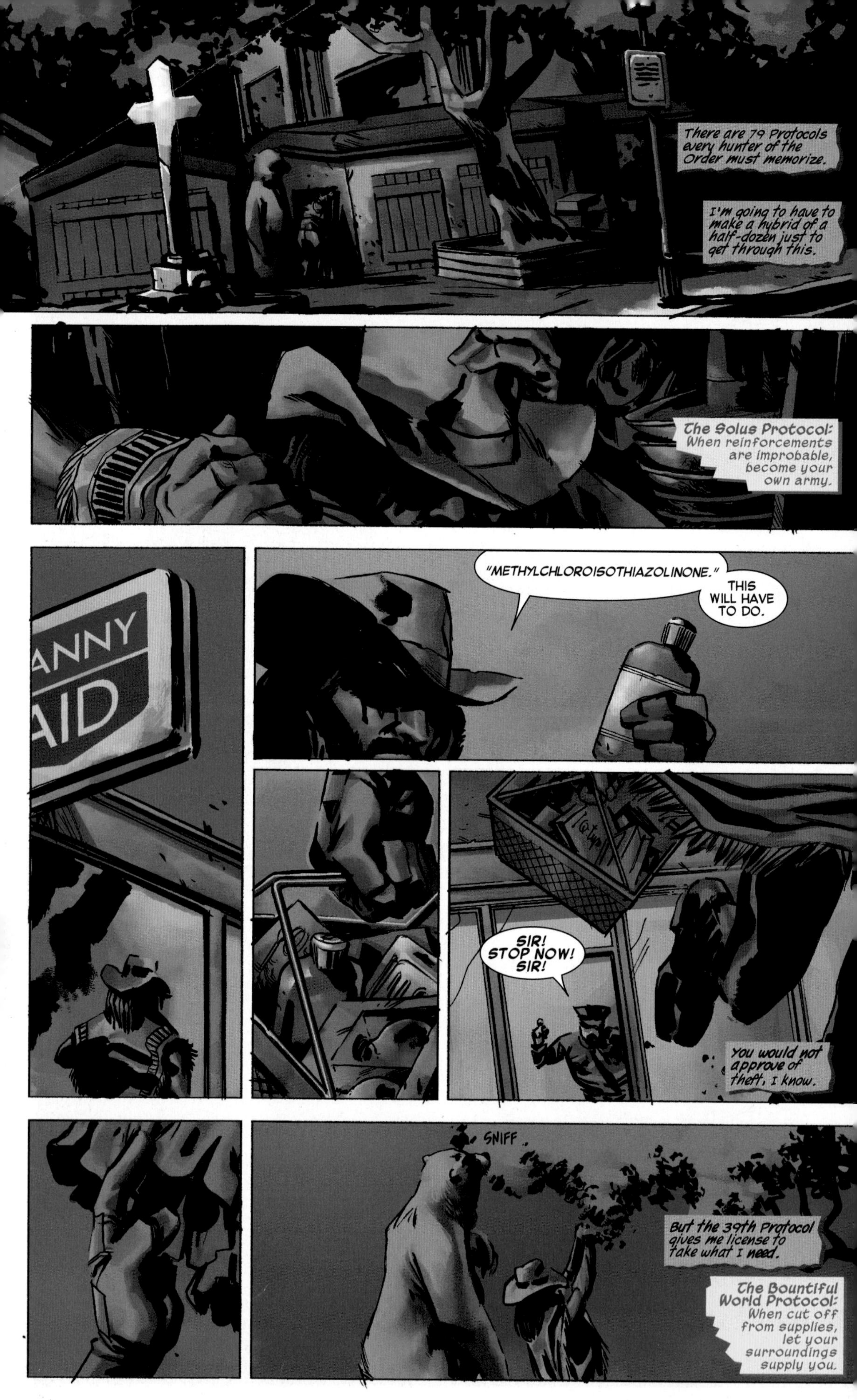
There are 79 Protocols every hunter of the Order must memorize.
I'm going to have to make a hybrid of a half-dozen just to get through this.
The Solus Protocol: When reinforcements are improbable, become your own army.
ANNY
AID
"METHYLCHLOROISOTHIAZOLINONE."
THIS WILL HAVE TO DO.
SIR! STOP NOW! SIR!
You would not approve of theft, I know.
SNIFF
But the 39th Protocol gives me license to take what I need.
The Bountiful World Protocol: When cut off from supplies, let your surroundings supply you.

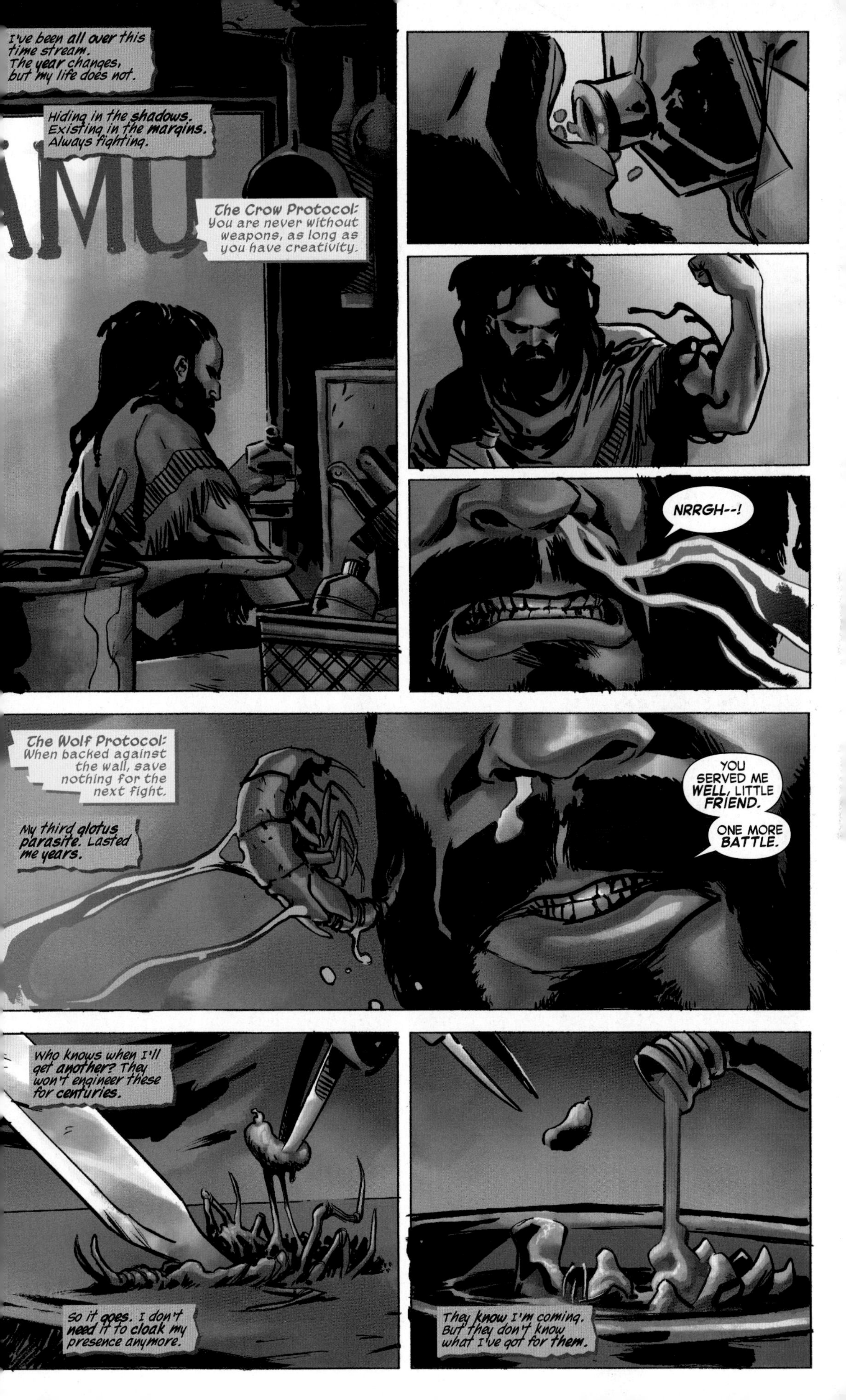
I've been all over this time stream. The year changes, but my life does not.
Hiding in the shadows. Existing in the margins. Always fighting.
AMU
The Crow Protocol: You are never without weapons, as long as you have creativity.
NRRGH--!
The Wolf Protocol: When backed against the wall, save nothing for the next fight.
My third glotus parasite. Lasted me years.
YOU SERVED ME WELL, LITTLE FRIEND.
ONE MORE BATTLE.
Who knows when I'll get another? They won't engineer these for centuries.
So it goes. I don't need it to cloak my presence anymore.
They know I'm coming. But they don't know what I've got for them.

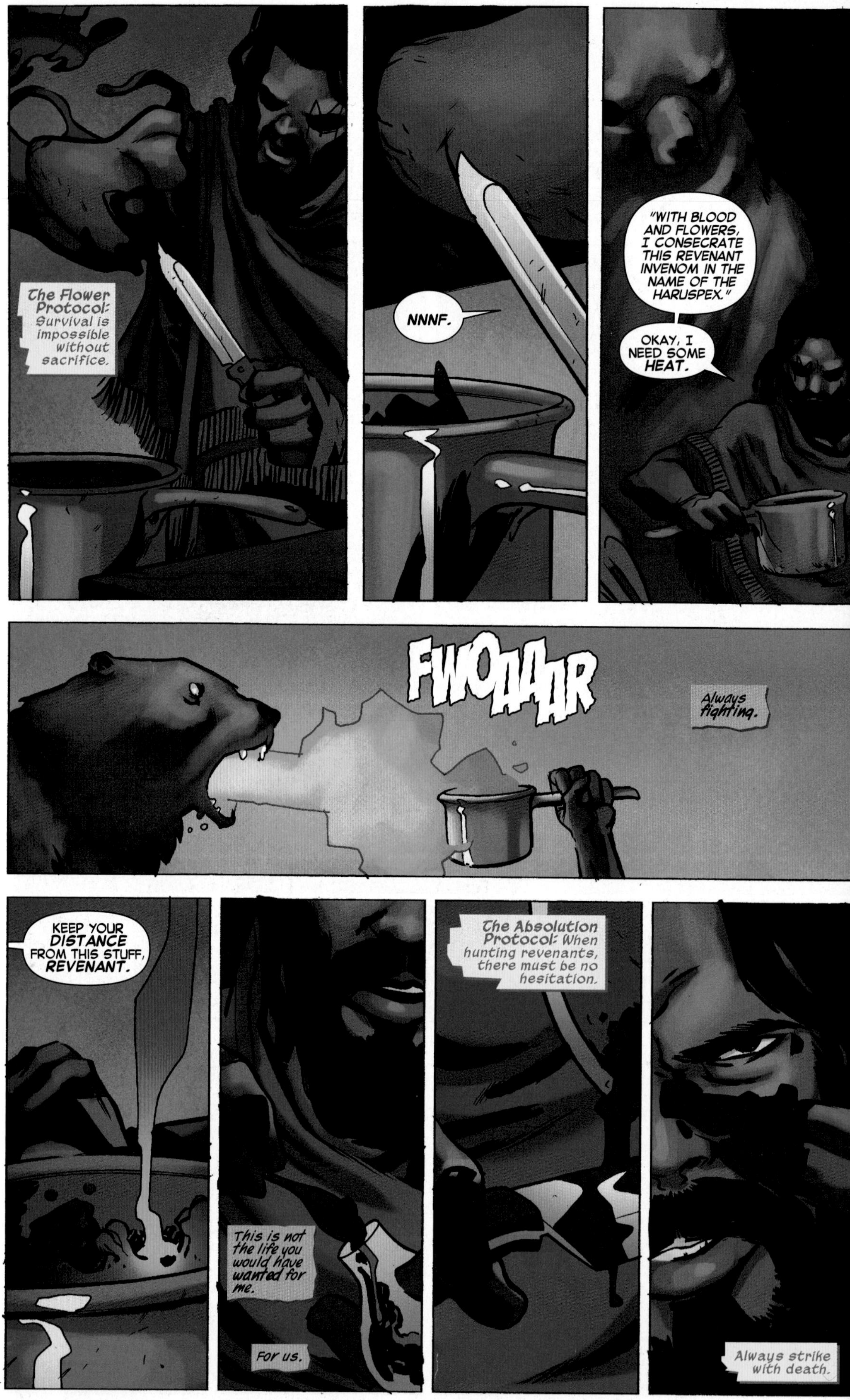
The Flower Protocol: Survival is impossible without sacrifice.
NNNF.
"WITH BLOOD AND FLOWERS, I CONSECRATE THIS REVENANT INVENOM IN THE NAME OF THE HARUSPEX."
OKAY, I NEED SOME HEAT.
FWOAAAR
Always fighting.
KEEP YOUR DISTANCE FROM THIS STUFF, REVENANT.
This is not the life you would have wanted for me.
For us.
The Absolution Protocol: When hunting revenants, there must be no hesitation.
Always strike with death.

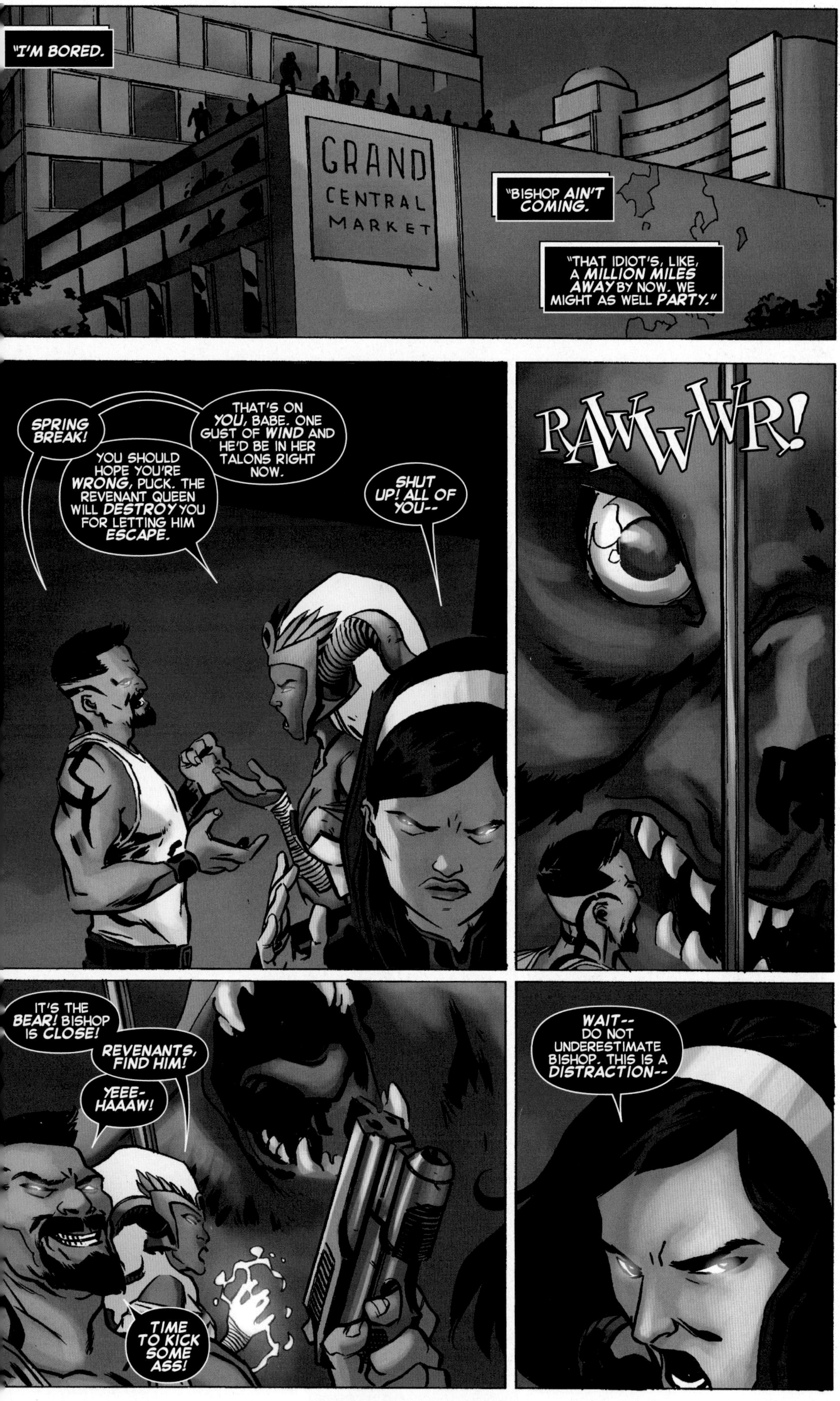

"I'M BORED.
GRAND CENTRAL MARKET
"BISHOP AIN'T COMING.
"THAT IDIOT'S, LIKE, A MILLION MILES AWAY BY NOW. WE MIGHT AS WELL PARTY."
SPRING BREAK!
THAT'S ON YOU, BABE. ONE GUST OF WIND AND HE'D BE IN HER TALONS RIGHT NOW.
YOU SHOULD HOPE YOU'RE WRONG, PUCK. THE REVENANT QUEEN WILL DESTROY YOU FOR LETTING HIM ESCAPE.
SHUT UP! ALL OF YOU--
RAWWWR!
IT'S THE BEAR! BISHOP IS CLOSE!
REVENANTS, FIND HIM!
YEEE-HAAAW!
TIME TO KICK SOME ASS!
WAIT-- DO NOT UNDERESTIMATE BISHOP. THIS IS A DISTRACTION--

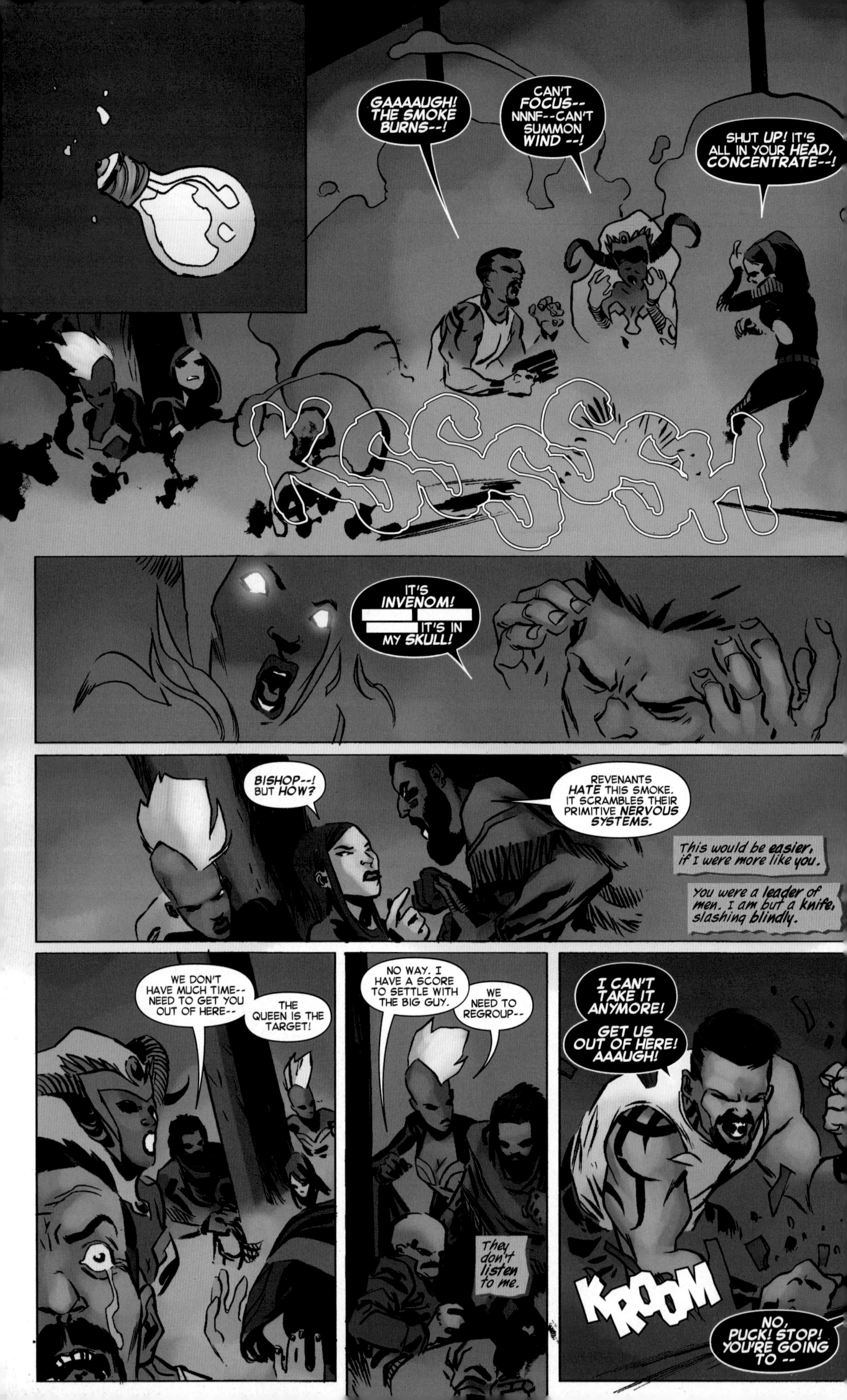

GAAAAUGH! THE SMOKE BURNS--!
CAN'T FOCUS--NNNF--CAN'T SUMMON WIND--!
SHUT UP! IT'S ALL IN YOUR HEAD, CONCENTRATE--!
KSSSSSH
IT'S INVENOM! [redacted] IT'S IN MY SKULL!
BISHOP--! BUT HOW?
REVENANTS HATE THIS SMOKE. IT SCRAMBLES THEIR PRIMITIVE NERVOUS SYSTEMS.
This would be easier, if I were more like you.
You were a leader of men. I am but a knife, slashing blindly.
WE DON'T HAVE MUCH TIME--NEED TO GET YOU OUT OF HERE--
THE QUEEN IS THE TARGET!
NO WAY. I HAVE A SCORE TO SETTLE WITH THE BIG GUY.
WE NEED TO REGROUP--
They don't listen to me.
I CAN'T TAKE IT ANYMORE!
GET US OUT OF HERE! AAAUGH!
KROOM
NO, PUCK! STOP! YOU'RE GOING TO--

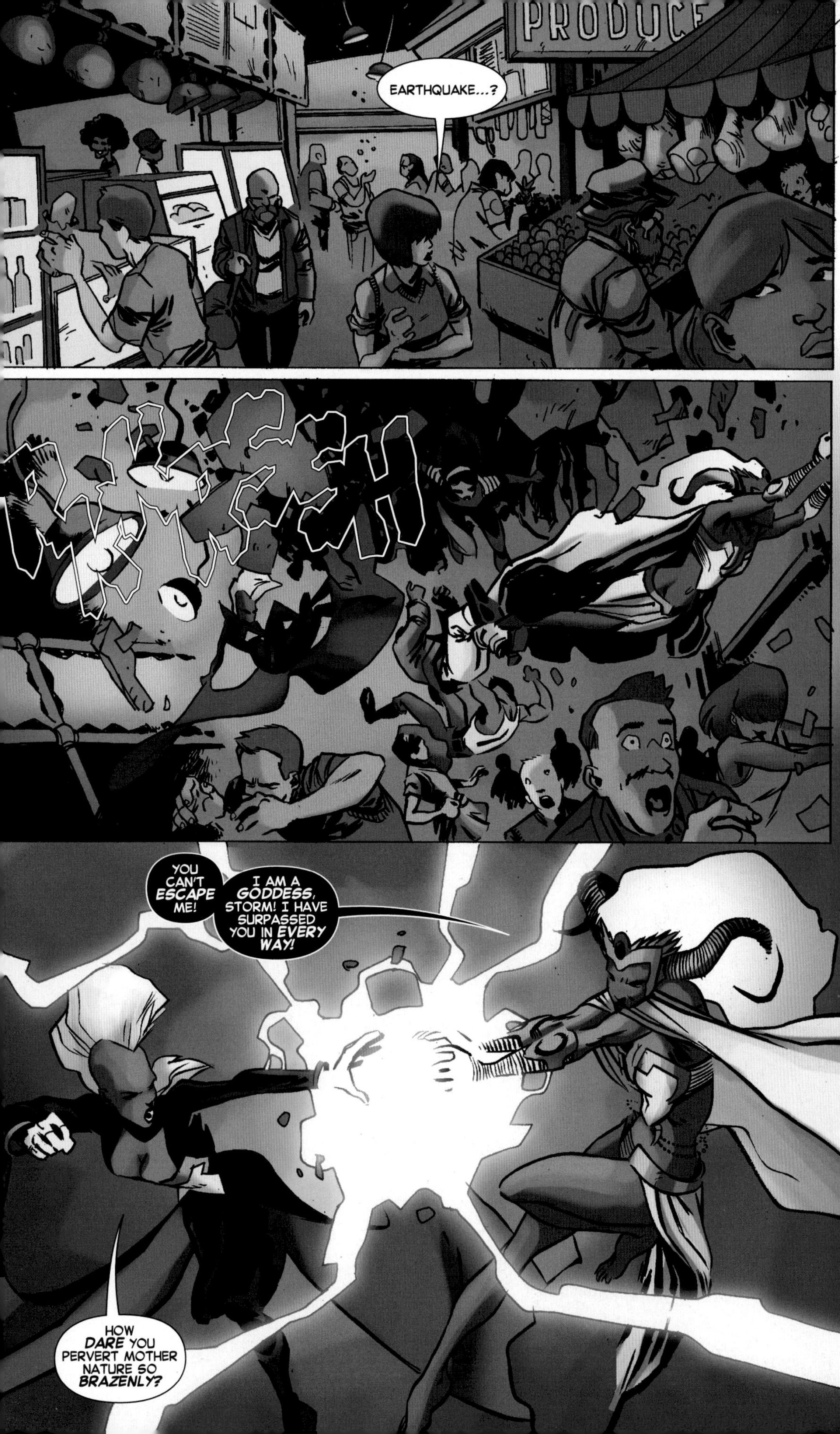
EARTHQUAKE...?
YOU CAN'T ESCAPE ME!
I AM A GODDESS, STORM! I HAVE SURPASSED YOU IN EVERY WAY!
HOW DARE YOU PERVERT MOTHER NATURE SO BRAZENLY?

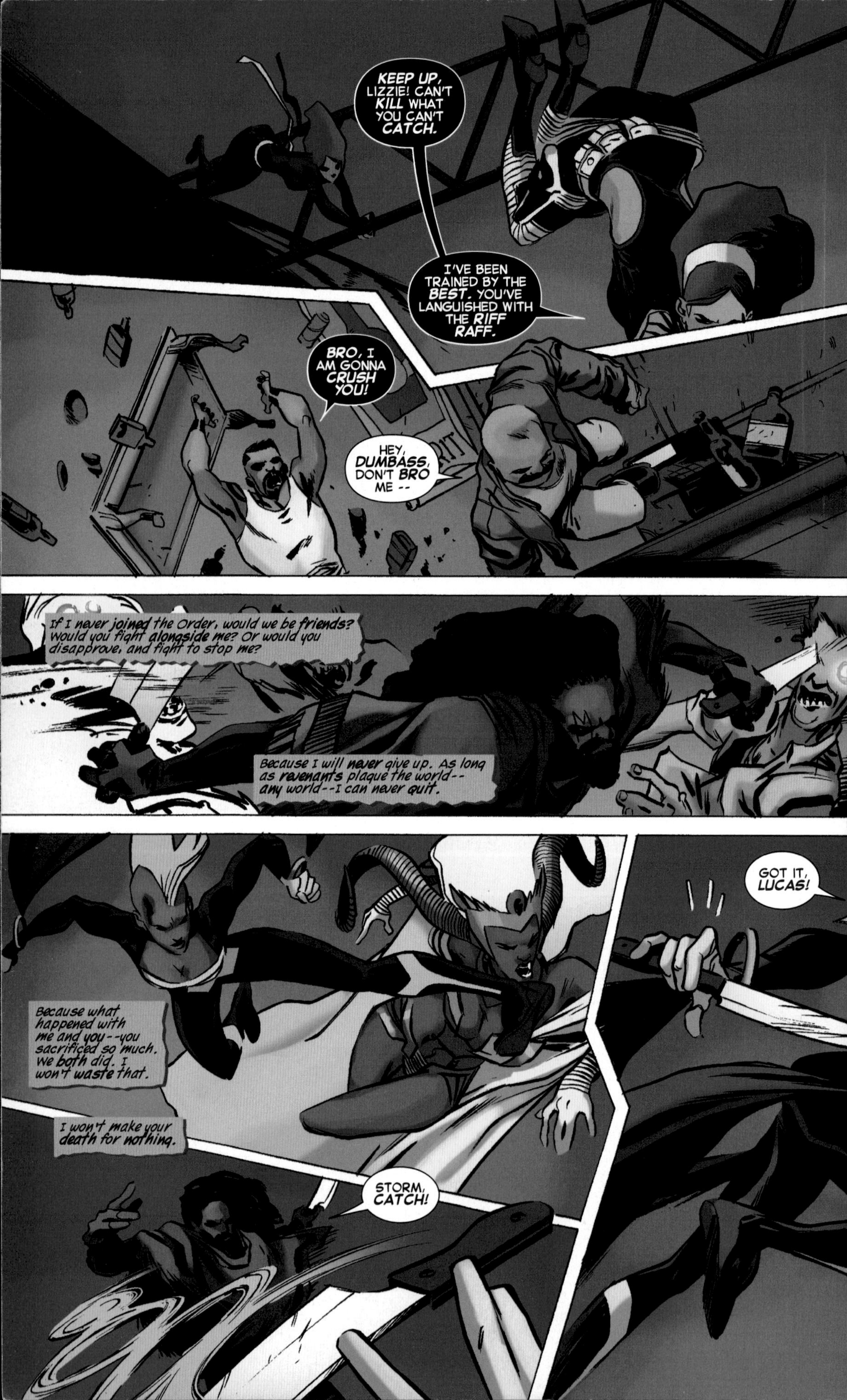
KEEP UP, LIZZIE! CAN'T KILL WHAT YOU CAN'T CATCH.
I'VE BEEN TRAINED BY THE BEST. YOU'VE LANGUISHED WITH THE RIFF RAFF.
BRO, I AM GONNA CRUSH YOU!
HEY, DUMBASS, DON'T BRO ME --
If I never joined the Order, would we be friends? Would you fight alongside me? Or would you disapprove, and fight to stop me?
Because I will never give up. As long as revenants plague the world-- any world--I can never quit.
Because what happened with me and you--you sacrificed so much. We both did. I won't waste that.
GOT IT, LUCAS!
I won't make your death for nothing.
STORM, CATCH!

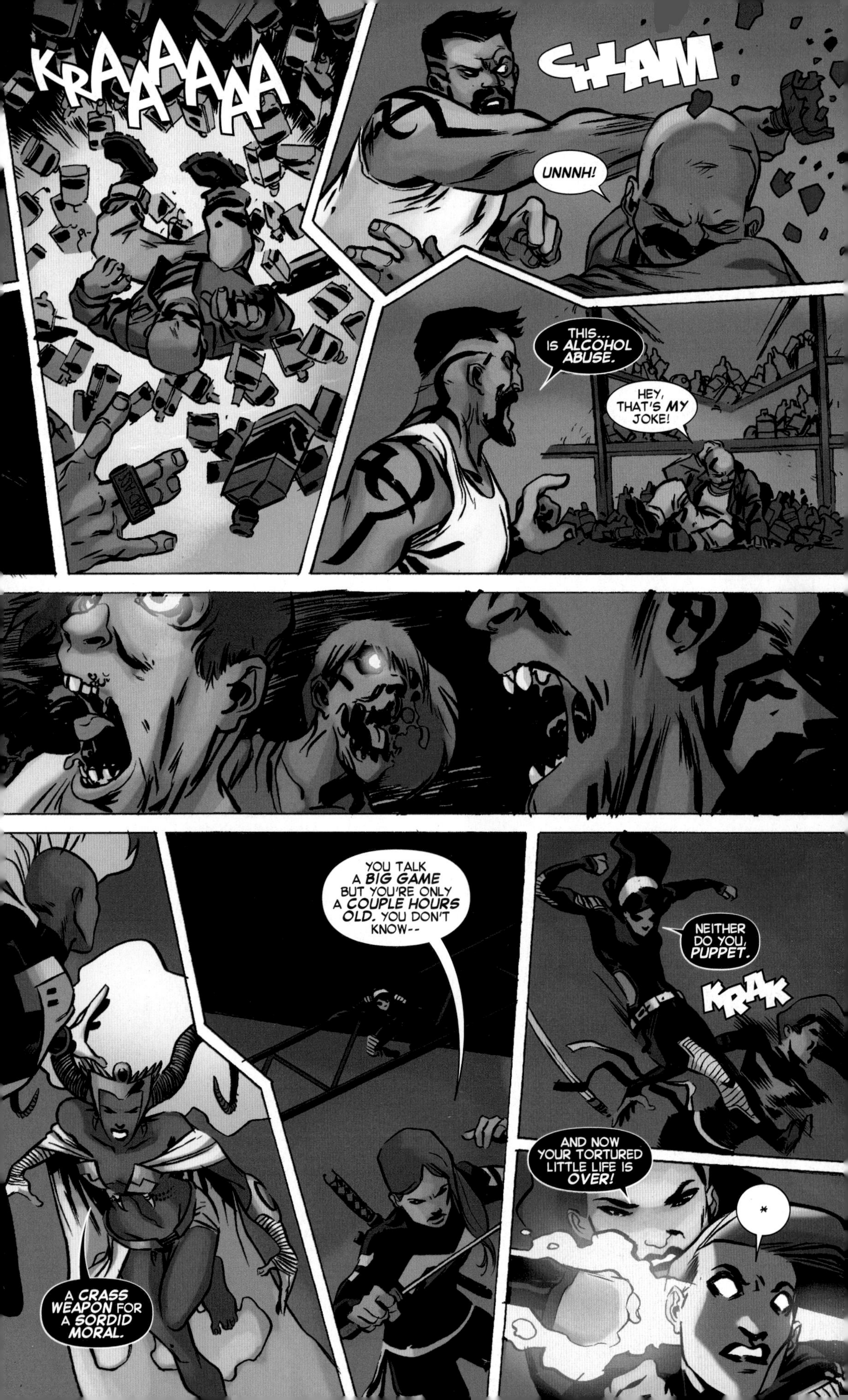
KRAAAAAAA
CHAM
UNNNH!
THIS... IS ALCOHOL ABUSE.
HEY, THAT'S MY JOKE!
YOU TALK A BIG GAME BUT YOU'RE ONLY A COUPLE HOURS OLD. YOU DON'T KNOW--
NEITHER DO YOU, PUPPET.
KRAK
A CRASS WEAPON FOR A SORDID MORAL.
AND NOW YOUR TORTURED LITTLE LIFE IS OVER!
*

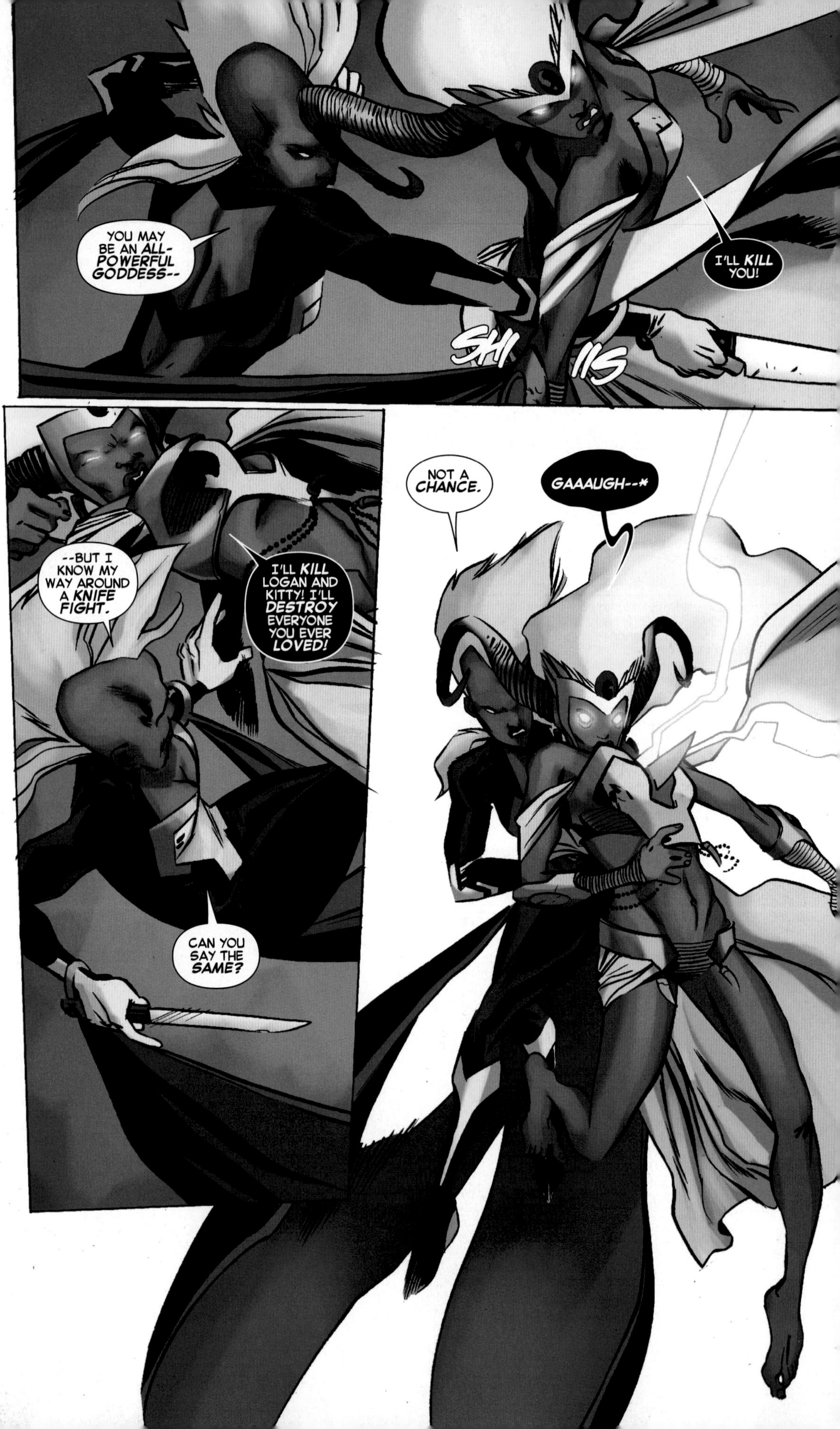
YOU MAY BE AN ALL-POWERFUL GODDESS--
I'LL KILL YOU!
SHIIS
--BUT I KNOW MY WAY AROUND A KNIFE FIGHT.
I'LL KILL LOGAN AND KITTY! I'LL DESTROY EVERYONE YOU EVER LOVED!
CAN YOU SAY THE SAME?
NOT A CHANCE.
GAAAUGH--*

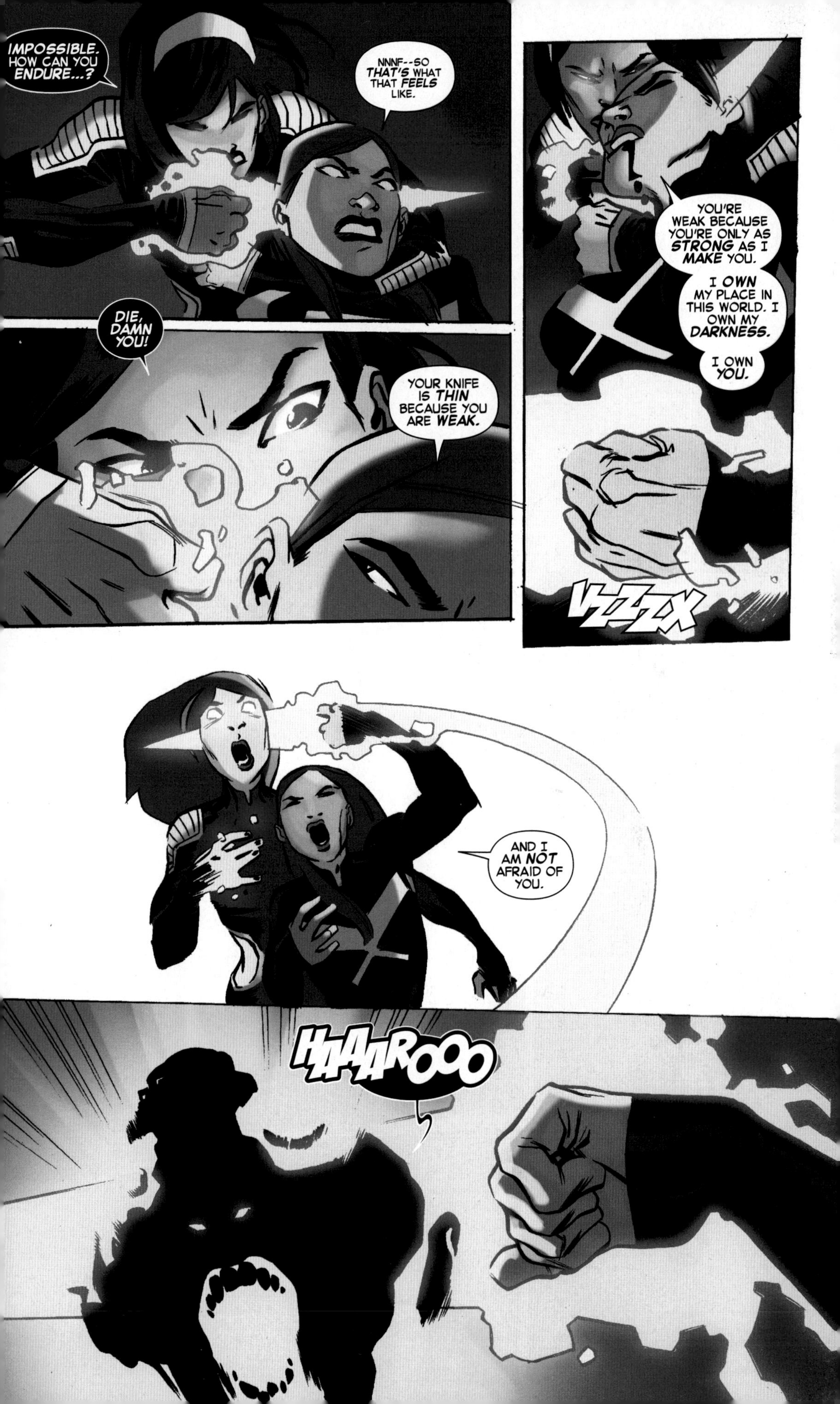
IMPOSSIBLE. HOW CAN YOU ENDURE...?
NNNF--SO THAT'S WHAT THAT FEELS LIKE.
DIE, DAMN YOU!
YOUR KNIFE IS THIN BECAUSE YOU ARE WEAK.
YOU'RE WEAK BECAUSE YOU'RE ONLY AS STRONG AS I MAKE YOU.
I OWN MY PLACE IN THIS WORLD. I OWN MY DARKNESS.
I OWN YOU.
VZZZX
AND I AM NOT AFRAID OF YOU.
HAAAROOO

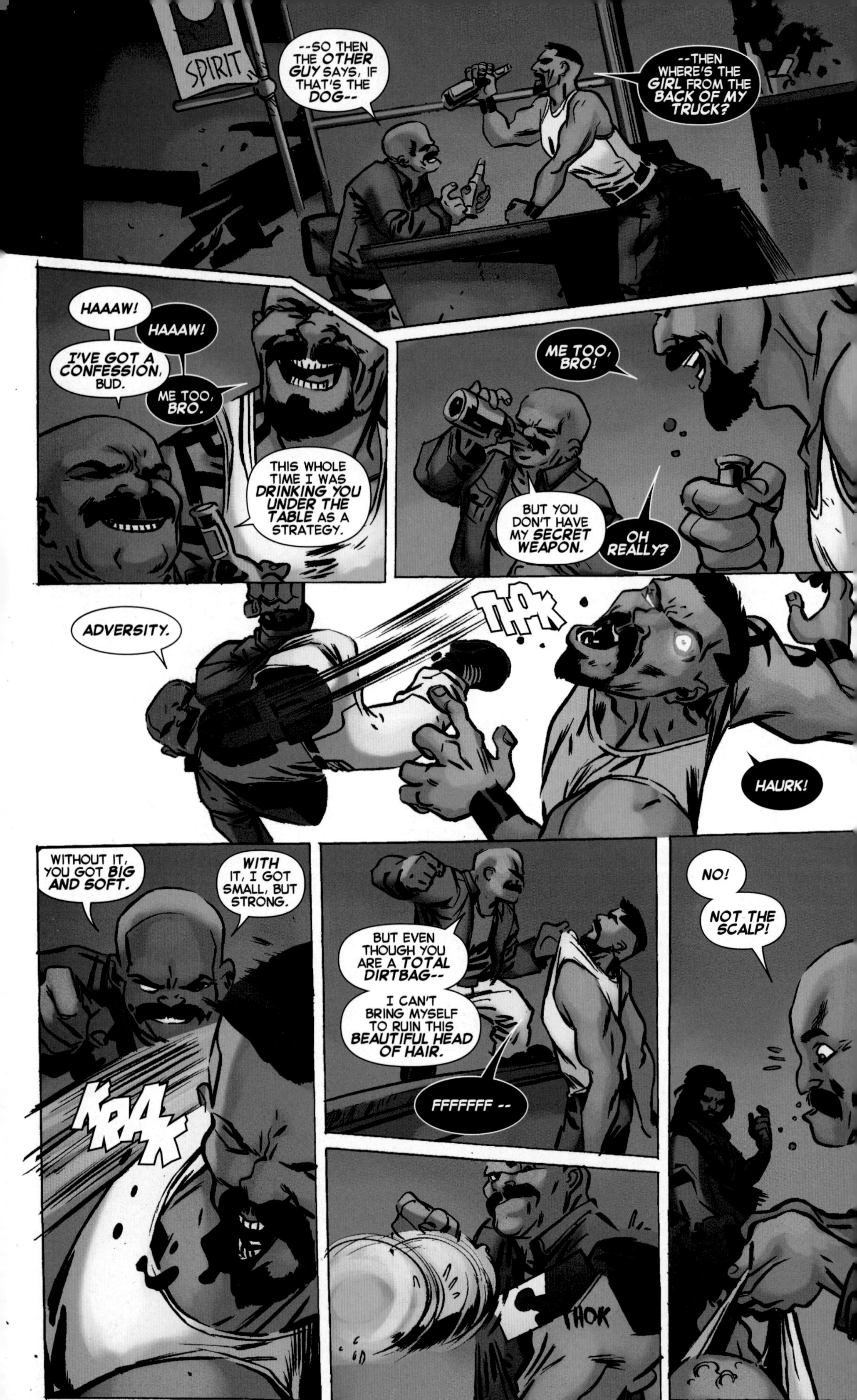

SPIRIT
--SO THEN THE OTHER GUY SAYS, IF THAT'S THE DOG--
--THEN WHERE'S THE GIRL FROM THE BACK OF MY TRUCK?
HAAAW!
HAAAW!
I'VE GOT A CONFESSION, BUD.
ME TOO, BRO.
THIS WHOLE TIME I WAS DRINKING YOU UNDER THE TABLE AS A STRATEGY.
ME TOO, BRO!
BUT YOU DON'T HAVE MY SECRET WEAPON.
OH REALLY?
ADVERSITY.
THOK
HAURK!
WITHOUT IT, YOU GOT BIG AND SOFT.
WITH IT, I GOT SMALL, BUT STRONG.
KRAK
BUT EVEN THOUGH YOU ARE A TOTAL DIRTBAG--
I CAN'T BRING MYSELF TO RUIN THIS BEAUTIFUL HEAD OF HAIR.
FFFFFFF --
THOK
NO!
NOT THE SCALP!

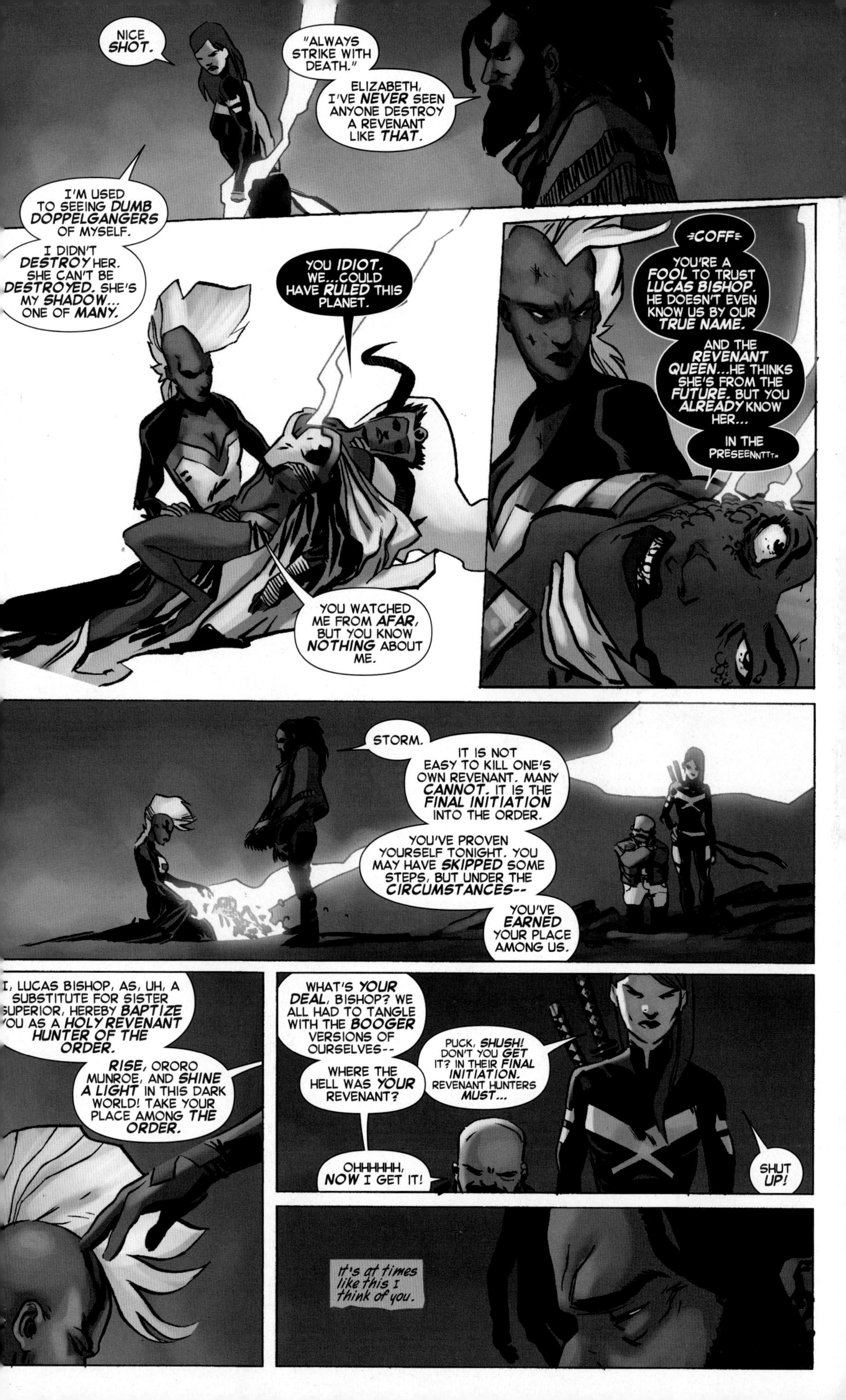
NICE SHOT.
"ALWAYS STRIKE WITH DEATH."
ELIZABETH, I'VE NEVER SEEN ANYONE DESTROY A REVENANT LIKE THAT.
I'M USED TO SEEING DUMB DOPPELGANGERS OF MYSELF.
I DIDN'T DESTROY HER. SHE CAN'T BE DESTROYED. SHE'S MY SHADOW... ONE OF MANY.
YOU IDIOT. WE...COULD HAVE RULED THIS PLANET.
YOU WATCHED ME FROM AFAR, BUT YOU KNOW NOTHING ABOUT ME.
COFF
YOU'RE A FOOL TO TRUST LUCAS BISHOP. HE DOESN'T EVEN KNOW US BY OUR TRUE NAME.
AND THE REVENANT QUEEN...HE THINKS SHE'S FROM THE FUTURE. BUT YOU ALREADY KNOW HER...
IN THE PRESEENNNTTT...
STORM.
IT IS NOT EASY TO KILL ONE'S OWN REVENANT. MANY CANNOT. IT IS THE FINAL INITIATION INTO THE ORDER.
YOU'VE PROVEN YOURSELF TONIGHT. YOU MAY HAVE SKIPPED SOME STEPS, BUT UNDER THE CIRCUMSTANCES--
YOU'VE EARNED YOUR PLACE AMONG US.
I, LUCAS BISHOP, AS, UH, A SUBSTITUTE FOR SISTER SUPERIOR, HEREBY BAPTIZE YOU AS A HOLY REVENANT HUNTER OF THE ORDER.
RISE, ORORO MUNROE, AND SHINE A LIGHT IN THIS DARK WORLD! TAKE YOUR PLACE AMONG THE ORDER.
WHAT'S YOUR DEAL, BISHOP? WE ALL HAD TO TANGLE WITH THE BOOGER VERSIONS OF OURSELVES--
WHERE THE HELL WAS YOUR REVENANT?
PUCK, SHUSH! DON'T YOU GET IT? IN THEIR FINAL INITIATION. REVENANT HUNTERS MUST...
OHHHHHH, NOW I GET IT!
SHUT UP!
It's at times like this I think of you.

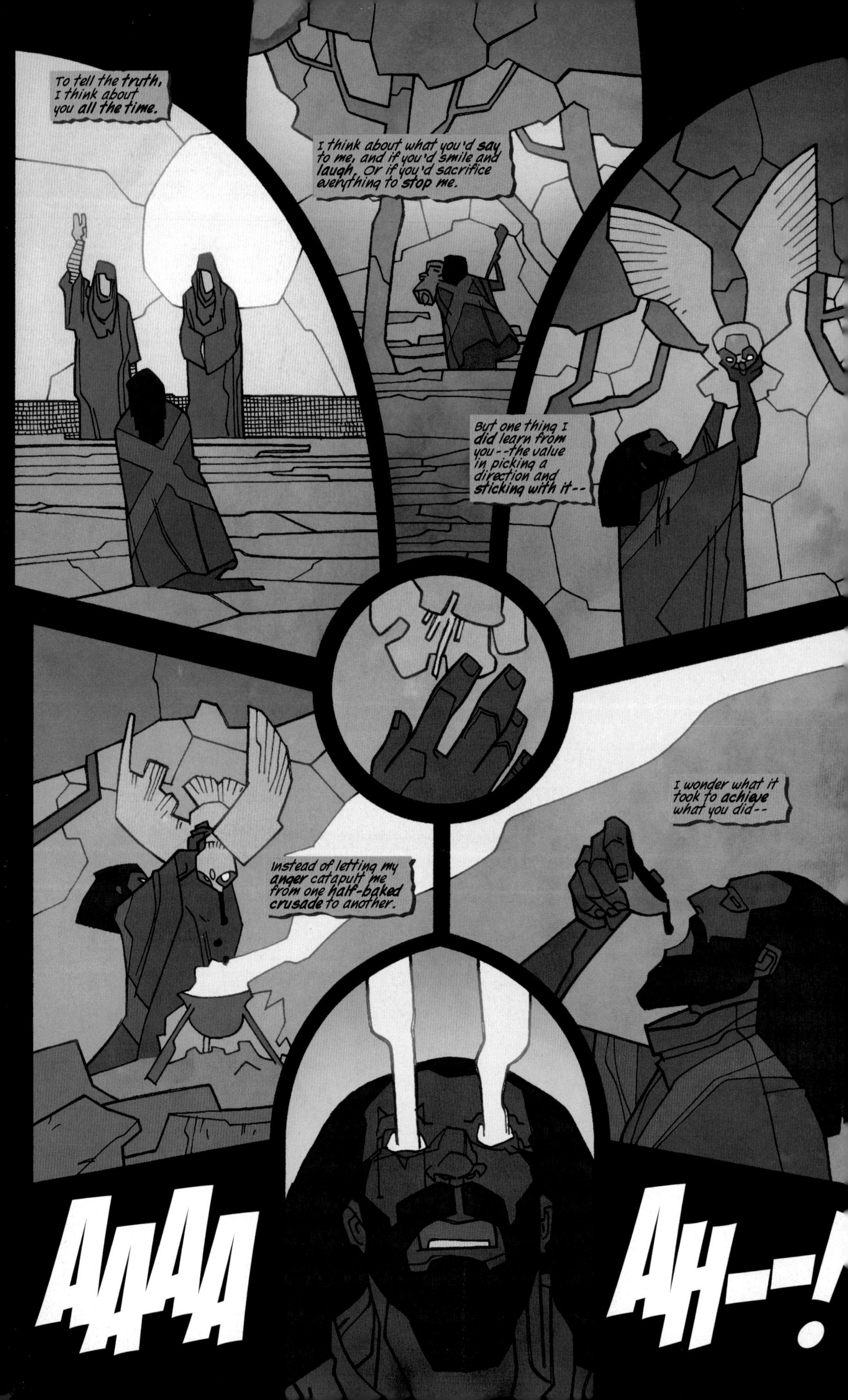
To tell the truth, I think about you all the time.
I think about what you'd say to me, and if you'd smile and laugh. Or if you'd sacrifice everything to stop me.
But one thing I did learn from you--the value in picking a direction and sticking with it--
Instead of letting my anger catapult me from one half-baked crusade to another.
I wonder what it took to achieve what you did--
AAAA AH--!

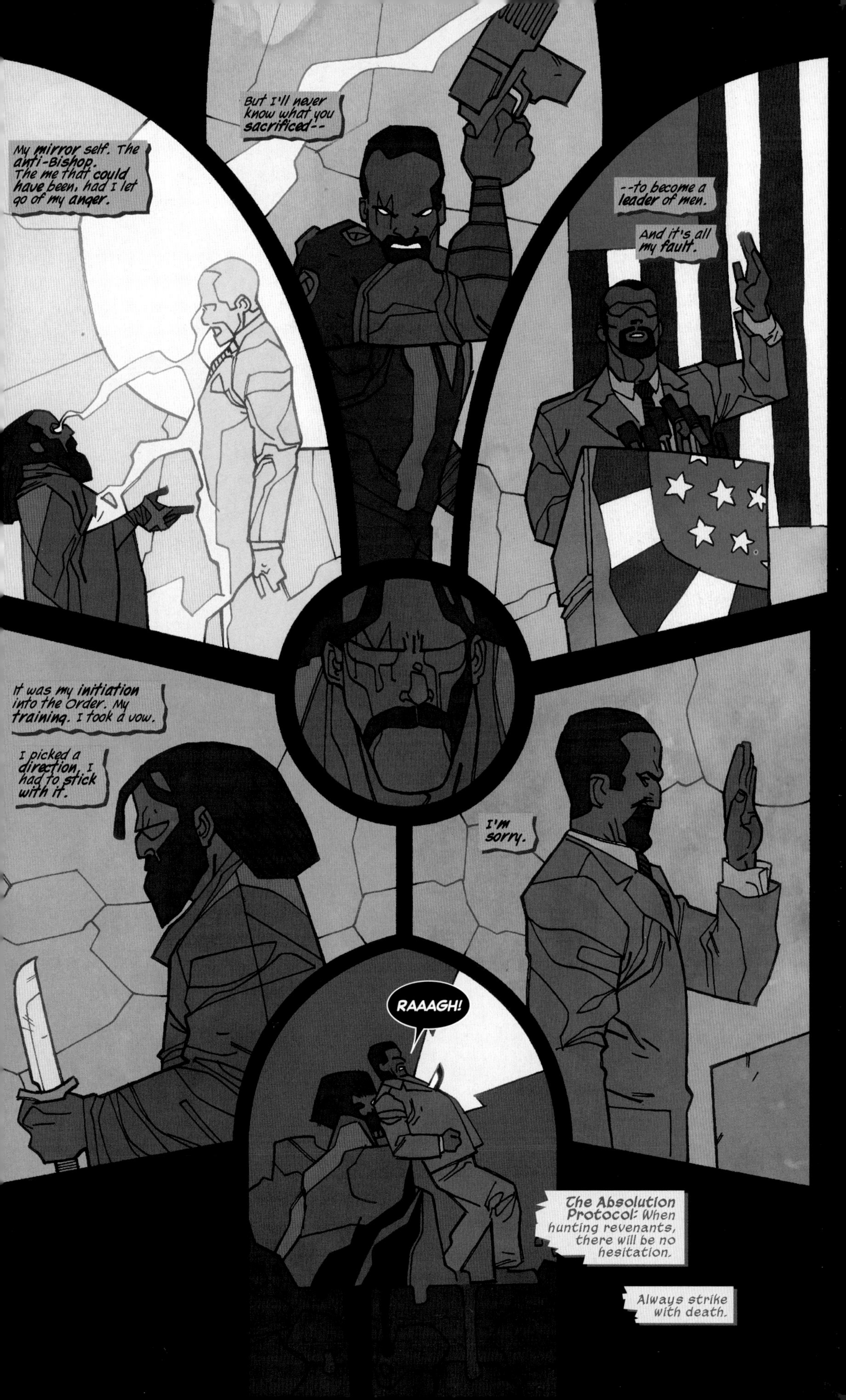

My mirror self. The anti-Bishop. The me that could have been, had I let go of my anger.
But I'll never know what you sacrificed--
--to become a leader of men.
And it's all my fault.
It was my initiation into the Order. My training. I took a vow.
I picked a direction, I had to stick with it.
I'm sorry.
RAAAGH!
The Absolution Protocol: When hunting revenants, there will be no hesitation.
Always strike with death.

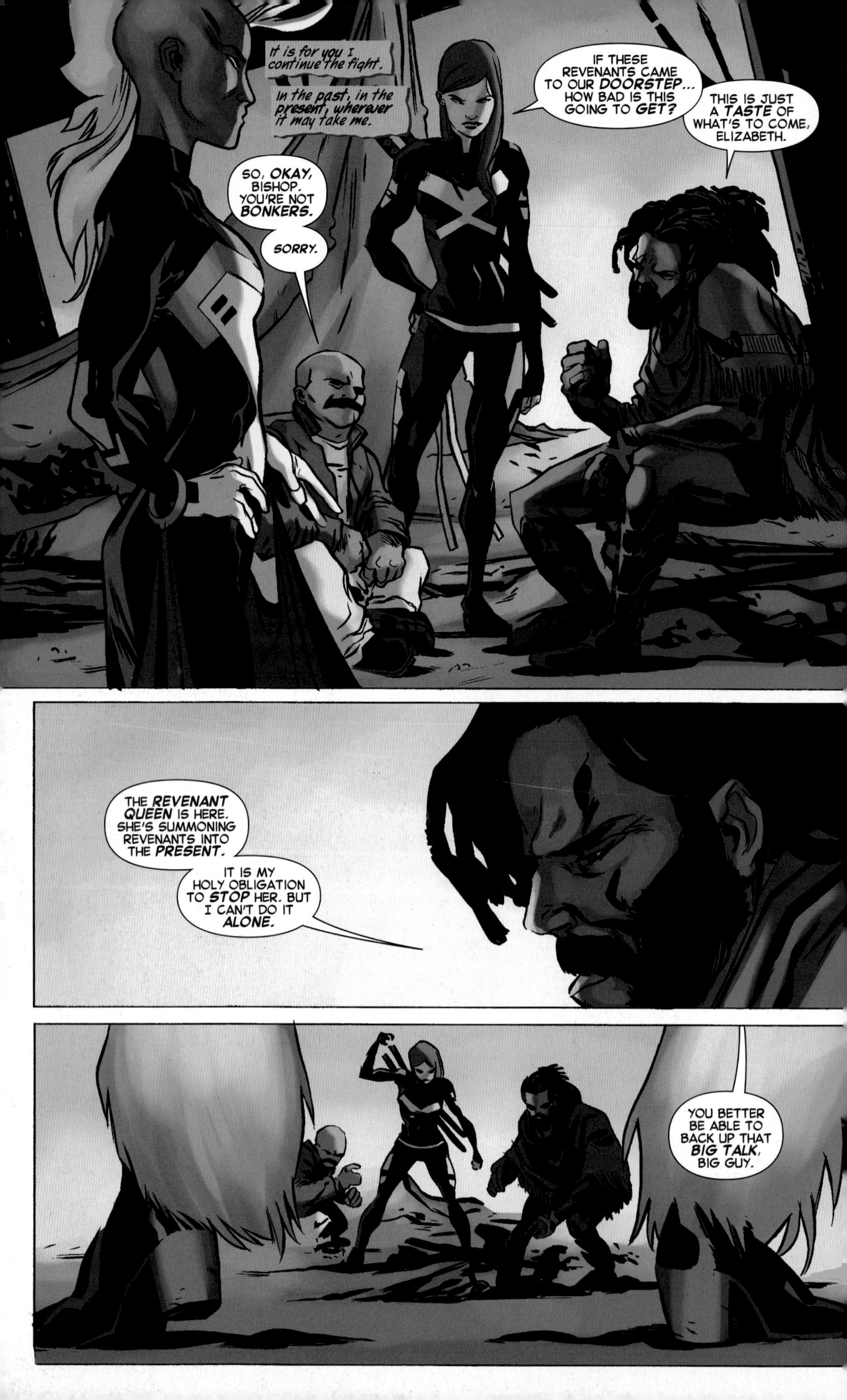
It is for you I continue the fight.
In the past, in the present, wherever it may take me.
IF THESE REVENANTS CAME TO OUR DOORSTEP... HOW BAD IS THIS GOING TO GET?
THIS IS JUST A TASTE OF WHAT'S TO COME, ELIZABETH.
SO, OKAY, BISHOP. YOU'RE NOT BONKERS.
SORRY.
THE REVENANT QUEEN IS HERE. SHE'S SUMMONING REVENANTS INTO THE PRESENT.
IT IS MY HOLY OBLIGATION TO STOP HER. BUT I CAN'T DO IT ALONE.
YOU BETTER BE ABLE TO BACK UP THAT BIG TALK, BIG GUY.

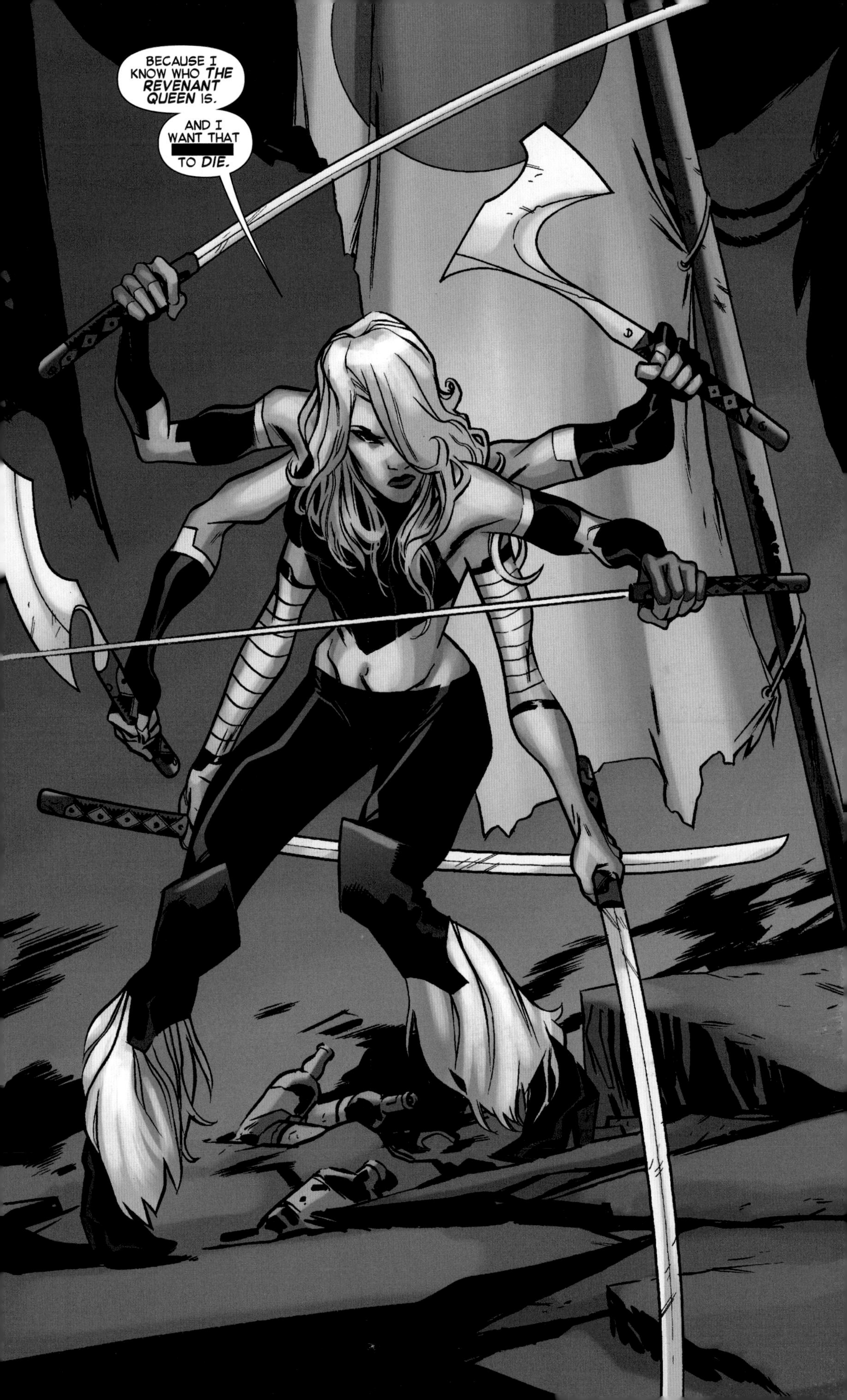
BECAUSE I KNOW WHO *THE REVENANT QUEEN* IS.
AND I WANT THAT [redacted] TO *DIE.*

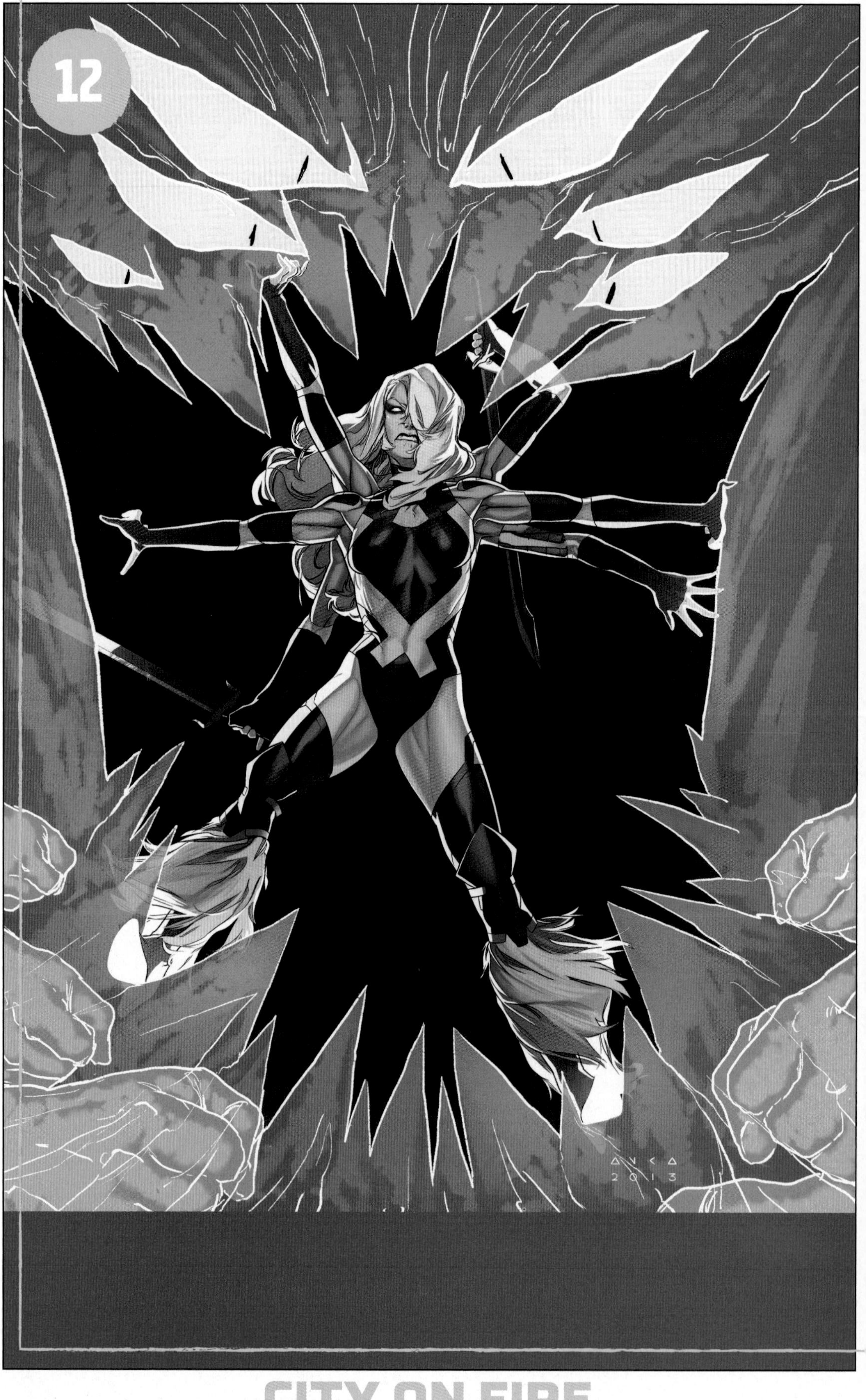
12
ANKA
2013

CITY ON FIRE

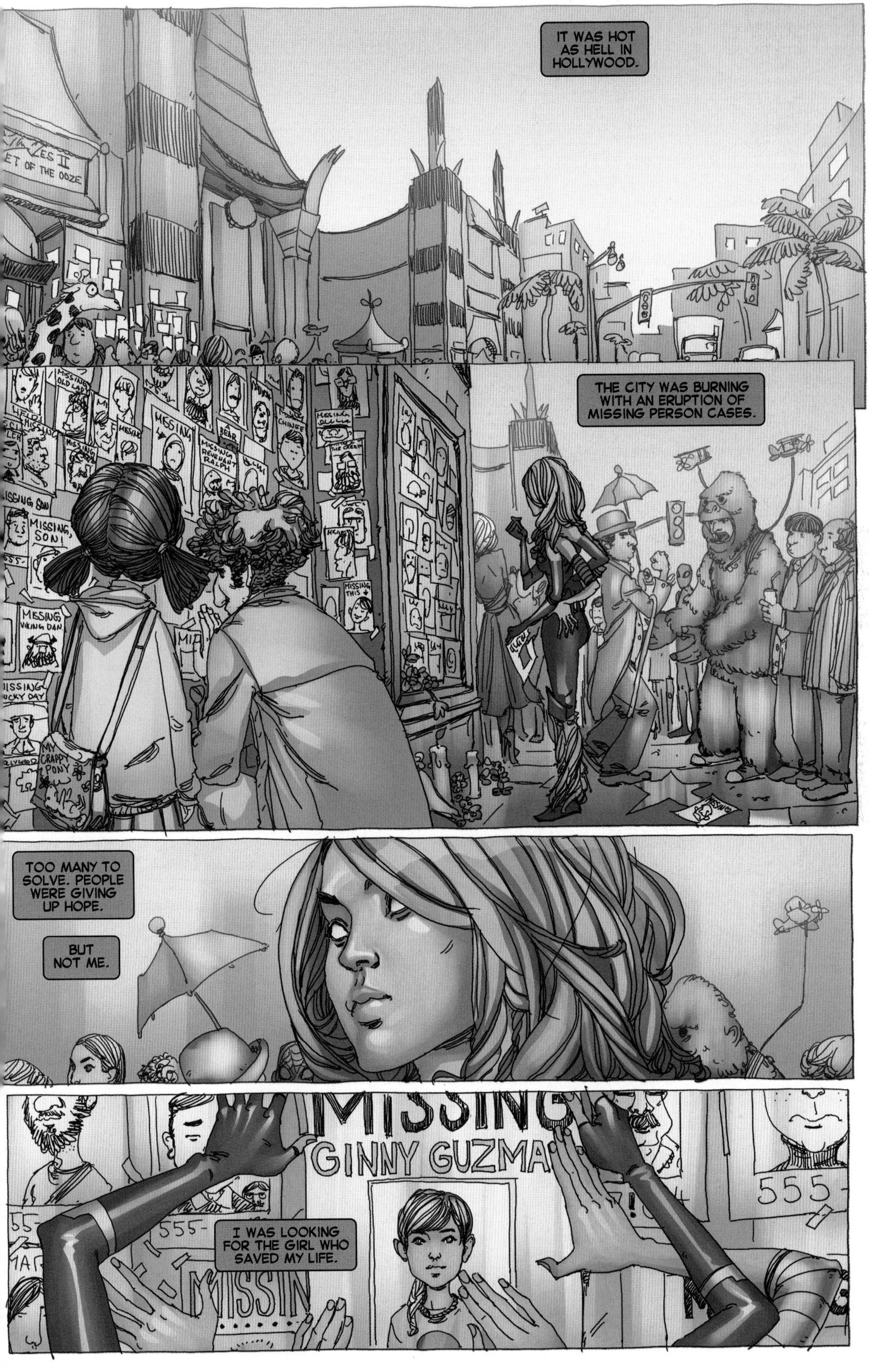
IT WAS HOT AS HELL IN HOLLYWOOD.
THE CITY WAS BURNING WITH AN ERUPTION OF MISSING PERSON CASES.
TOO MANY TO SOLVE. PEOPLE WERE GIVING UP HOPE.
BUT NOT ME.
MISSING
GINNY GUZMA
I WAS LOOKING FOR THE GIRL WHO SAVED MY LIFE.

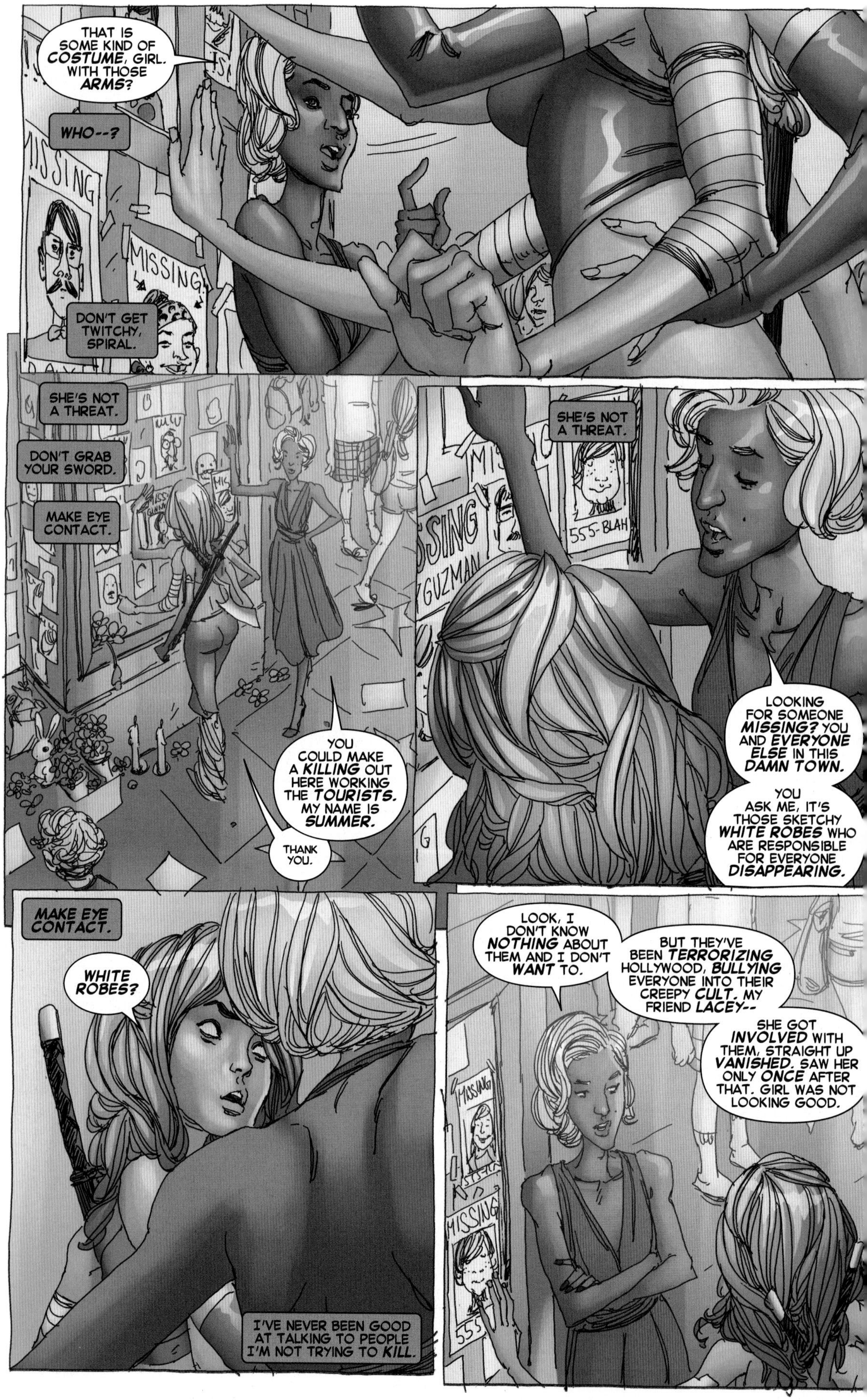
THAT IS SOME KIND OF COSTUME, GIRL. WITH THOSE ARMS?
WHO--?
DON'T GET TWITCHY, SPIRAL.
SHE'S NOT A THREAT.
DON'T GRAB YOUR SWORD.
MAKE EYE CONTACT.
YOU COULD MAKE A KILLING OUT HERE WORKING THE TOURISTS. MY NAME IS SUMMER.
THANK YOU.
SHE'S NOT A THREAT.
LOOKING FOR SOMEONE MISSING? YOU AND EVERYONE ELSE IN THIS DAMN TOWN.
YOU ASK ME, IT'S THOSE SKETCHY WHITE ROBES WHO ARE RESPONSIBLE FOR EVERYONE DISAPPEARING.
MAKE EYE CONTACT.
WHITE ROBES?
I'VE NEVER BEEN GOOD AT TALKING TO PEOPLE I'M NOT TRYING TO KILL.
LOOK, I DON'T KNOW NOTHING ABOUT THEM AND I DON'T WANT TO.
BUT THEY'VE BEEN TERRORIZING HOLLYWOOD, BULLYING EVERYONE INTO THEIR CREEPY CULT. MY FRIEND LACEY--
SHE GOT INVOLVED WITH THEM, STRAIGHT UP VANISHED. SAW HER ONLY ONCE AFTER THAT. GIRL WAS NOT LOOKING GOOD.

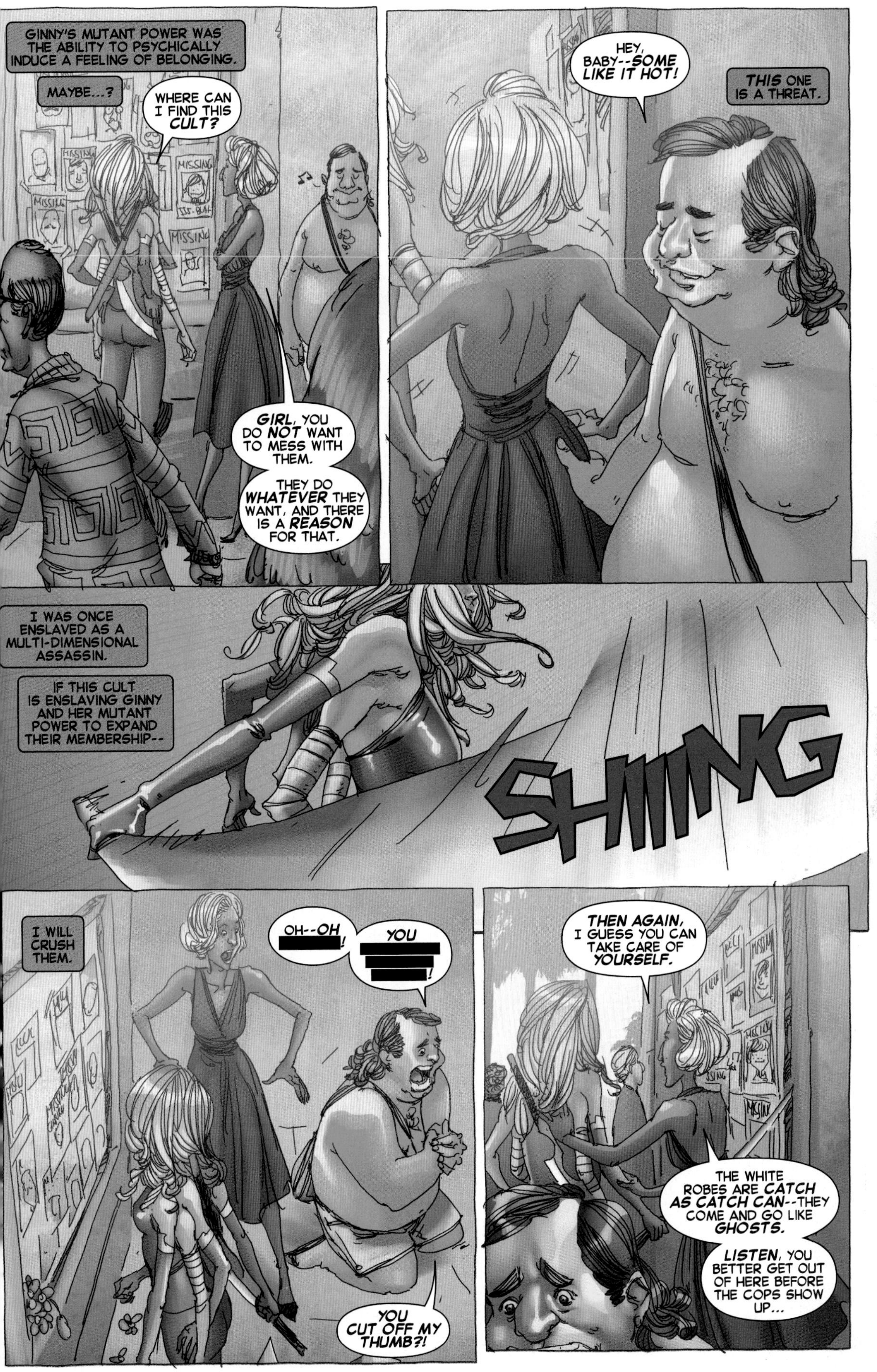
GINNY'S MUTANT POWER WAS THE ABILITY TO PSYCHICALLY INDUCE A FEELING OF BELONGING.
MAYBE...?
WHERE CAN I FIND THIS CULT?
GIRL, YOU DO NOT WANT TO MESS WITH THEM.
THEY DO WHATEVER THEY WANT, AND THERE IS A REASON FOR THAT.
HEY, BABY--SOME LIKE IT HOT!
THIS ONE IS A THREAT.
I WAS ONCE ENSLAVED AS A MULTI-DIMENSIONAL ASSASSIN.
IF THIS CULT IS ENSLAVING GINNY AND HER MUTANT POWER TO EXPAND THEIR MEMBERSHIP--
SHIIIING
I WILL CRUSH THEM.
OH--OH [redacted]!
YOU [redacted]!
YOU CUT OFF MY THUMB?!
THEN AGAIN, I GUESS YOU CAN TAKE CARE OF YOURSELF.
THE WHITE ROBES ARE CATCH AS CATCH CAN--THEY COME AND GO LIKE GHOSTS.
LISTEN, YOU BETTER GET OUT OF HERE BEFORE THE COPS SHOW UP...

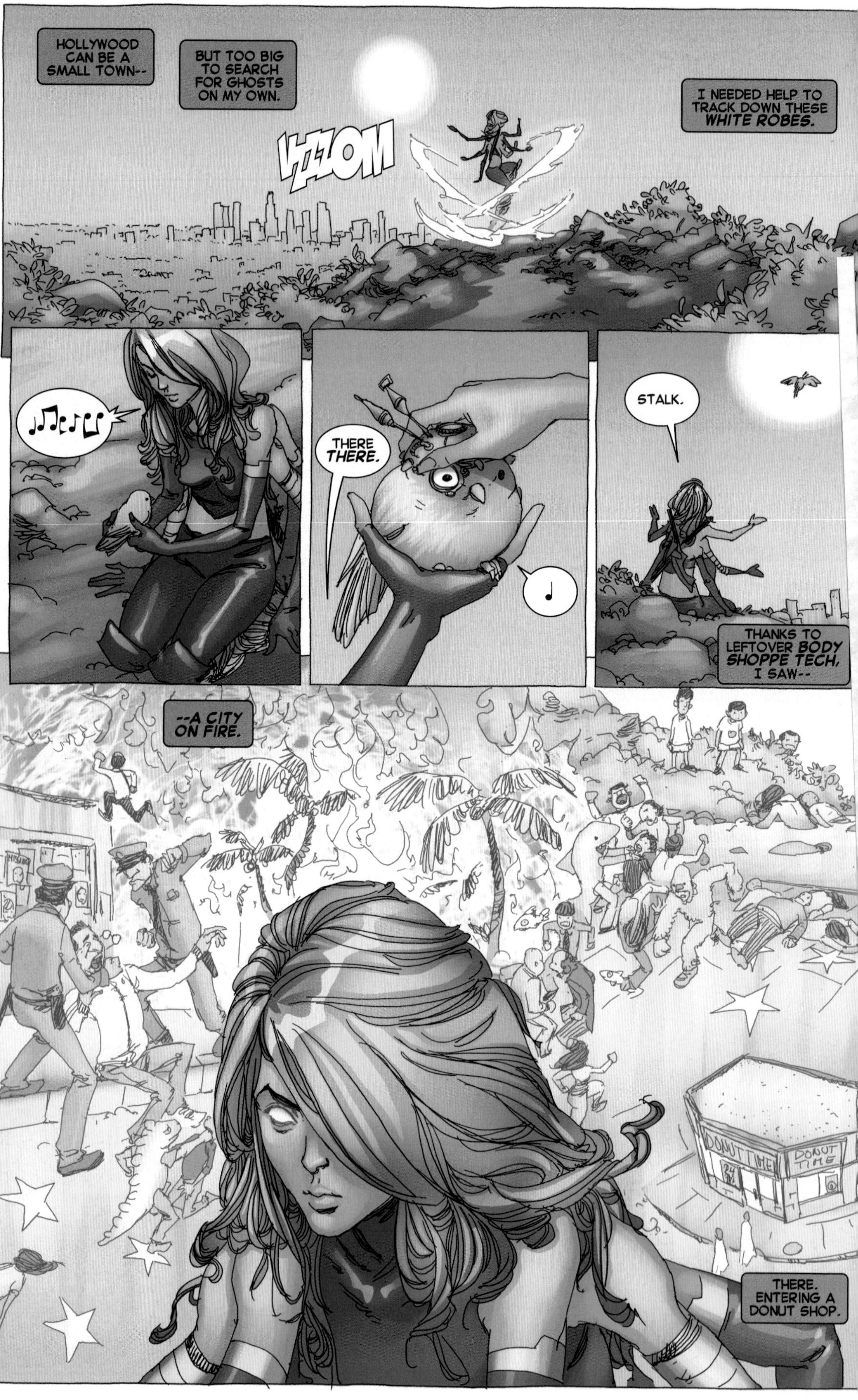
HOLLYWOOD CAN BE A SMALL TOWN--
BUT TOO BIG TO SEARCH FOR GHOSTS ON MY OWN.
I NEEDED HELP TO TRACK DOWN THESE WHITE ROBES.
VZZZOM
THERE THERE.
STALK.
THANKS TO LEFTOVER BODY SHOPPE TECH, I SAW--
--A CITY ON FIRE.
DONUT TIME
DONUT TIME
THERE. ENTERING A DONUT SHOP.

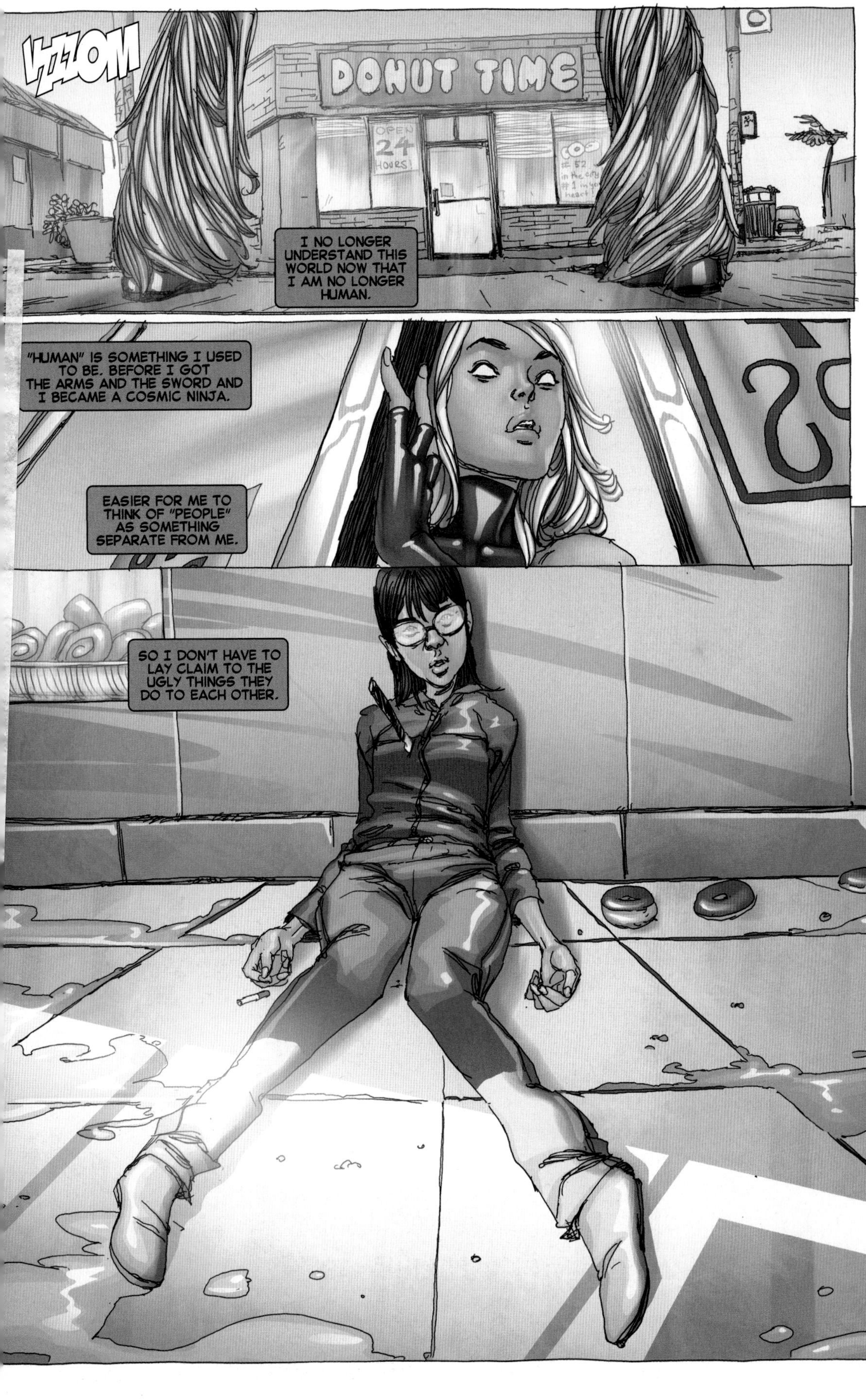
VZZZOM
DONUT TIME
OPEN 24 HOURS!
I NO LONGER UNDERSTAND THIS WORLD NOW THAT I AM NO LONGER HUMAN.
"HUMAN" IS SOMETHING I USED TO BE. BEFORE I GOT THE ARMS AND THE SWORD AND I BECAME A COSMIC NINJA.
EASIER FOR ME TO THINK OF "PEOPLE" AS SOMETHING SEPARATE FROM ME.
SO I DON'T HAVE TO LAY CLAIM TO THE UGLY THINGS THEY DO TO EACH OTHER.

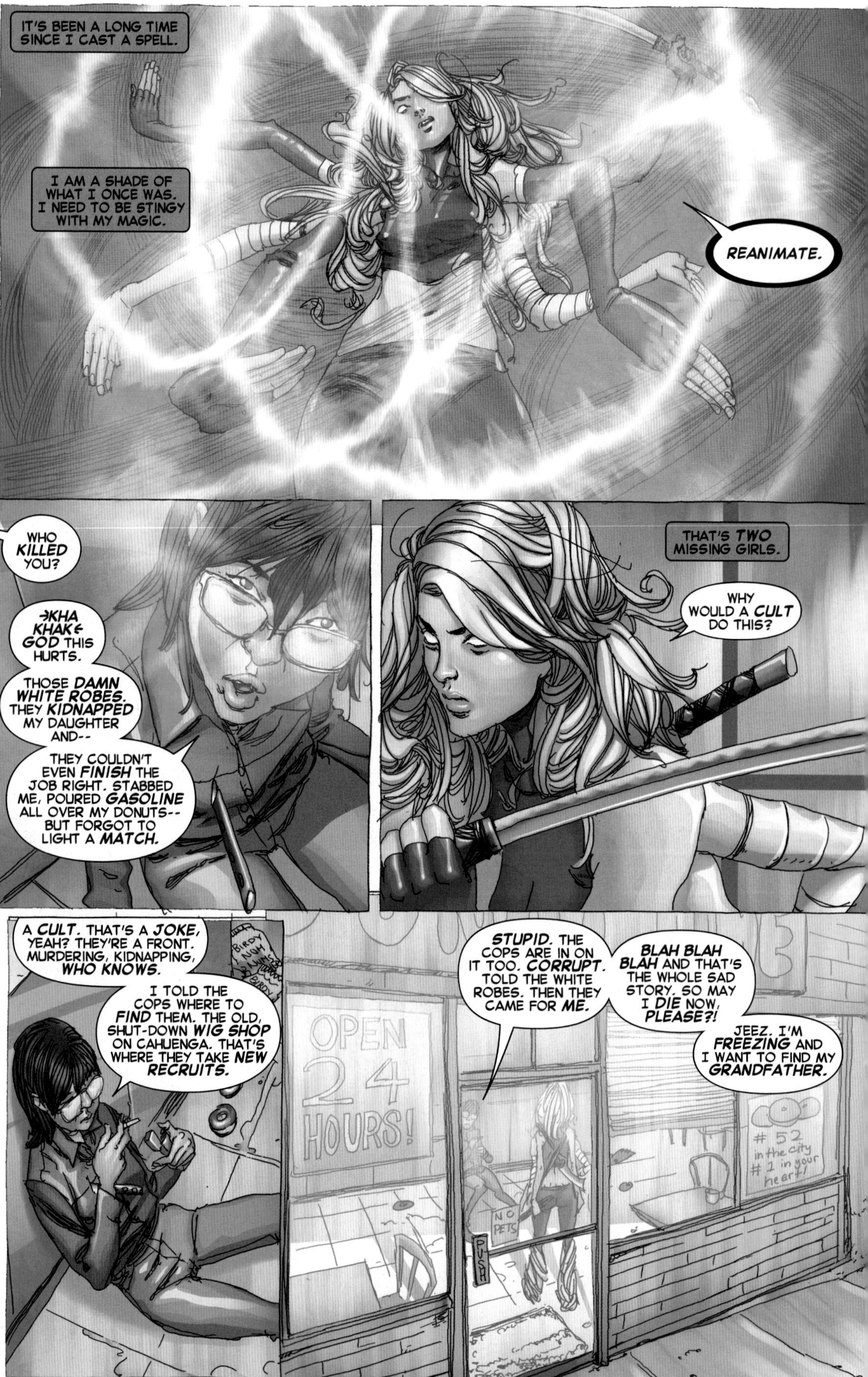

IT'S BEEN A LONG TIME SINCE I CAST A SPELL.
I AM A SHADE OF WHAT I ONCE WAS. I NEED TO BE STINGY WITH MY MAGIC.
REANIMATE.
WHO KILLED YOU?
→KHA KHAK← GOD THIS HURTS.
THOSE DAMN WHITE ROBES. THEY KIDNAPPED MY DAUGHTER AND--
THEY COULDN'T EVEN FINISH THE JOB RIGHT. STABBED ME, POURED GASOLINE ALL OVER MY DONUTS-- BUT FORGOT TO LIGHT A MATCH.
THAT'S TWO MISSING GIRLS.
WHY WOULD A CULT DO THIS?
A CULT. THAT'S A JOKE, YEAH? THEY'RE A FRONT. MURDERING, KIDNAPPING, WHO KNOWS.
I TOLD THE COPS WHERE TO FIND THEM. THE OLD, SHUT-DOWN WIG SHOP ON CAHUENGA. THAT'S WHERE THEY TAKE NEW RECRUITS.
STUPID. THE COPS ARE IN ON IT TOO. CORRUPT. TOLD THE WHITE ROBES. THEN THEY CAME FOR ME.
BLAH BLAH BLAH AND THAT'S THE WHOLE SAD STORY. SO MAY I DIE NOW, PLEASE?!
JEEZ. I'M FREEZING AND I WANT TO FIND MY GRANDFATHER.
OPEN 24 HOURS!
NO PETS
PUSH
#52 in the city #1 in your heart!

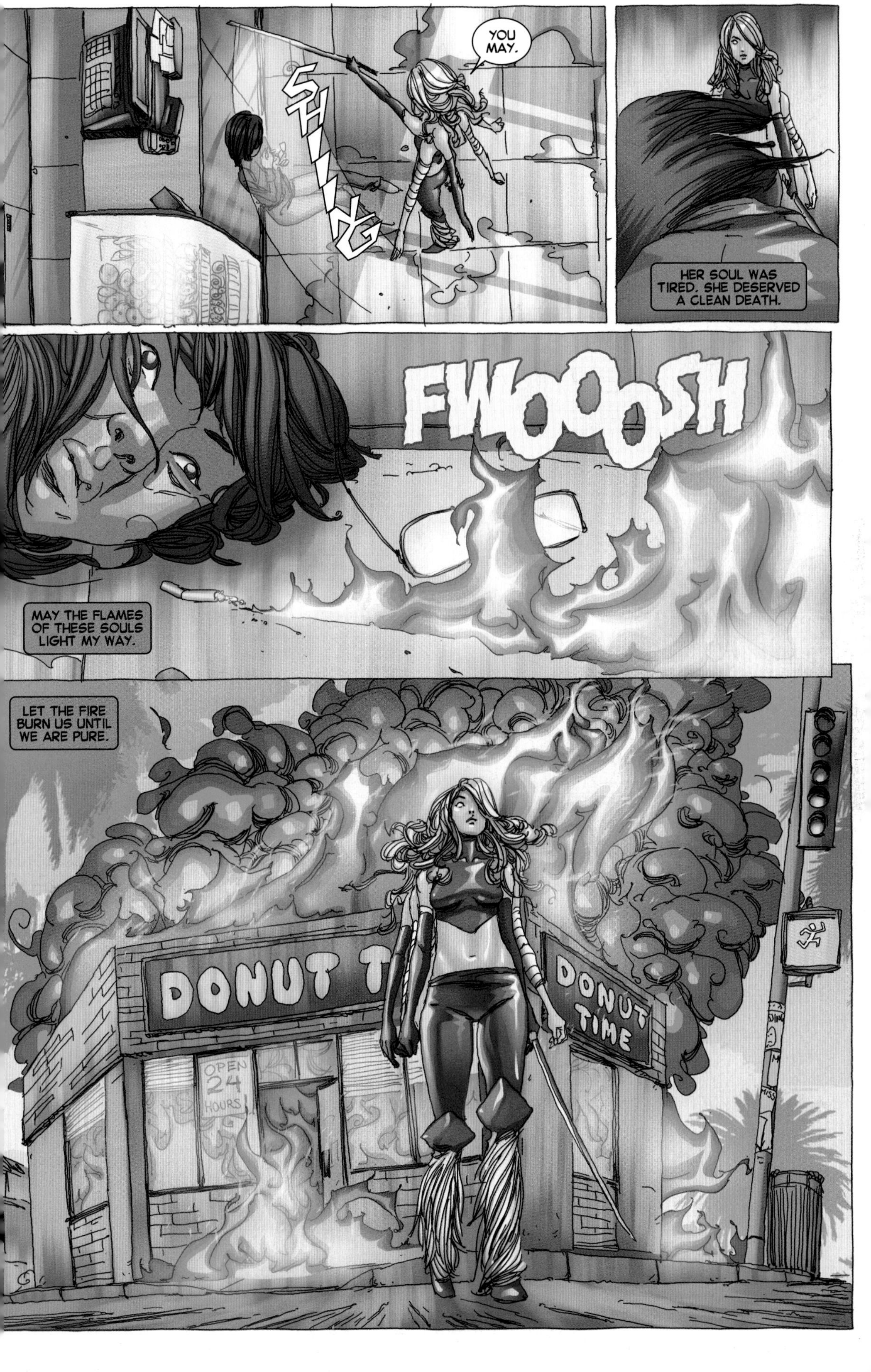
YOU MAY.
SHHING
HER SOUL WAS TIRED. SHE DESERVED A CLEAN DEATH.
FWOOOSH
MAY THE FLAMES OF THESE SOULS LIGHT MY WAY.
LET THE FIRE BURN US UNTIL WE ARE PURE.
DONUT T
DONUT TIME
OPEN 24 HOURS

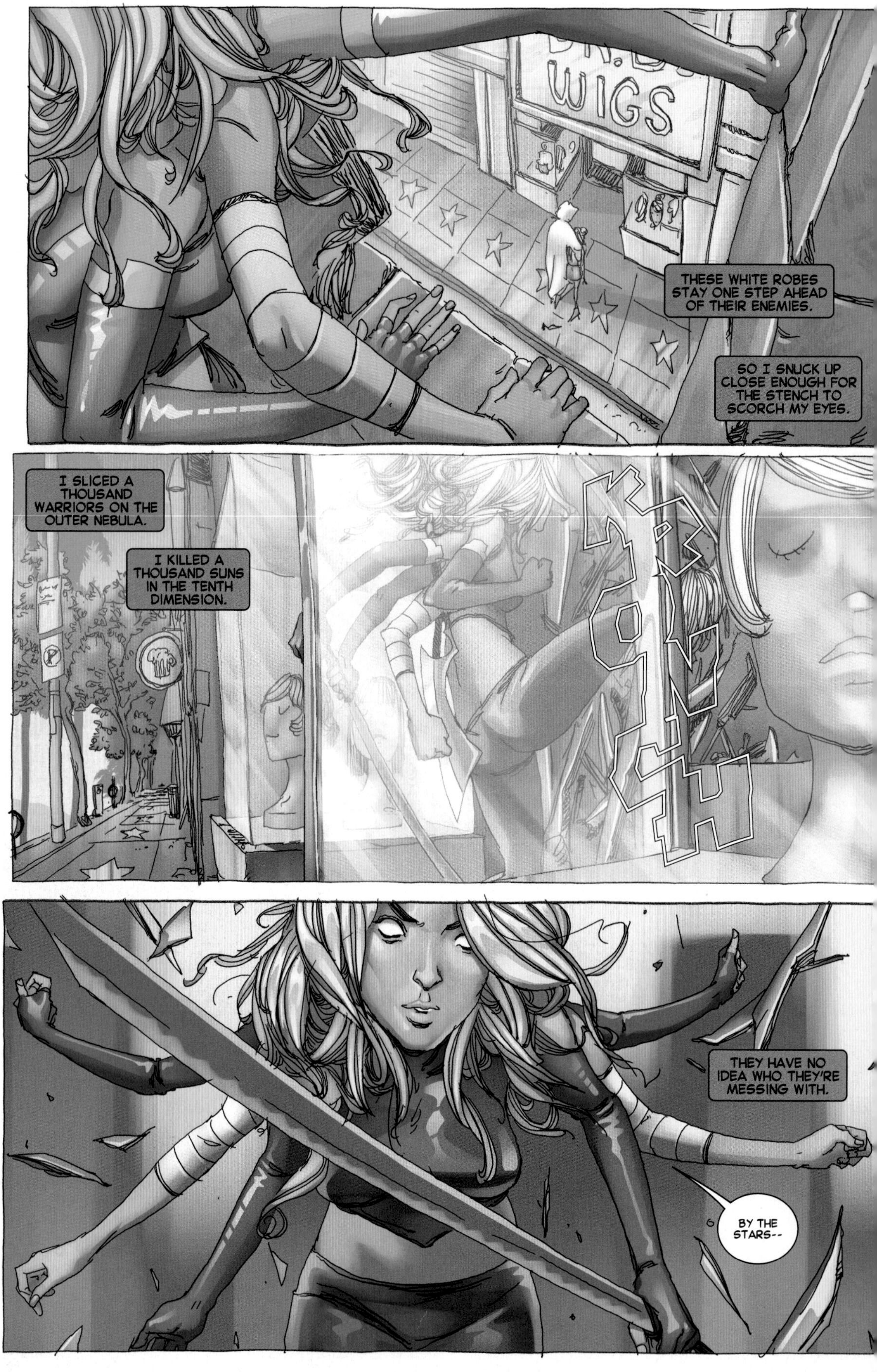
WIGS
THESE WHITE ROBES STAY ONE STEP AHEAD OF THEIR ENEMIES.
SO I SNUCK UP CLOSE ENOUGH FOR THE STENCH TO SCORCH MY EYES.
I SLICED A THOUSAND WARRIORS ON THE OUTER NEBULA.
I KILLED A THOUSAND SUNS IN THE TENTH DIMENSION.
KRAKOOSH
THEY HAVE NO IDEA WHO THEY'RE MESSING WITH.
BY THE STARS--

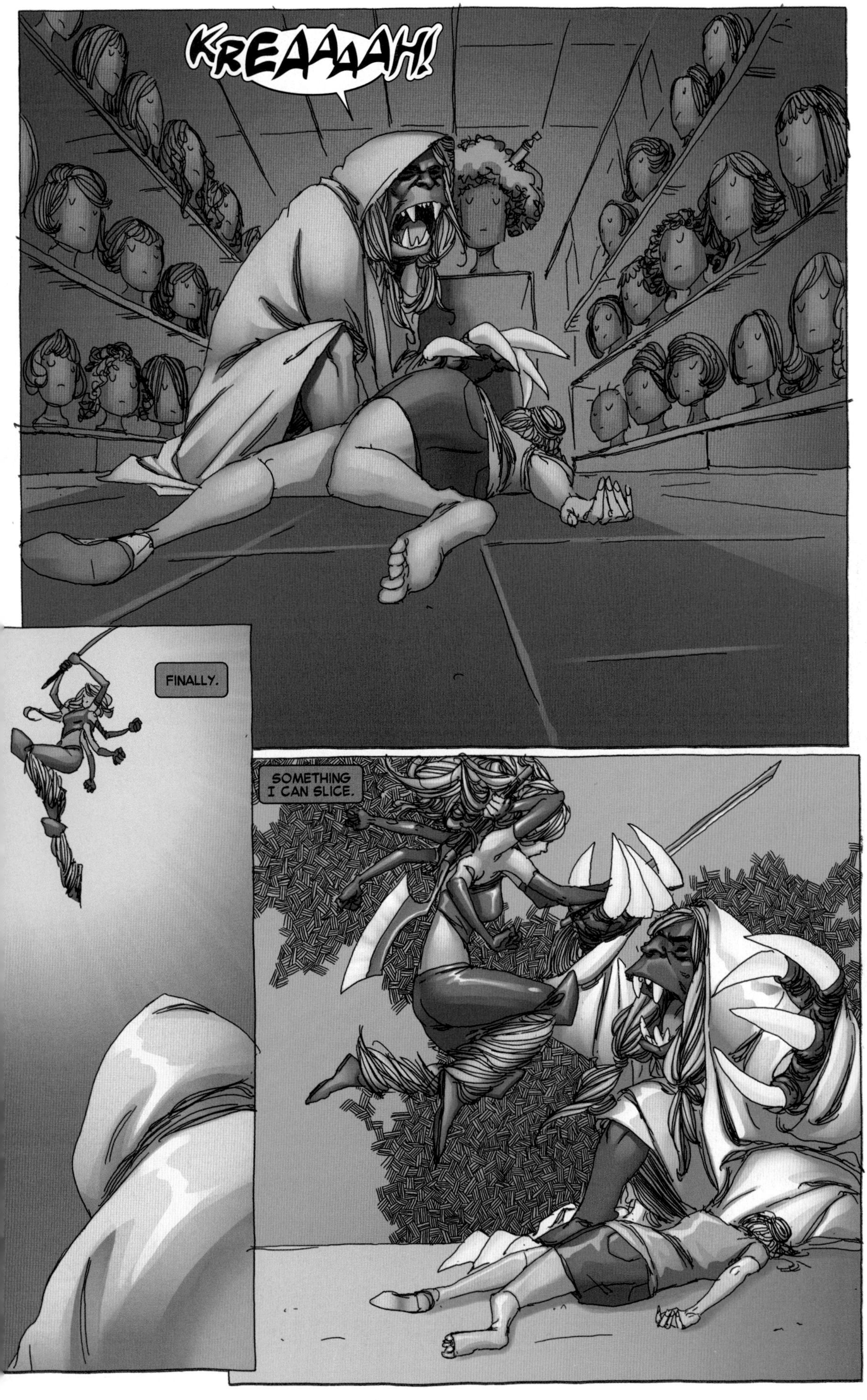
KREAAAAAH!
FINALLY.
SOMETHING I CAN SLICE.

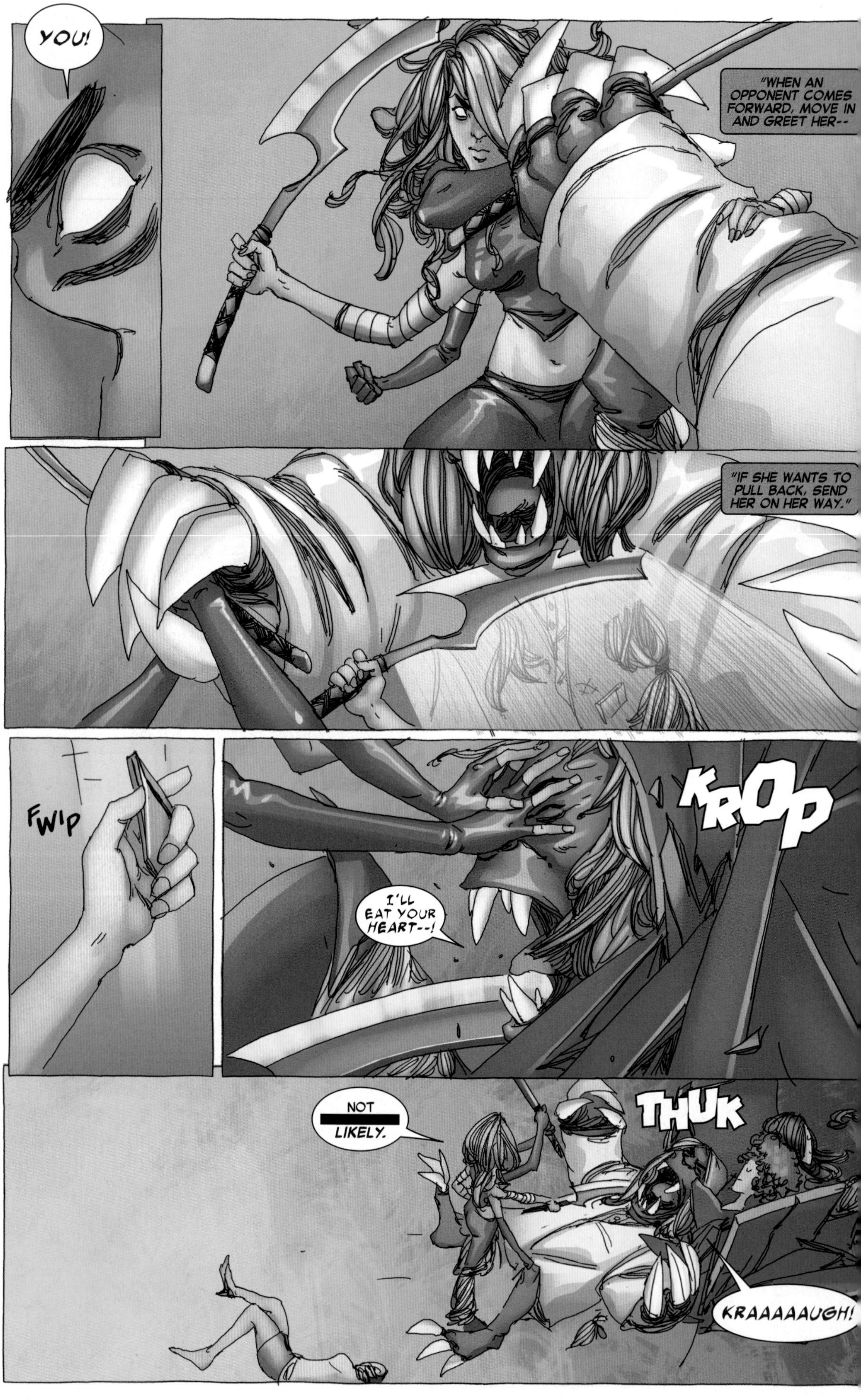
YOU!
"WHEN AN OPPONENT COMES FORWARD, MOVE IN AND GREET HER--
"IF SHE WANTS TO PULL BACK, SEND HER ON HER WAY."
FWIP
KROP
I'LL EAT YOUR HEART--!
THUK
NOT [redacted] LIKELY.
KRAAAAAUGH!

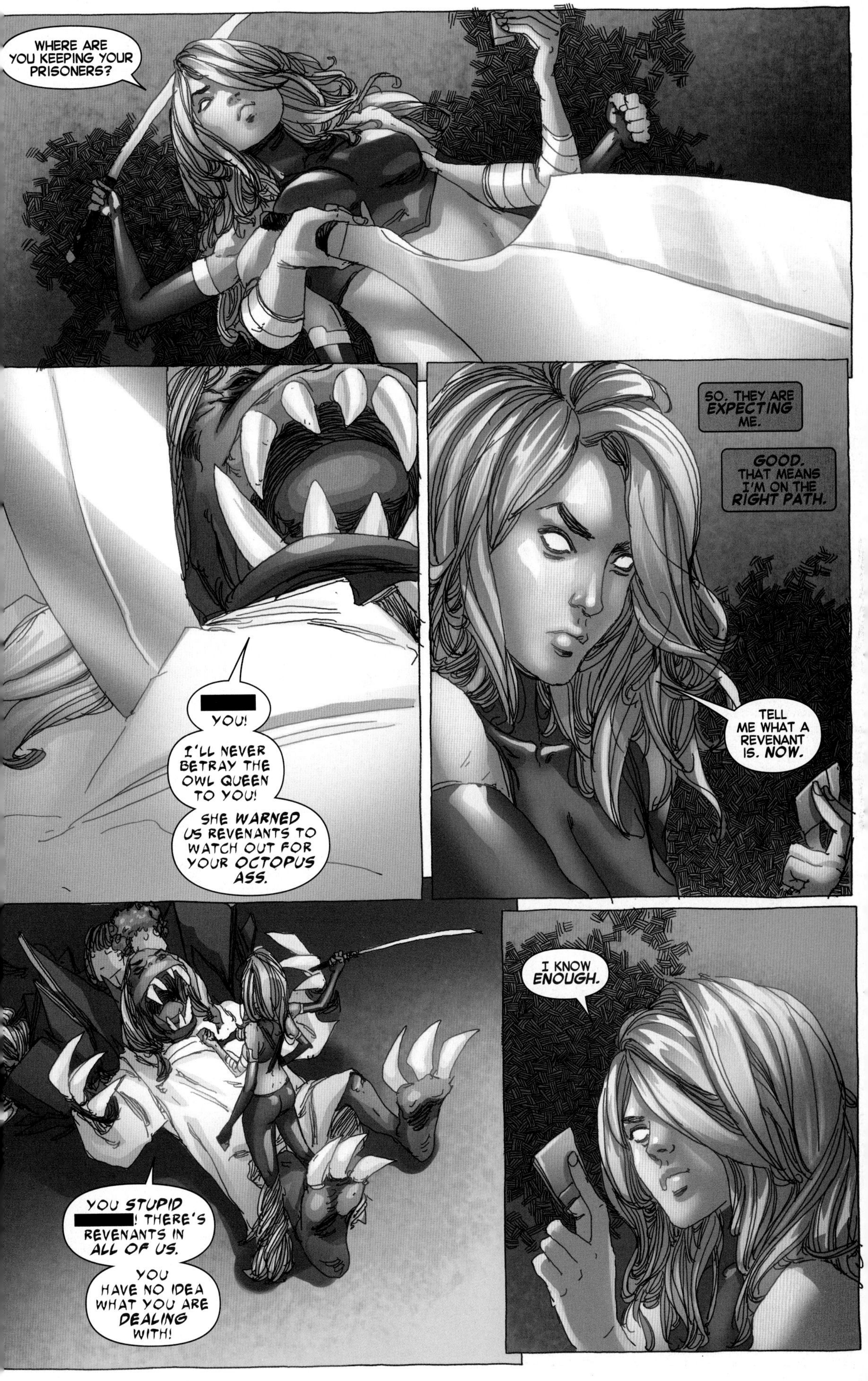
WHERE ARE YOU KEEPING YOUR PRISONERS?
[redacted] YOU!
I'LL NEVER BETRAY THE OWL QUEEN TO YOU!
SHE WARNED US REVENANTS TO WATCH OUT FOR YOUR OCTOPUS ASS.
SO, THEY ARE EXPECTING ME.
GOOD. THAT MEANS I'M ON THE RIGHT PATH.
TELL ME WHAT A REVENANT IS. NOW.
YOU STUPID [redacted]! THERE'S REVENANTS IN ALL OF US.
YOU HAVE NO IDEA WHAT YOU ARE DEALING WITH!
I KNOW ENOUGH.

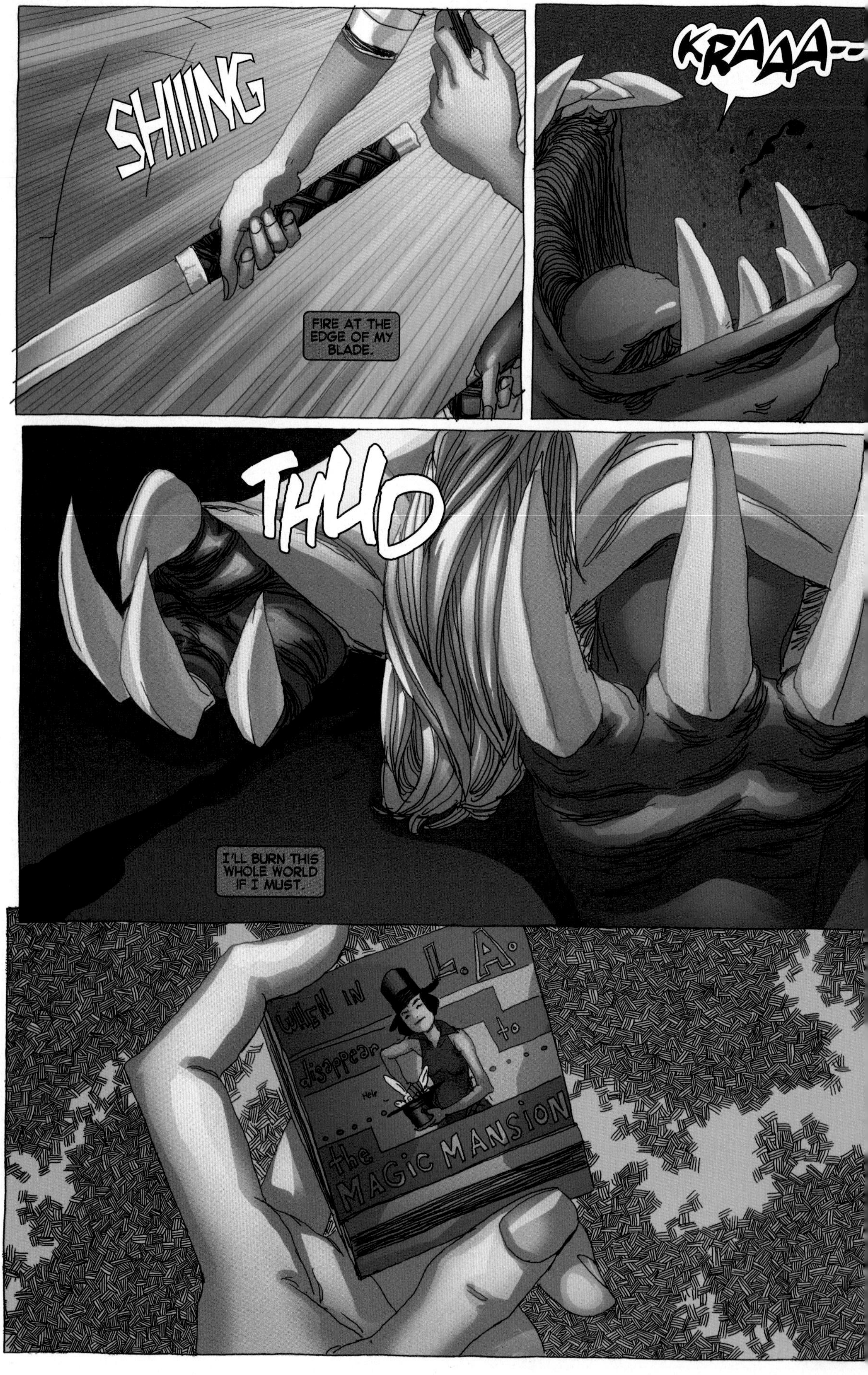
SHIIING
FIRE AT THE EDGE OF MY BLADE.
KRAAA--
THUD
I'LL BURN THIS WHOLE WORLD IF I MUST.
WHEN IN L.A.
to
disappear
the
MAGIC MANSION

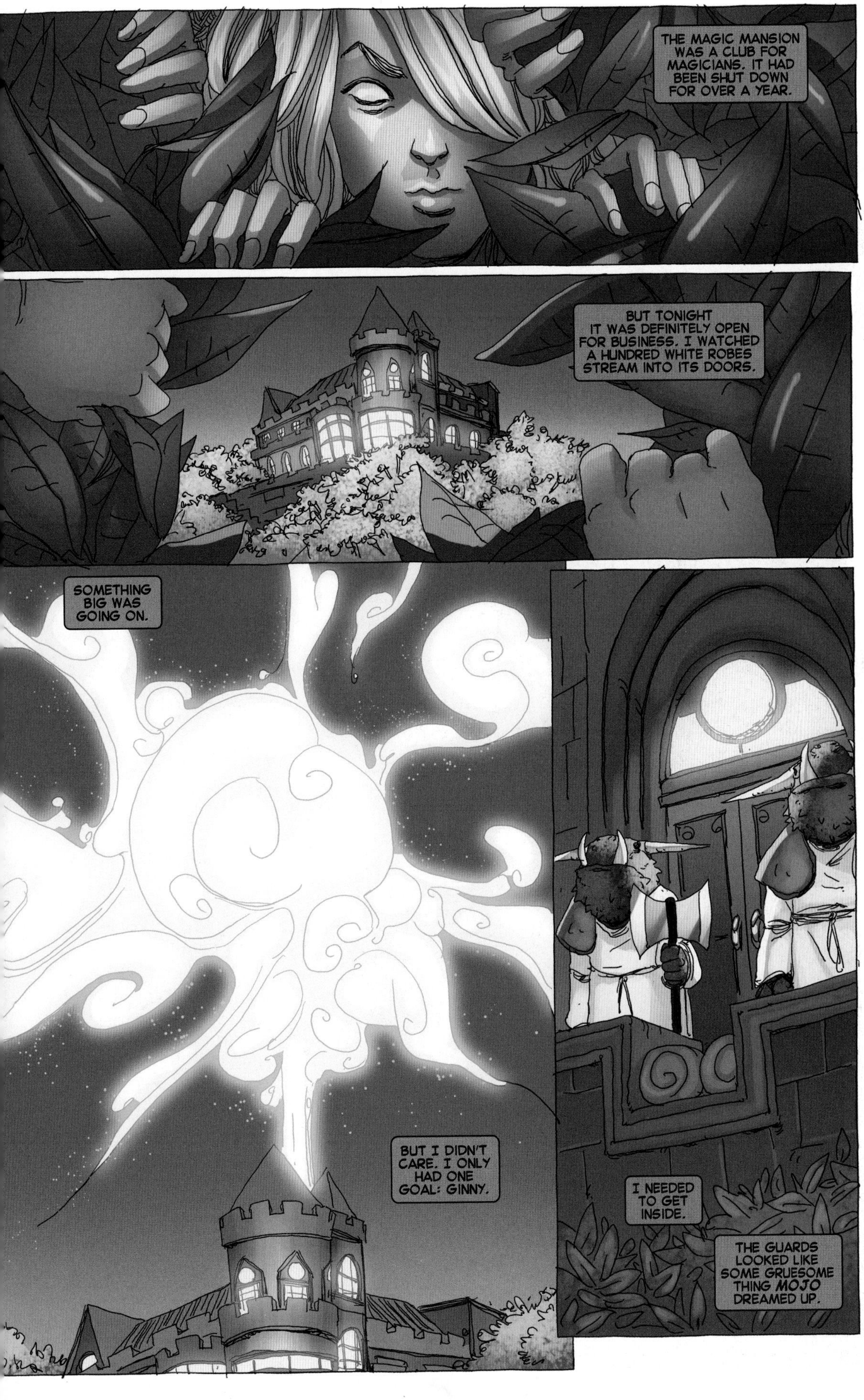
THE MAGIC MANSION WAS A CLUB FOR MAGICIANS. IT HAD BEEN SHUT DOWN FOR OVER A YEAR.
BUT TONIGHT IT WAS DEFINITELY OPEN FOR BUSINESS. I WATCHED A HUNDRED WHITE ROBES STREAM INTO ITS DOORS.
SOMETHING BIG WAS GOING ON.
BUT I DIDN'T CARE. I ONLY HAD ONE GOAL: GINNY.
I NEEDED TO GET INSIDE.
THE GUARDS LOOKED LIKE SOME GRUESOME THING MOJO DREAMED UP.

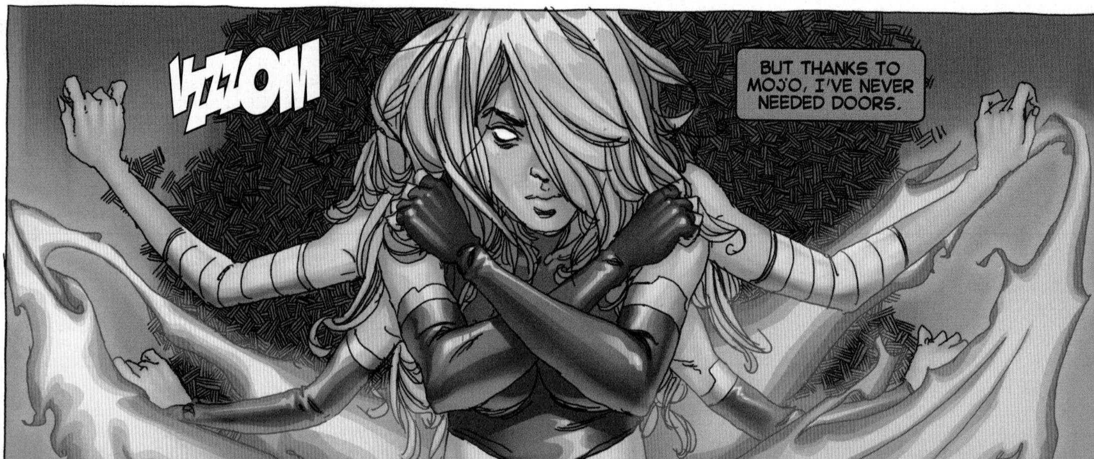
VZZZOM
BUT THANKS TO MOJO, I'VE NEVER NEEDED DOORS.

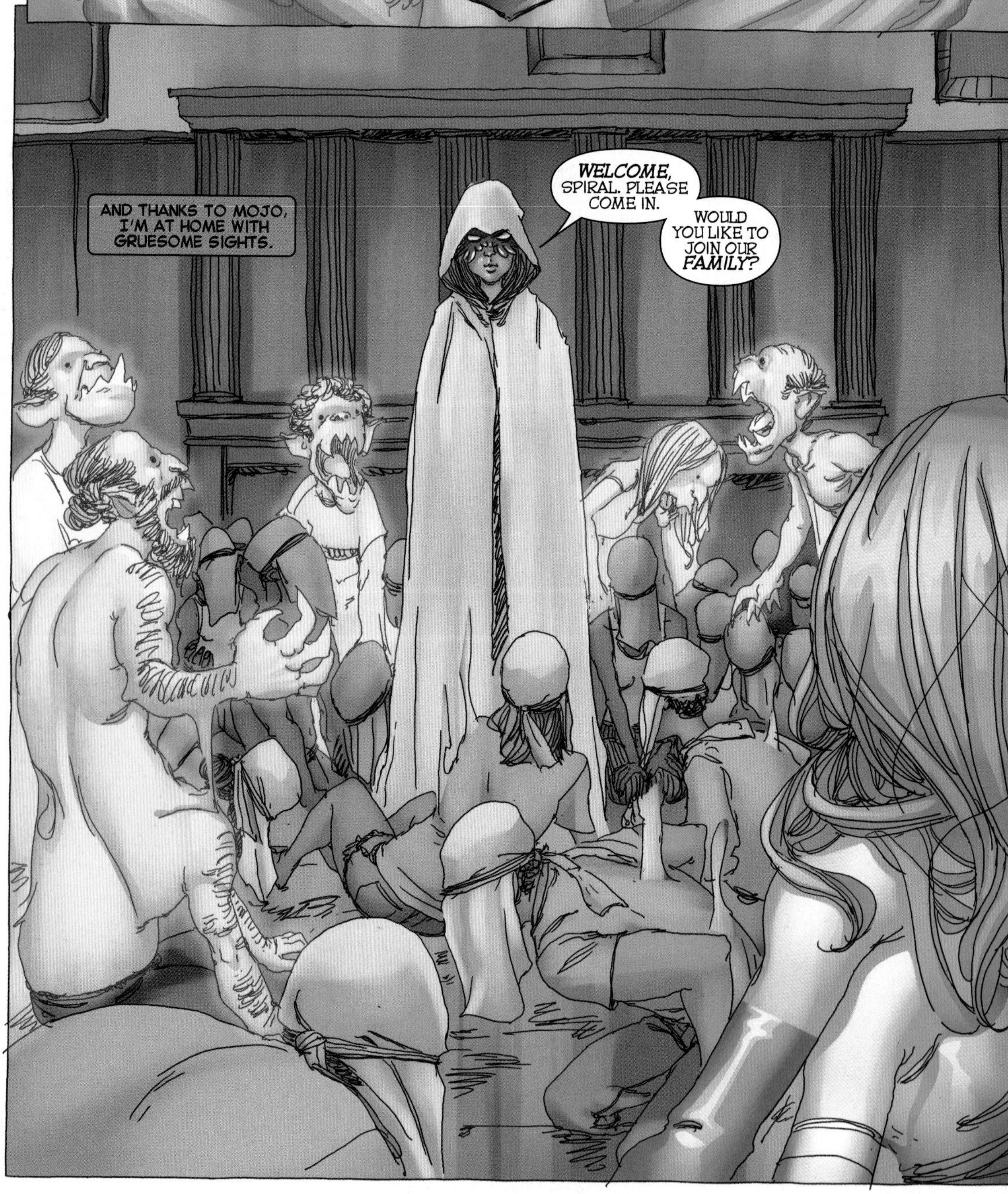
AND THANKS TO MOJO, I'M AT HOME WITH GRUESOME SIGHTS.
WELCOME, SPIRAL. PLEASE COME IN.
WOULD YOU LIKE TO JOIN OUR FAMILY?

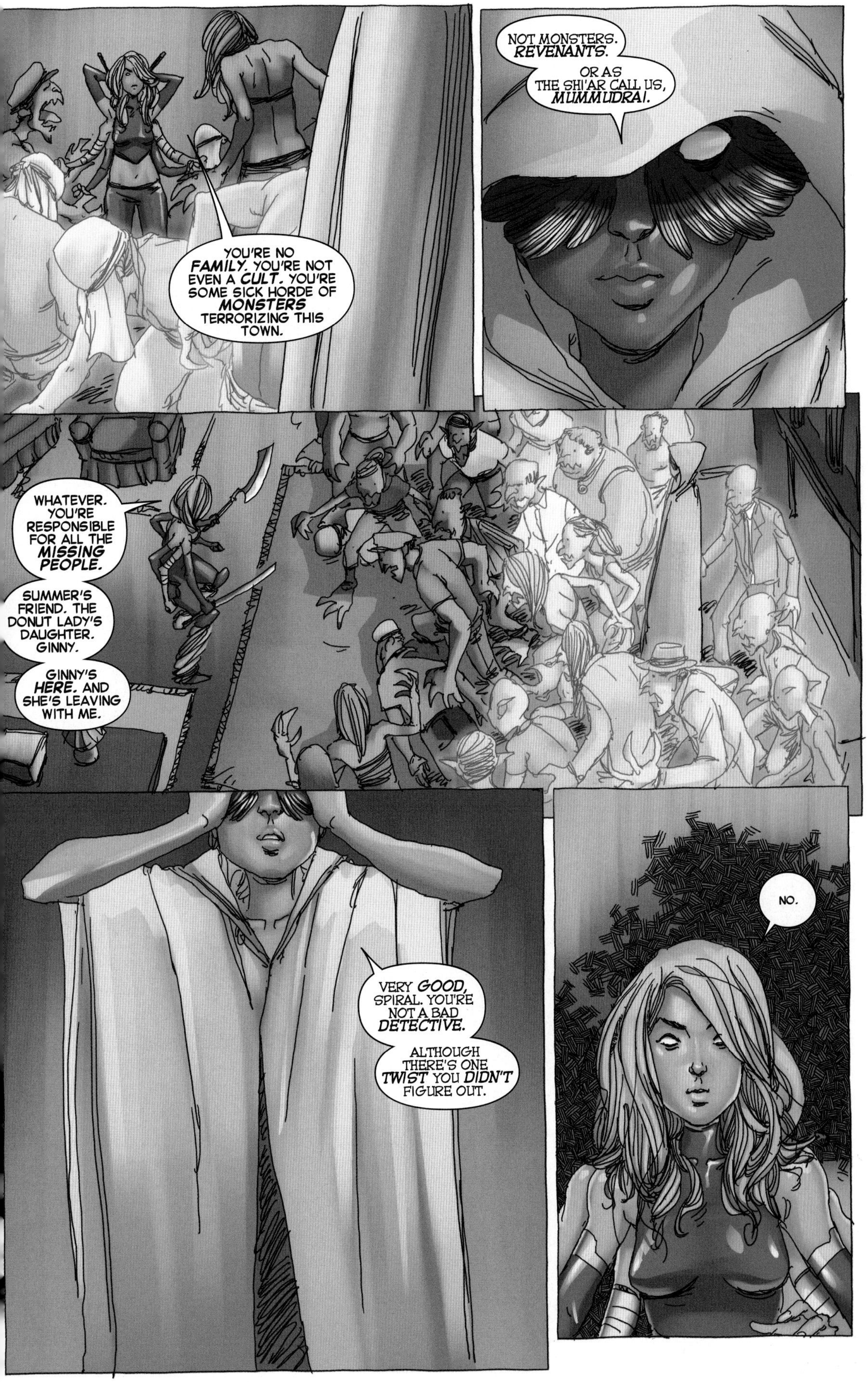
YOU'RE NO FAMILY. YOU'RE NOT EVEN A CULT. YOU'RE SOME SICK HORDE OF MONSTERS TERRORIZING THIS TOWN.
NOT MONSTERS. REVENANTS.
OR AS THE SHI'AR CALL US, MUMMUDRAI.
WHATEVER. YOU'RE RESPONSIBLE FOR ALL THE MISSING PEOPLE.
SUMMER'S FRIEND. THE DONUT LADY'S DAUGHTER. GINNY.
GINNY'S HERE. AND SHE'S LEAVING WITH ME.
VERY GOOD, SPIRAL. YOU'RE NOT A BAD DETECTIVE.
ALTHOUGH THERE'S ONE TWIST YOU DIDN'T FIGURE OUT.
NO.

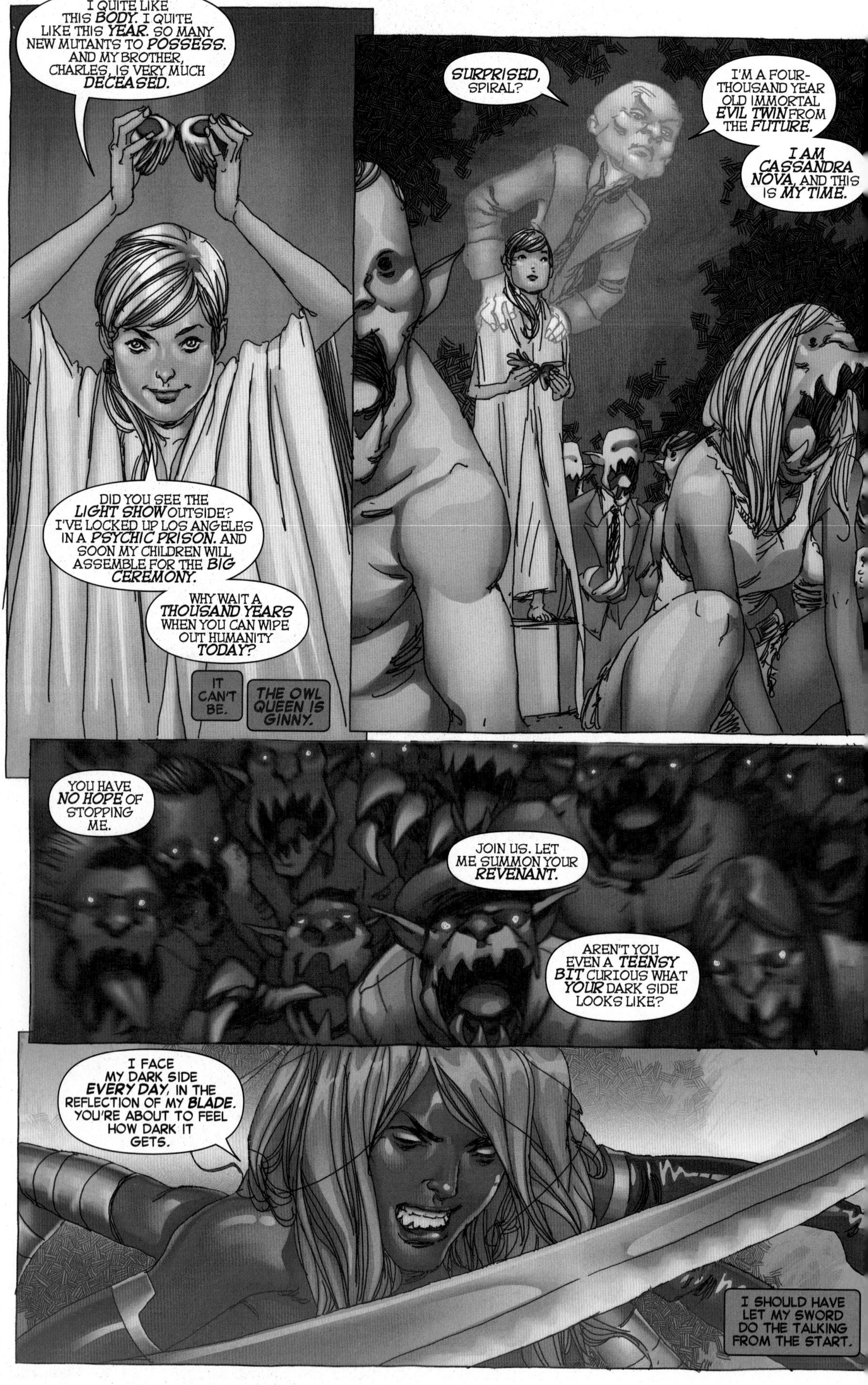
I QUITE LIKE THIS BODY. I QUITE LIKE THIS YEAR. SO MANY NEW MUTANTS TO POSSESS. AND MY BROTHER, CHARLES, IS VERY MUCH DECEASED.
SURPRISED, SPIRAL?
I'M A FOUR-THOUSAND YEAR OLD IMMORTAL EVIL TWIN FROM THE FUTURE.
I AM CASSANDRA NOVA, AND THIS IS MY TIME.
DID YOU SEE THE LIGHT SHOW OUTSIDE? I'VE LOCKED UP LOS ANGELES IN A PSYCHIC PRISON. AND SOON MY CHILDREN WILL ASSEMBLE FOR THE BIG CEREMONY.
WHY WAIT A THOUSAND YEARS WHEN YOU CAN WIPE OUT HUMANITY TODAY?
IT CAN'T BE.
THE OWL QUEEN IS GINNY.
YOU HAVE NO HOPE OF STOPPING ME.
JOIN US. LET ME SUMMON YOUR REVENANT.
AREN'T YOU EVEN A TEENSY BIT CURIOUS WHAT YOUR DARK SIDE LOOKS LIKE?
I FACE MY DARK SIDE EVERY DAY, IN THE REFLECTION OF MY BLADE. YOU'RE ABOUT TO FEEL HOW DARK IT GETS.
I SHOULD HAVE LET MY SWORD DO THE TALKING FROM THE START.

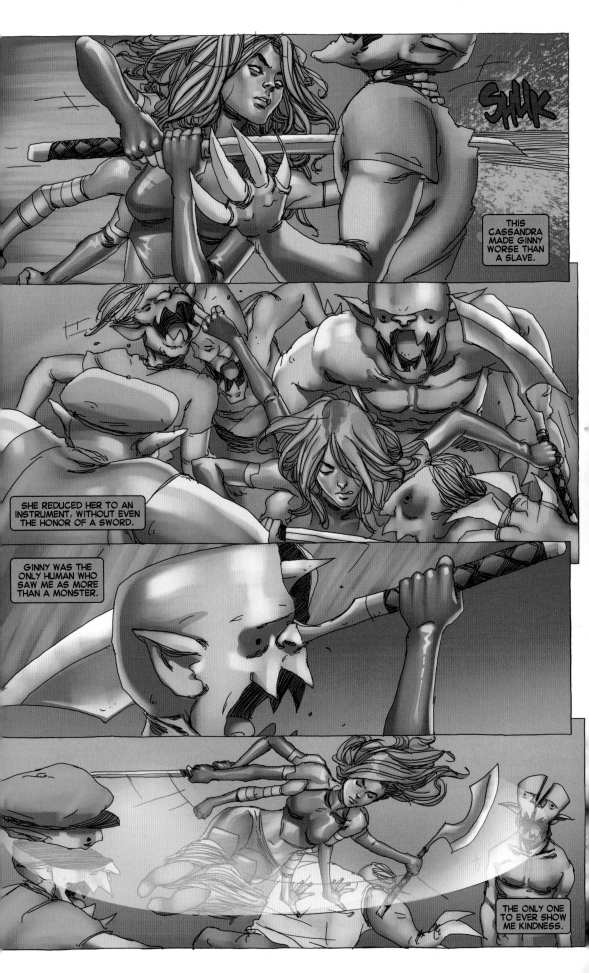

SHUK

THIS CASSANDRA MADE GINNY WORSE THAN A SLAVE.

SHE REDUCED HER TO AN INSTRUMENT, WITHOUT EVEN THE HONOR OF A SWORD.

GINNY WAS THE ONLY HUMAN WHO SAW ME AS MORE THAN A MONSTER.

THE ONLY ONE TO EVER SHOW ME KINDNESS.

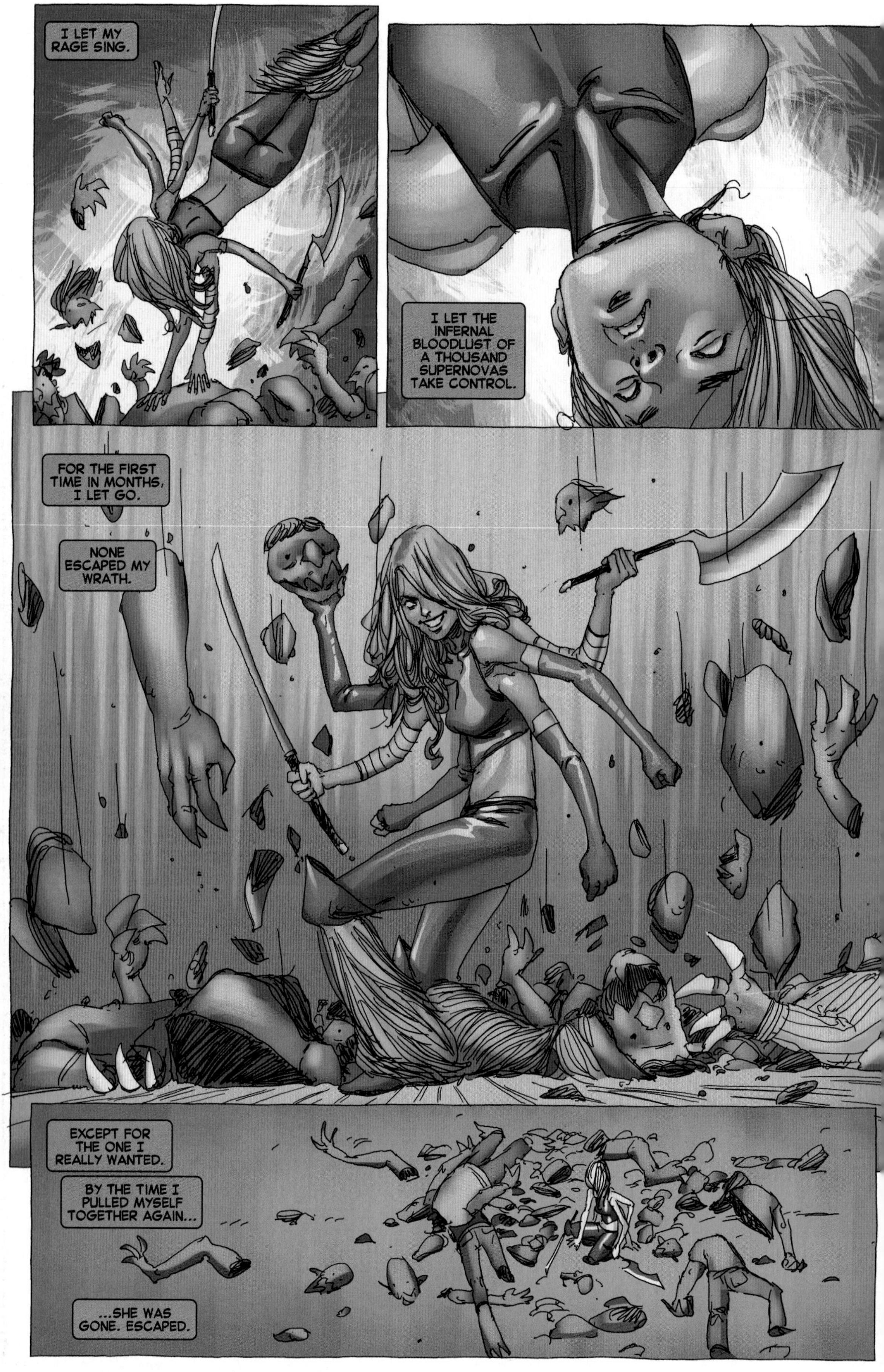
I LET MY RAGE SING.
I LET THE INFERNAL BLOODLUST OF A THOUSAND SUPERNOVAS TAKE CONTROL.
FOR THE FIRST TIME IN MONTHS, I LET GO.
NONE ESCAPED MY WRATH.
EXCEPT FOR THE ONE I REALLY WANTED.
BY THE TIME I PULLED MYSELF TOGETHER AGAIN...
...SHE WAS GONE. ESCAPED.

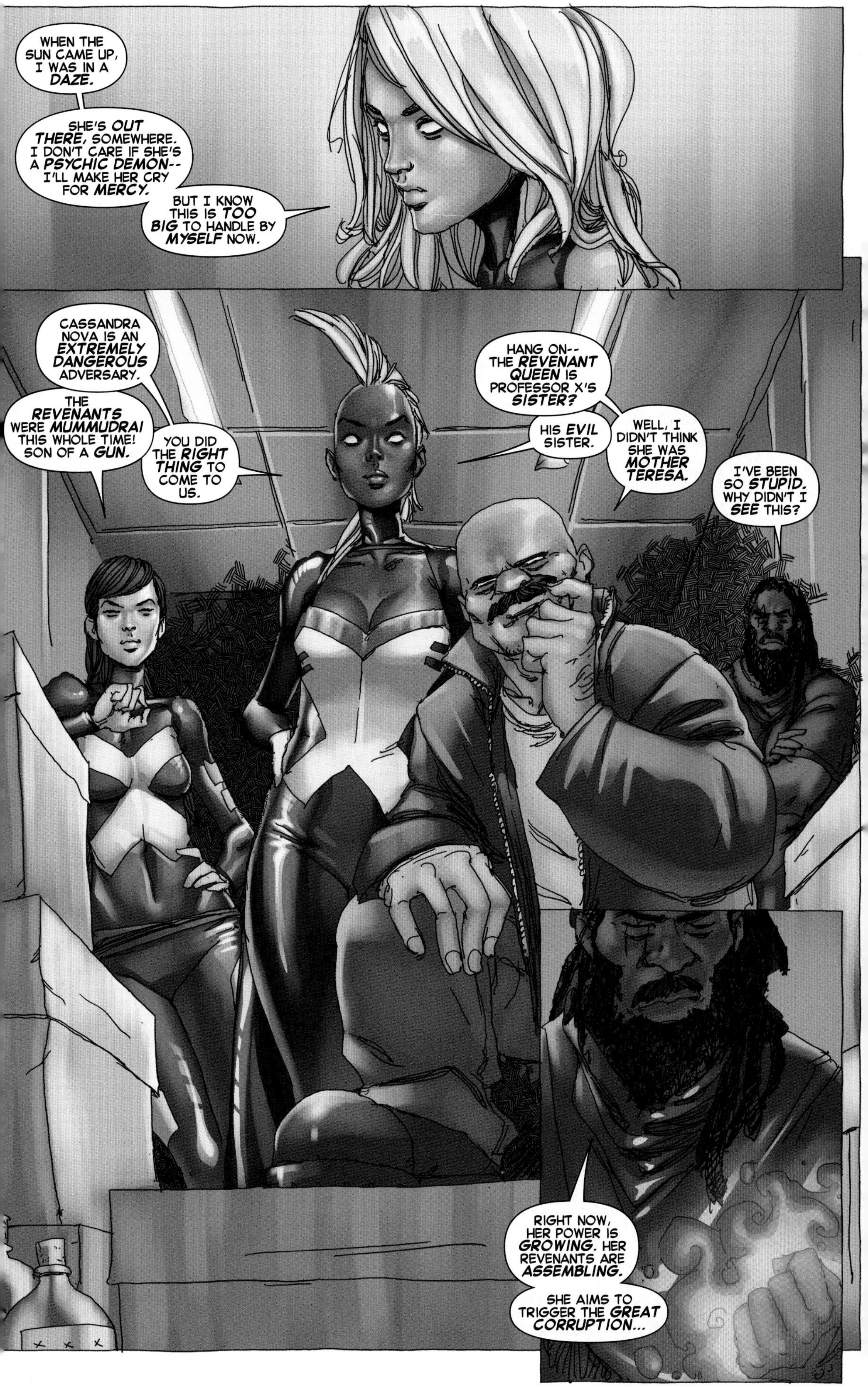
WHEN THE SUN CAME UP, I WAS IN A DAZE.
SHE'S OUT THERE, SOMEWHERE. I DON'T CARE IF SHE'S A PSYCHIC DEMON-- I'LL MAKE HER CRY FOR MERCY.
BUT I KNOW THIS IS TOO BIG TO HANDLE BY MYSELF NOW.
CASSANDRA NOVA IS AN EXTREMELY DANGEROUS ADVERSARY.
THE REVENANTS WERE MUMMUDRAI THIS WHOLE TIME! SON OF A GUN.
YOU DID THE RIGHT THING TO COME TO US.
HANG ON-- THE REVENANT QUEEN IS PROFESSOR X'S SISTER?
HIS EVIL SISTER.
WELL, I DIDN'T THINK SHE WAS MOTHER TERESA.
I'VE BEEN SO STUPID. WHY DIDN'T I SEE THIS?
RIGHT NOW, HER POWER IS GROWING. HER REVENANTS ARE ASSEMBLING.
SHE AIMS TO TRIGGER THE GREAT CORRUPTION...

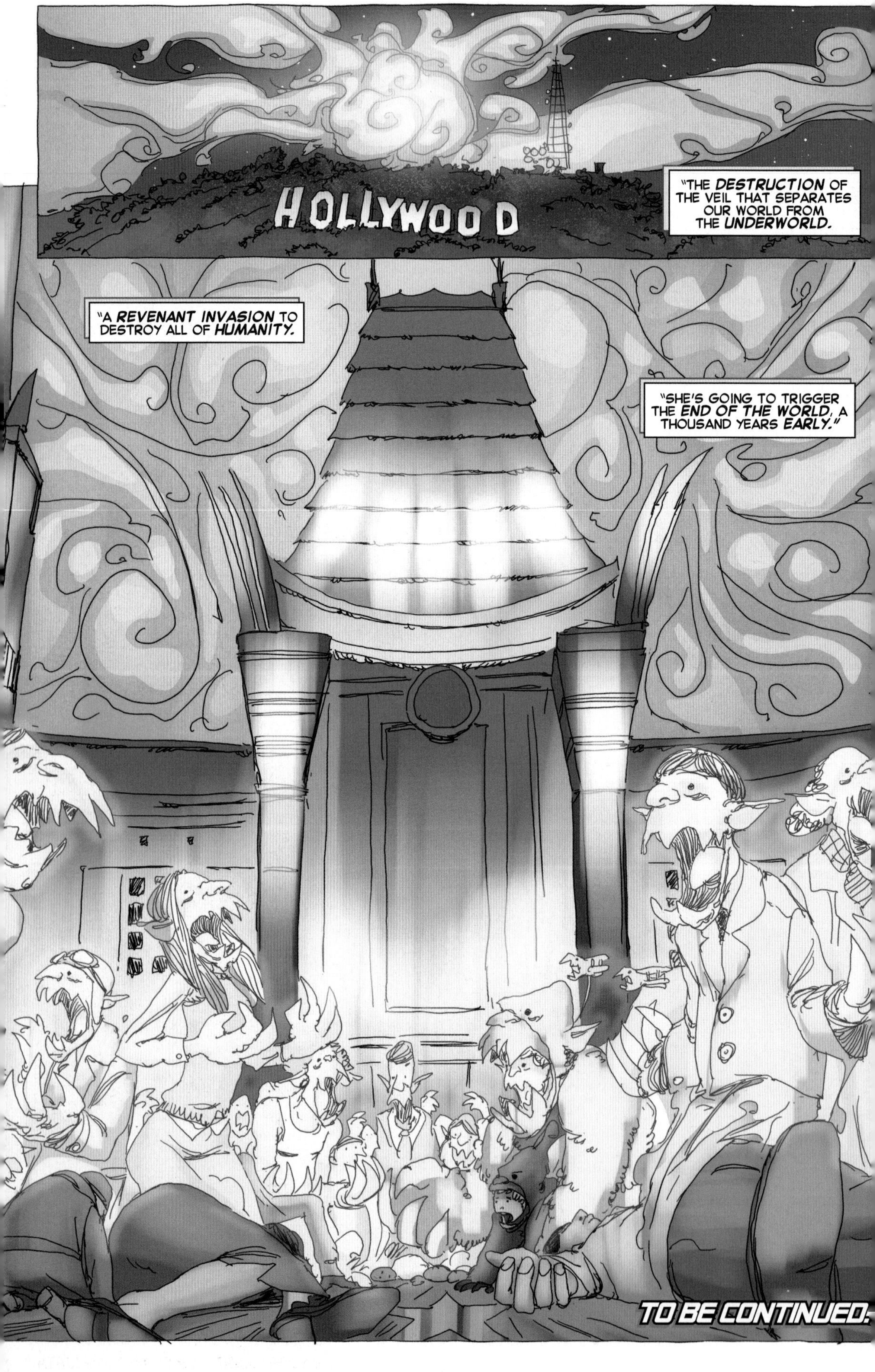
HOLLYWOOD
"THE DESTRUCTION OF THE VEIL THAT SEPARATES OUR WORLD FROM THE UNDERWORLD.
"A REVENANT INVASION TO DESTROY ALL OF HUMANITY.
"SHE'S GOING TO TRIGGER THE END OF THE WORLD, A THOUSAND YEARS EARLY."
TO BE CONTINUED...

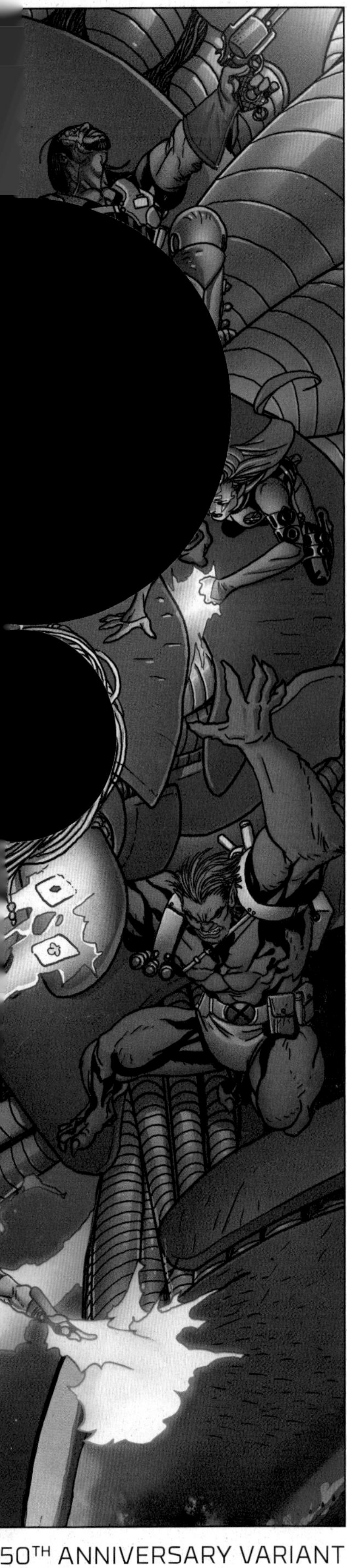

50TH ANNIVERSARY VARIANT
SALVADOR LARROCA & FRANK D'ARMATA

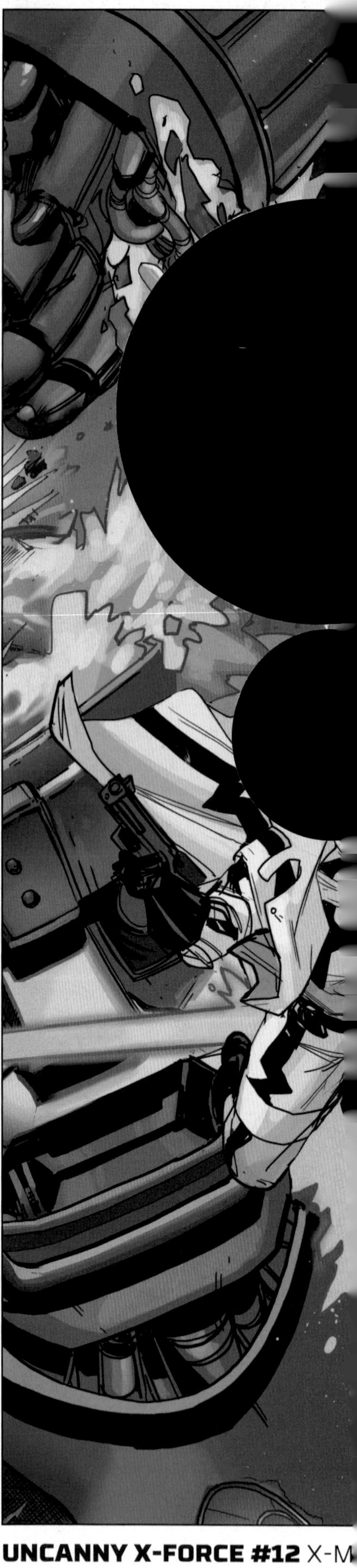

UNCANNY X-FORCE #12 X-M
BY PHIL NOTO

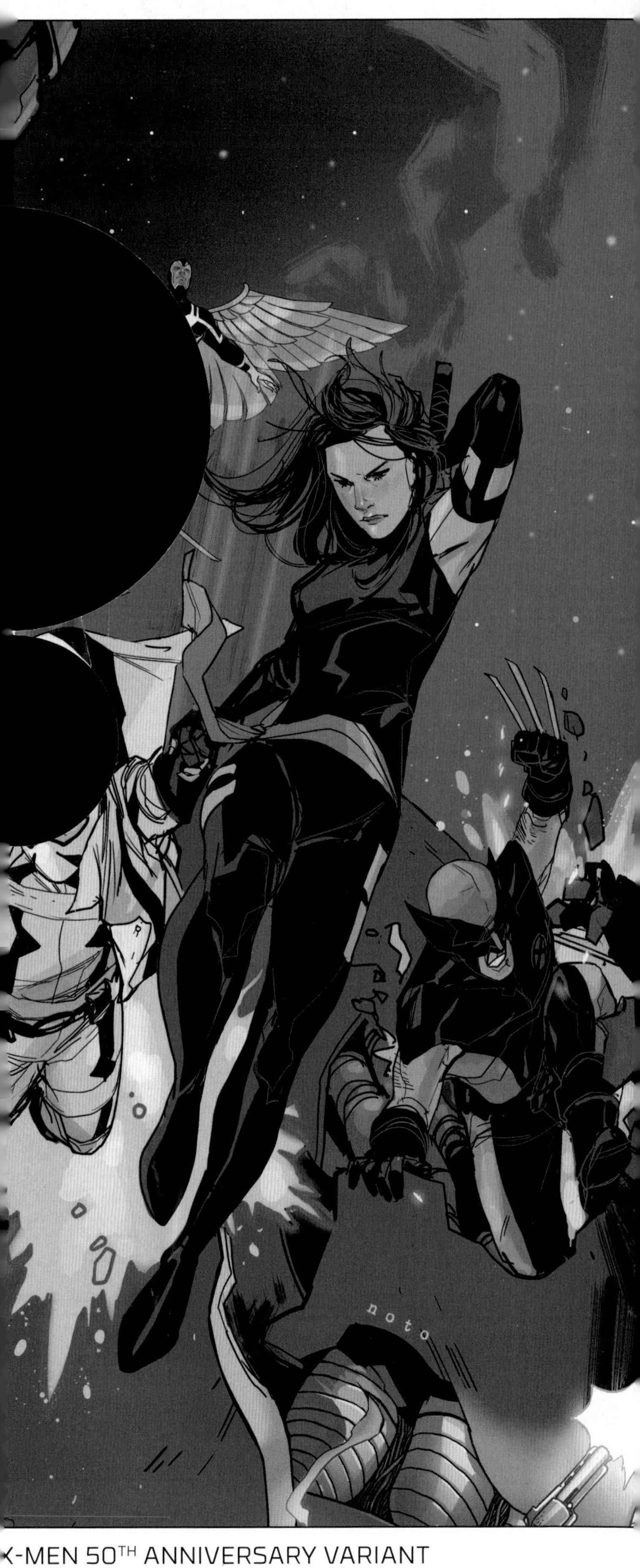
noto

X-MEN 50TH ANNIVERSARY VARIANT

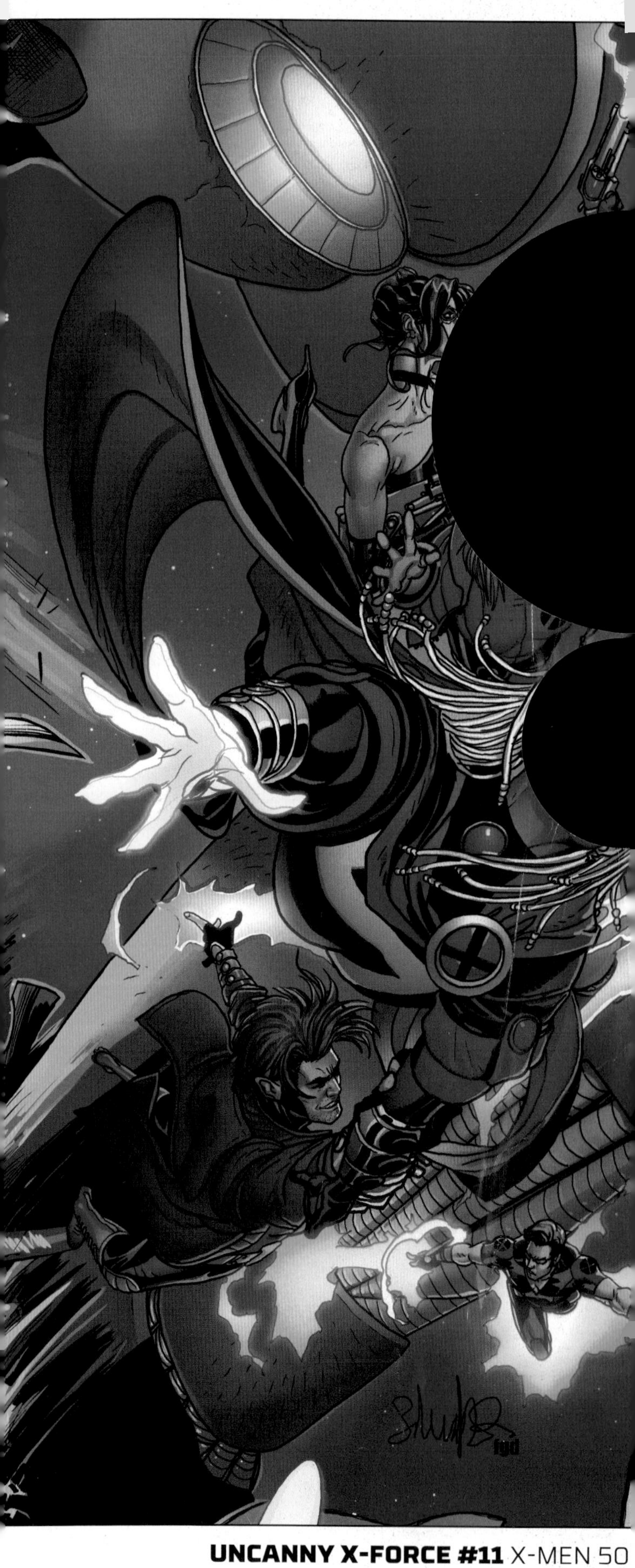

UNCANNY X-FORCE #11 X-MEN 50
BY SALV

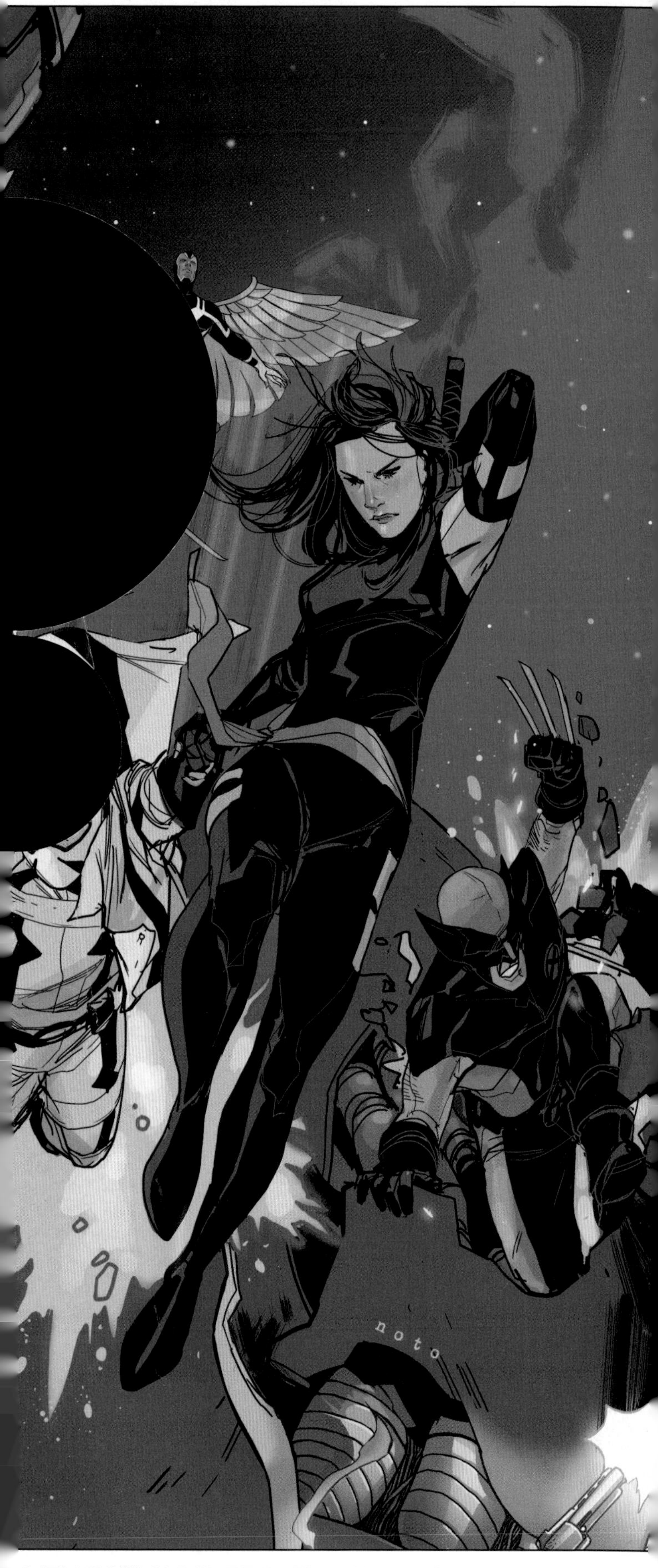
noto

MEN 50TH ANNIVERSARY VARIANT

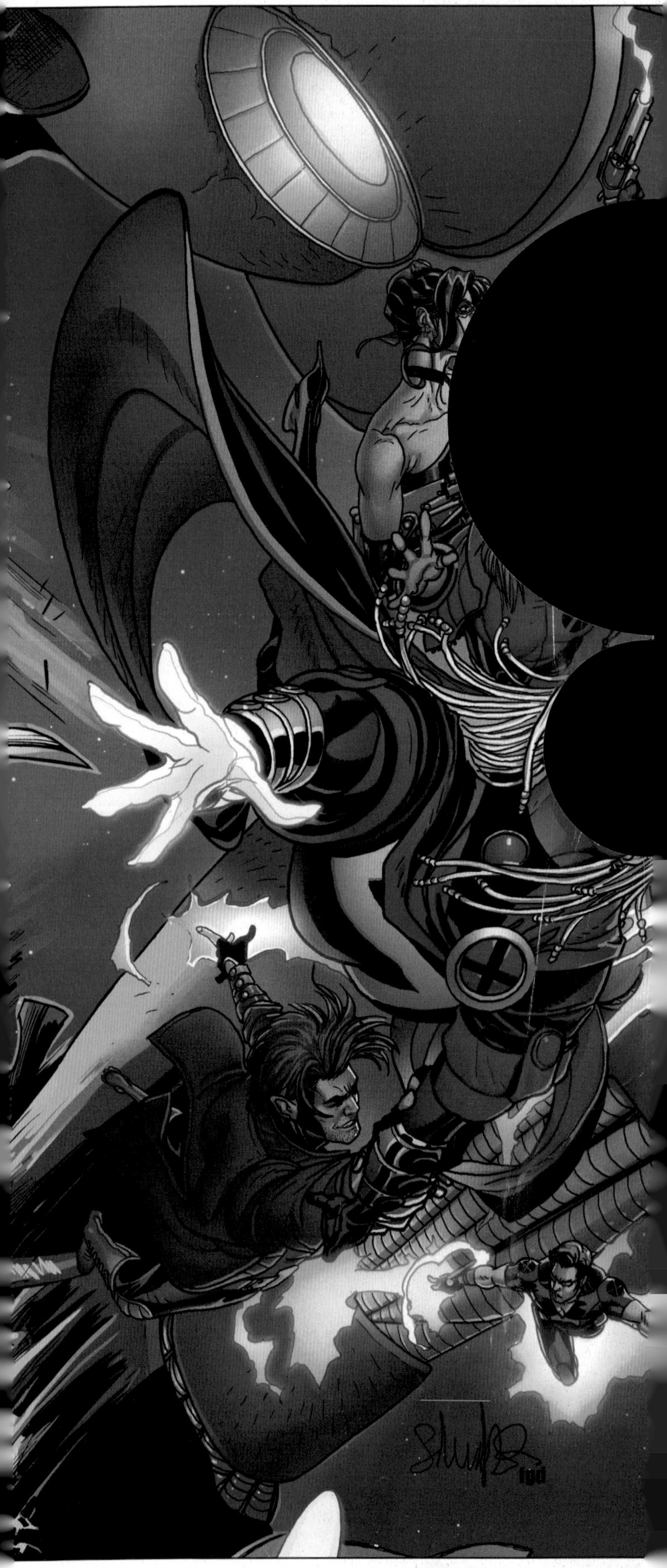

UNCANNY X-FORCE #11 X-MEN 5

BY SA

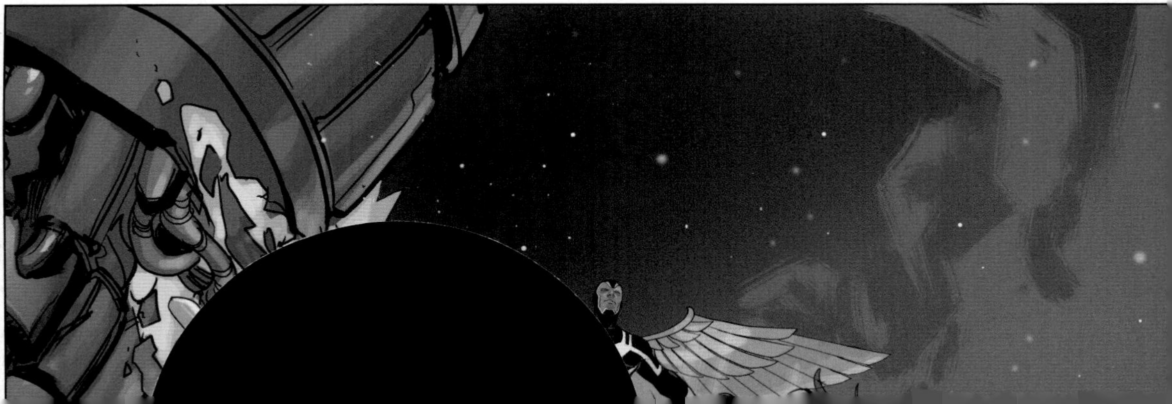

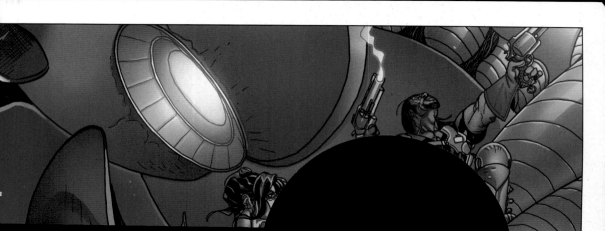

CHARACTER SKETCHES BY ADRIAN ALPHONA

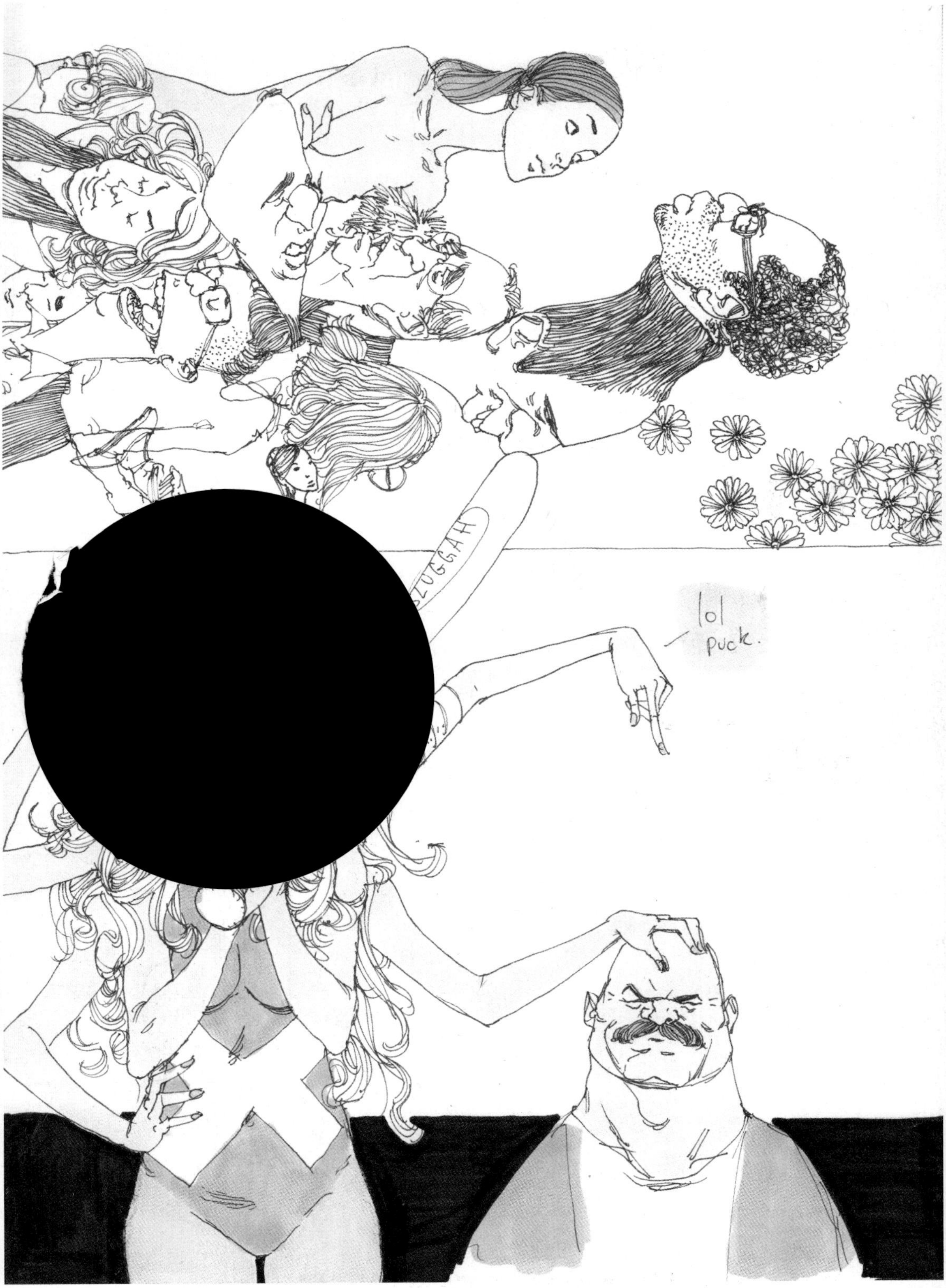
SLUGGAH
lol puck.

COVER SKETCHES BY KRIS ANKA

#8 SKETCHES

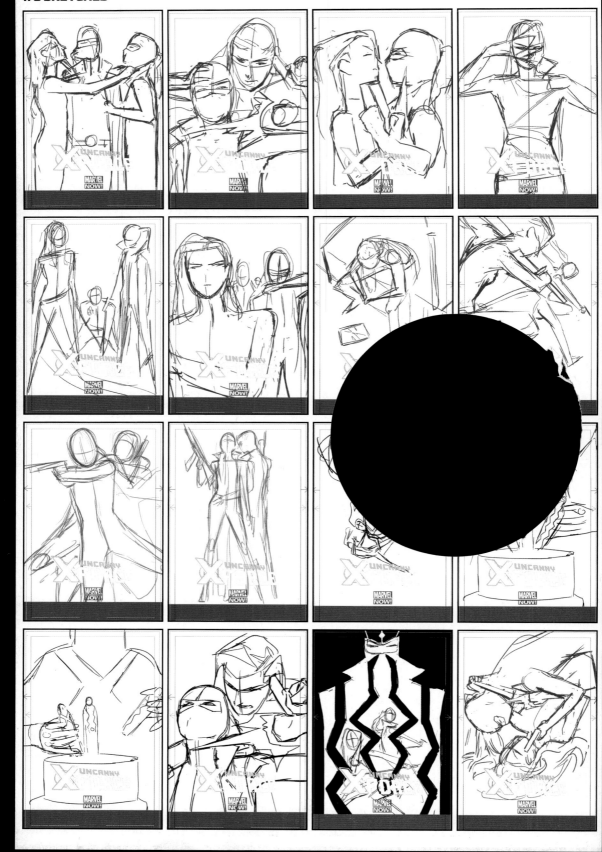

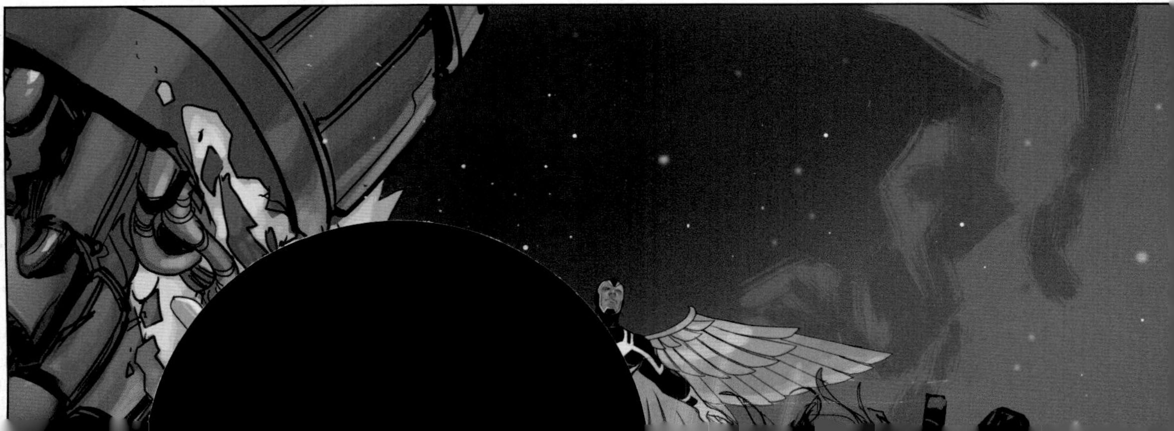

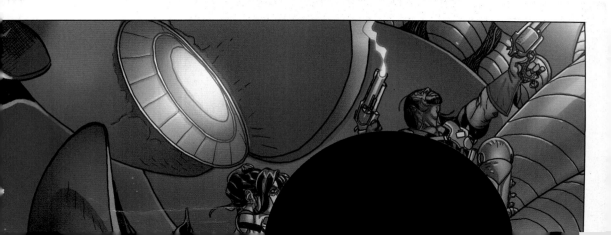

#9

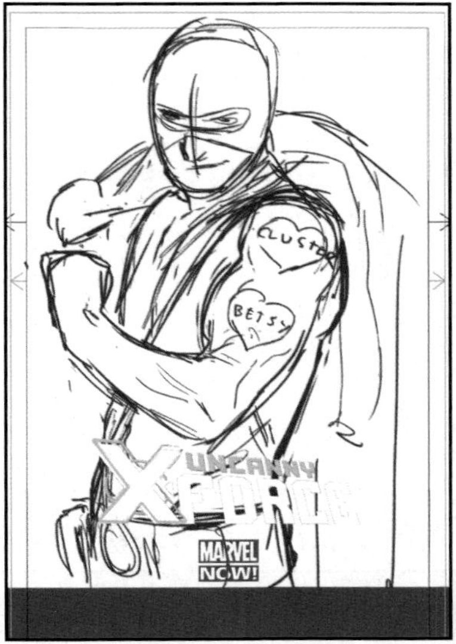
BETSY
UNCANNY
X-FORCE
MARVEL
NOW!

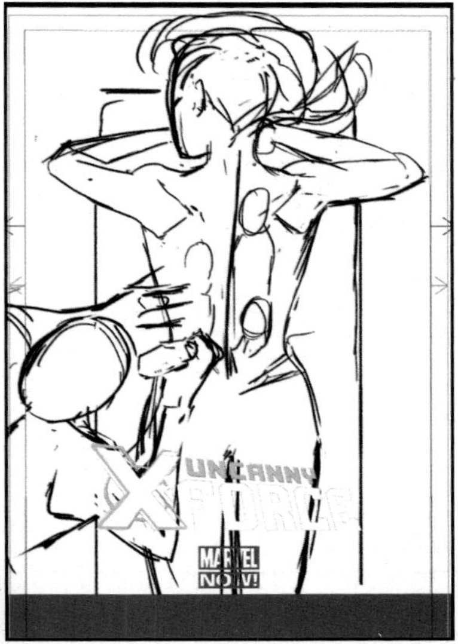
UNCANNY
X-FORCE
MARVEL
NOW!

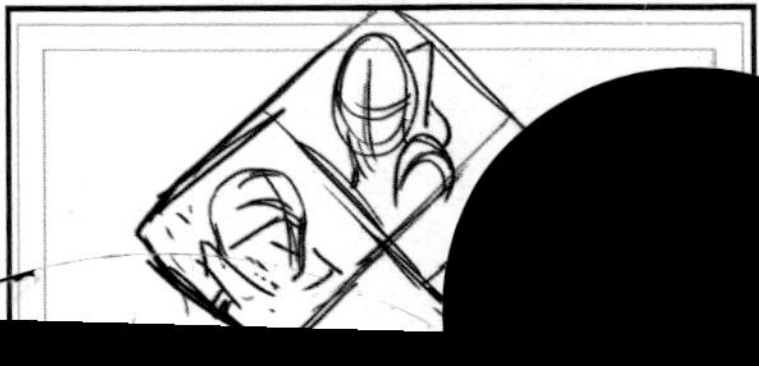

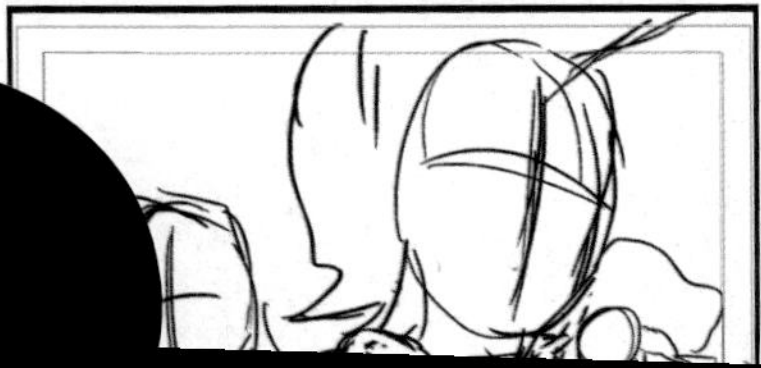